The Origins
of Central Banking
in the United States

The Origins
of Central Banking
in the United States

RICHARD H. TIMBERLAKE, JR.

Harvard University Press
Cambridge, Massachusetts
and London, England *1978*

Library of Congress Cataloging in Publication Data

Timberlake, Richard Henry, 1922-
  The origins of central banking in the United States.

  Includes index.
  1. Banks and banking, Central—United States—
History. 2. Monetary policy—United States—History.
I. Title.
HG2461.T55   332.1′1′0973   78-4622
ISBN 0-674-64480-8

To Tommy, Chris, Megan, Dave, and Dick

Preface

While many books have been written about central banking in the United States, few have been concerned with central banking before the incorporation of the Federal Reserve System; and none, so far as I can tell, has explicitly treated the central banking function as a general institutional development not bounded by the creation or destruction of a particular institution, such as the Second Bank of the United States.

The work that led to this book began twenty years ago when I decided to write a doctoral dissertation on nineteenth-century Treasury monetary policy. My research focused on the period between 1830 and 1860. As I read the works of scholars, the congressional debates, and other government documents covering this period, I became aware that the central banking concept had been fully understood and appreciated by the time of Andrew Jackson. Therefore, I presumed, it must have first appeared much earlier. So as a postdoctoral continuation of my dissertation, I traced back through the primary sources to see where the central banking idea had originated and who was responsible for it. Much to my surprise, I could find no trace of its formal initiation. On the contrary, all the evidence pointed to proscription of any kind of conscious deliberative control of the monetary system. I then decided that the whole subject of central banking origins, growth, thought, and institutions needed further treatment.

My sources of primary materials for this work were *The Annals of Congress*, *The Register of Debates in Congress*, *The Congressional Globe*, and *The Congressional Record*. These documents compose the serial record of congressional debates since 1789. In addition, executive documents, executive replies to congressional inquiries, reports of commissions, and annual reports of secretaries of the Treasury, comptrollers of the currency, and other government officials, have been used extensively.

I treat the central banking idea as the belief that deliberate control over the monetary and banking system could be undertaken by delegated authority in order to provide a more rational monetary structure. Thus, this book is a type of intellectual history. I also use statistical data, but primarily to emphasize institutional developments.

The traditional wisdom admits the central banking nature of the First and Second Banks of the United States, but presumes a chaotic monetary Dark Ages between the end of the Second Bank (as a government institution) in 1836 and the formation of the Federal Reserve System seventy-eight years later. The probable reason for this hiatus is that some central banking institutions of the era—for example, the independent treasury—did not take the outward and visible form of a bank. They were therefore dismissed as freakish and undesirable accidents even though they reflected the notion of positive control over the monetary system.

The principal conclusion of this study is that central banking was made, not born, and that it evolved as a pragmatic and opportunistic action when favorable circumstances set the stage. Whether this evolution resulted in good or evil for society is a matter of opinion. Ironically enough, many of the central banking institutions that appeared were sanctioned in order to reduce political tampering with the monetary system. But human manipulation of the system, despite the strictures of the Constitution, was not to be denied. Each successive institution developed its own pattern of intervention.

In spite of the appearance of central banks and quasi-central banks, the dominant monetary institution during the period I examine was the self-regulatory specie standard—first the bimetallic standard, and after 1900 the monometallic gold standard. Since central banking institutions had to operate within these formal frameworks, their scope for action was limited. Only in the twentieth century did specie standards fade away like the Cheshire Cat. Discretionary central banks became the dominant form of monetary control, and not even the "grin" of metallic standards remained. Governments actually forbade the monetary use of gold; but the recent development of free world markets for commodity-gold suggests some possibility that the metal may return as a commodity-money. This possibility will become stronger if central banks continue their inflationary ways.

Much of this book is drawn from articles I have had published in various professional journals since 1960. Chapter 2 is largely derived from an article that appeared in the *Revue Internationale d'Histoire de la Banque* 2(1969): 209-225. A less detailed version of Chapter 5 appeared in the *Journal of Political Economy* 68(April 1960): 109-117 (copyright © 1960 by the University of Chicago; all rights reserved). Parts of Chapter 6 are drawn from an article in the *Southern Economic Journal* 27 (October 1960): 92-103. Chapters 7, 8, and 9 include material that appeared in the *Journal of Economic History* 24 (March 1964): 29-52; and 34 (December 1974): 835-850. Chapter 8 also incorporates research done for an article published in the *Journal of Monetary Economics* 1 (1975): 343-354. Chapter 11 is reprinted by permission from the *Journal of Money, Credit, and Banking* 10 (February 1978): 27-45 (copyright © 1978 by the Ohio University Press; all rights reserved). Part of Chapter 12 was first written as an article for the *Quarterly Journal of Economics* 77 (February 1963): 40-54.

Most of these articles have been reworked extensively and supplemented with additional research material before incorporation in this book. The high quality of professional criticism provided by these journal editors and their referees has been of inestimable value to me in synthesizing these parts into a whole. I also want to include in this group the editorial staff of the Harvard University Press. I thank these helpful critics one and all for their time, their competence, and their constructive suggestions.

Some other critics and contributors deserve special mention. I am especially indebted to Earl J. Hamilton and Milton Friedman of the University of Chicago, who were instrumental in guiding the initial phase of this work and who have made additional constructive comments at various times since. I also have had worthwhile suggestions and encouragement over a considerable span of time from Clark Warburton, Leland Yeager, Anna J. Schwartz, the late Ross Robertson, Frank W. Fetter, Murray Rothhard, Alfred Bornemann, Thomas Humphrey, my wife, Hildegard, and others. I accept the responsibility for its remaining imperfections, and I feel confident that subsequent investigators ultimately will set all matters right.

Contents

The Origins
of Central Banking
in the United States

1. The Genesis of Monetary Control

> Whereas it is conceived that the establishment of a bank for the United States, . . . will be very conducive to the successful conducting of the national finances; will tend to give facility to the obtaining of loans, for the use of the Government, . . . and will be productive of considerable advantage to trade and industry in general: Therefore, *Be it enacted*, etc. That a Bank of the United States shall be established . . . (*Annals of Congress*, 25 February 1791)

Contemporary societies accept the institutional presence of central banks without understanding what they are and how or where they originated. The almost universal ignorance of central banking by the layman and its unquestioned acceptance by most economists prompts the questions: How did central banking come about? What was the origin of this powerful institution? How did central banking, as opposed to commercial banking, evolve? Was central banking simply an offshoot of commercial banking, or were other institutions involved in its development? Was the institution so necessary after all?

Specie standards were the common means for formalizing monetary systems in most countries during the eighteenth and nineteenth centuries. Gold and silver were the usual commodities on which these systems were based. Metallic currency foundations were then supplemented by institutions now known as central banks. These earlier institutions were private banking corporations with loose and ill-defined relationships to their governments.[1] Whatever they were as institutions, their operations were strictly subordinate to the workings of specie standards. In the twentieth century this position has been reversed. Central banks have become dominant institutions, while metallic standards are hardly more than vestigial and functionless facades.

That the central bank proper has become the recognized agency for controlling the community's stock of money seems to imply that central banks were appointed by executive or legislative decree to carry out this task. Yet if this implication has a grain of truth, it is only a grain. By and large, central banks as recognized official manipulators of the money stock evolved; they grew into their role, they were not born to it. A stronger argument can be made that they were originally enjoined from discretionary operations to effect changes in the quantity of money or influence the volume of trade or credit and that they were officially obliterated if they showed too much enthusiasm for monetary regulation. The story of how and why their original proscriptions became their ultimate prescriptions constitutes the political economy of central banking.

An institution is not necessarily bound by a particular physical structure. Control of the money supply in the United States is a good example of an institutional function that has been carried out by physical establishments of divergent forms.[2] The gold and silver (specie) monetary standards, the commercial banking system, the First and Second Banks of the United States, the independent treasury system, the national banking system, clearinghouse associations, and the Federal Reserve system have all been instrumental in altering the quantity of money at different times and by various means. The one first in force and largely fundamental to the others was the metallic standard system.

A typical metallic standard system is automatic and self-regulating after the original rules or conditions for its operation have been established. The first rule is that the government should define the unit of account in terms of a weight of precious metal—gold, for example.[3] Between 1834 and 1934 in the United States, 232.2 grains of pure gold were defined as equal to an abstract ten-dollar gold piece, nominally a gold eagle.[4] This relationship would be meaningless, except that by the second rule the government must be ready, willing, and able to convert gold bullion (bulk metal) into coined money at this ratio. The third rule is that the coined metal must be legal tender for all debts, public and private. Any legal tender provision of government is made operational by the enforcing agencies of the government, that is, by the judicial and penal systems. Without the power of decree any government is a figurehead, and its money may be refused either in payment of debts or in transacting ordinary business.

Specific economic conditions are also necessary for the operational efficacy of the self-regulating gold standard. The money supply has to be responsive to the quantity of monetary gold; prices must be sensitive to changes in the quantity of money; and gold must be allowed to flow freely in or out of the economy in response to private demands. Given a depression in business activity, for example, prices of goods and services in terms of the unit of account (dollar) fall. Since the money price of gold is fixed by statute, it remains constant; so the purchasing power of gold

—its real value—increases. New gold for monetization could then be obtained in three ways: (1) Nonmonetary gold, that is, "plate" and ornaments, could be monetized. (2) Additional quantities of gold could be mined if the economy contained a gold-mining industry. (3) Gold from foreign monetary stocks could be shipped in to purchase the now lower-priced domestic goods. Any of these actions would tend to restore prices, incomes, employment, and business activity.

A "perfect" specie (or gold) standard has been described as a system in which the "proportionate increment of [the economy's] revenue . . . [is] always as great as the proportionate increment of its aggregate quantity of gold."[5] Actual working models have not usually followed this blueprint. Whether or not the economic prerequisites exist in the real world to the degree necessary, the fact remains that the world's gold mines cannot be relied on for a relatively smooth flow of gold. Mining is an extractive industry acutely subject to diminishing returns. Fresh discoveries of gold may buoy the world's monetary systems for a time, from time to time. But diminished rates of gold output tend to produce a secular drag on the growth in the quantity of money, and to depress money prices and business activity, until another big discovery repeats the process. This pattern might be repeated indefinitely except that gold discoveries are subject to diminishing returns on a limited earth.

A second infelicity of the gold standard system is that the use of gold as money involves a real cost. The gold, either in the form of bank reserves or as money balances of individuals, must be stored. Gold is a commodity as well as a money. Means for economizing its apparent idleness, for reducing its wear and tear as a currency, and for minimizing the costs of transporting it are sought by the people who must bear the costs of handling. Both paper currency and bank deposits are economically cheaper substitutes for gold, and both have been used extensively in response to gold-economizing motives.

Another drawback to a gold standard is the belt-tightening discipline the system occasionally imposes on the economy. When a business boom triggered by a relatively large influx of gold languishes because of the subsequent decline of the gold inflow, then prices, wages, incomes, and general business activity all decline commensurately. This process, painful for many people, must be endured until a new cost-price equilibrium is reestablished or until a new source of gold is discovered.

Metallic standard systems with both their good and their bad qualities continued for centuries simply because no other system was self-regulating, and therefore no other system could be trusted. Despite occasional debasements of the currency by irresponsible political authorities, a monetary system of rules, such as the gold standard, seemed to offer less opportunity for evil practices than any other system. Delegating to individual authorities a control as vital to society's well-being as that of altering the quantity of money was too obvious a way to further the capricious power of despots. Once political power seemed to be constrained by constitutional principles and no longer too subject to usurpation by uncontrollable regencies, the economization of media of exchange could proceed more confidently. Whether this confidence was well-founded remains problematical.

The first change from a purely metallic money system to a mixed money system was the substitution of paper money for either gold coin or gold bullion, even though gold was still required as a redemption medium for the paper. This mutation, effected principally during the eighteenth century, resulted primarily from the development of commercial banking. Banking was a natural offspring of goldsmithing, and banks and bank notes grew together. The growth of banks raised the complementary question of how banks were to fit politically into the social structure. The Bank of England was incorporated under a charter from the crown in 1694, but in the United States three state banks were chartered before Congress incorporated the First Bank of the United States. Still, the activities of the First Bank marked the real beginning of the government's more positive relationship to monetary control.

The First Bank was not intended to be a central bank; it was not to control the quantity of money. Nor was it to act as a centralized depository, an office of discount for commercial banks, or a lender of last resort. All these latter-day responsibilities of central banks were originally denied it—not even considered possibilities—for two principal reasons. First, the new Constitution specified that *Congress* should have the power to coin money and regulate its value. Even though this stipulation presumed a simple, self-adjusting, specie standard and limited the power of Congress to setting the legal tender value of metal, it "gave the government . . . the near-absolute authority over currency and coinage that has always been considered the necessary consequence of national sovereignty."[6] Second, the four banks in existence in 1791 did not need a central bank in any of its manifestations. In fact, each of these banks approached the model of a single isolated banking system. Transportation was primitive. Not only were collections of specie for outstanding notes and checks slow, but notes and checks did not move very far beyond the local financial circle served by a given bank.[7] The raison d'être for this bank had to be established on other grounds.

Alexander Hamilton, acting in his capacity as secretary of the Treasury, was the first to describe in detail the kind of institution the First Bank was to be. His "Report on a National Bank," delivered to Congress in 1790, reads remarkably like Adam Smith's normative account for the Bank of England published fourteen years earlier in *The Wealth of Na-*

tions.[8] The Bank of England, Smith said, "acts, not only as an ordinary bank, but as a great engine of state." Its duties, he continued, include receiving taxes, paying interest on the government debt, circulating temporary currency (monetary debt) of the government, and discounting bills for banks in England and sometimes for banks in Hamburg and Holland. "In those different operations," Smith added somewhat undiplomatically, "its duty to the public may sometimes have obliged it, without any fault of its directors, to overstock the circulation with paper money."[9] Hamilton wrote similarly: "It is to be considered that such a bank is not a mere matter of private property, but a political machine of greatest importance to the State." A public bank would give "facility to the Government in obtaining pecuniary aids," that is, loans. It would aid in sales of public lands; its profits would accrue to the government; and it would eventually provide a uniform paper currency.[10]

Both Smith and Hamilton defended banking in general as a means for "augmenting the active or productive capital of a country." The judicious operations of banking, they alleged, converted the "dead stock of gold and silver" into active and productive capital by substituting paper in place of metal. Paper money, being easier to transport, "economized" specie while it made possible the "quickening of circulation."[11] Smith cautioned that commerce and business were less secure when "suspended upon the Daedalian wings of paper money, [than] when they travel about upon the solid ground of gold and silver."[12] Hamilton, too, recognized that banks could furnish "temptations to overtrading," and thereby banish gold and silver from the country. But the force of his objection rested "on their being an engine [sic] of paper credit."[13] So long as the paper money was "payable upon demand without any condition, and . . . readily paid as soon as presented," the dangers of overissue would be obviated, Smith wrote in optimistic answer to his own caveat.[14] To his warning on how banking excesses might lead to overtrading Hamilton replied: "If the abuses of a beneficial thing are to determine its condemnation, there is scarcely a source of public prosperity [sic] which will not speedily be closed."[15]

Hamilton perceived that another necessary step in the formation of a public or national bank was minimization of the risk of possible abuses. While he did not want the State to participate in the executive direction of the bank, nor "to own the whole or a principal part of the stock, . . . the ordinary rules of prudence require that the Government should possess the means of ascertaining . . . that so delicate a trust is executed with fidelity and care."[16] To this end, the State should hold some of the stock and be able to check on the bank's affairs at any instant.

The bank Hamilton foresaw was a national or public bank as well as an extra-large bank. It was required, he thought, as an auxiliary to the fiscal operations of a federal state. Unlike the state banks, it would not be subject to the constraints of any one set of state laws; it would have branches in the states. It could therefore issue a uniform national currency that would greatly facilitate the payments and receipts required of a national government. The privately owned, publicly operated bank would also be a commercial bank, still subject to the discipline of redeeming its notes in gold and silver on demand. A government-owned bank, while able to furnish a uniform paper currency, would have only its own discretion to limit emissions of currency. This discretion could not always be trusted because of the "temptation of momentary exigencies" that the government might face.[17]

The final and most important function of the public bank was that of bulwarking government credit. To this end, the bulk of its capitalization would be based on government debt. The new federal government had taken over much of the states' Revolutionary War debts as its own responsibility. It was understandably concerned about the management and repayment of the debt and wished to insure the possibility of additional flotations if they became necessary. Capital stock of the bank would be payable one-fourth in specie and three-fourths in the 6 percent public debt. The specie would serve as reserves; the debt would allow a capital structure "sufficiently large to be the basis of an extensive [note] circulation, and an adequate security for it."[18]

A public bank might take up only a small fraction of the debt. (The First Bank originally held $6.20 million of a total national debt of $75.5 million.) However, even a minor holding could strengthen the total market for the debt so that interest rates could be kept "low." Hamilton gave the "low" interest issue its obvious due: (1) Interest was a cost to the government; for the sake of fiscal economy it should be minimized. (2) Low interest rates promoted national growth. His final argument was that the debt would be respectable collateral for the uniform paper currency the bank would issue.[19]

The writings of Adam Smith and Hamilton clarified the case for a paper currency based on specie and redeemable in the same on demand. Indeed, the course of the Bank of England throughout the eighteenth century demonstrated the reconciliation between a paper currency based on specie and the classic specie standard. The issue of exchequer bills by the British government and the issue of notes by the Bank of England were examples of this evolution.[20]

The chartering of the First Bank aroused a controversy in Congress, a controversy that was concentrated in the House of Representatives. One Congressman, James Jackson of Georgia, noted that a geographical line separated those who were for the bank from those who were against it. All representatives to the "eastward" were for it and all to the "southward" were against it, almost without exception.[21] The principal spokesman for the group against the bank was James Madison of Virginia. Madison did not believe that the bank would have an appreciable effect on "raising the value of stock" because the government "stock" absorbed by the bank would be replaced in the market by bank stock. Madison cited Smith's *Wealth of Nations* to show that bank paper would "banish the precious metals by substituting another medium to perform their office."[22]

Madison's chief arguments were not economic but political and legal. They focused on the constitutionality of such a bank and the possible conflict between the states' interests and the federal interest. A national bank issuing notes on a national basis "would directly interfere with the rights of the states to prohibit as well as to establish Banks, and [it would also interfere with] the circulation of [state] bank notes."[23] Madison was correct that the states would not be able to prohibit the paper of the national bank; but they could (and did) continue to charter their own banks to issue "local" paper.

The other half of the state-federal argument, given by John Laurence of New York, was that if the law for a national bank interfered with state laws, "the particular interest of a State must give way to the general interest."[24] Not much more can be said on either side of this argument except that each event involving a conflict of interests must be decided on its own merits. In the case of paper currency issue, hindsight would support the efficacy in exchanges that results from a uniform currency. Whether such issues must or should be made by a national bank is yet another question.

Madison had additional, powerful arguments. The right of Congress to establish a bank, he stated, was a logical precedent for Congress to incorporate any other business. Then, in a passage notable especially for its insight into the kind of expansion central banks might one day assume, he said: "If . . . Congress, by virtue of the power to borrow, can create the means of lending, and, in pursuance of these means, can incorporate a Bank, they may do any thing whatever creative of like means . . . If again, Congress by virtue of the power to borrow money, can create the ability to lend, they may, by virtue of the power to levy money, create the ability to pay it."[25]

The proponents of the bank rested their case on the powers implied by the Constitution. The principal clauses cited were the powers of Congress to borrow money and to lay and collect taxes. Especially important was the aid the bank would furnish in making available quick credit to the Treasury in time of emergency. "If we have not the power to establish [the bank]," said Fisher Ames of Massachusetts, "our social compact is incomplete, we want the means of self-preservation."[26]

The only monetary power implied by the Constitution is the clause instructing Congress to coin money and regulate its value. "Money" at that time and for a good while afterward was presumed to include only gold and silver coin. Since bank paper was not money, Congress did not have the power to regulate it.[27] The pretense of this syllogism was carried on until about 1830, and for much longer by some purists. Nevertheless, a uniform paper currency could be promoted in 1790 without an implication of treason; and several statements in support of this function by the First Bank, including Hamilton's "Report," were made. Adam Smith's authority was cited twice in the House debate in favor of the bank-issued currency and once against it. The debates demonstrated a sharp distinction between paper currency issued as an economical substitute for specie, based on specie, and convertible into specie, and paper money issued in order to regulate trade. The issue of specie-based currency need be nothing more than the substitution of an economical medium of exchange for a more expensive one; but the issue of currency to control trade is a true central banking operation. Some congressmen had cited the power of Congress to regulate trade as an argument for the bank. "But what has this bill to do with trade? Would any plain man suppose that this bill had anything to do with trade?" Madison asked rhetorically.[28] The same disclaimer was made by Fisher Ames, an outspoken supporter of the bank. While he was much in favor of the bank's possible utility in furnishing a national currency, "he would not pause to examine" its power to regulate inland bills of exchange and bank paper as the instruments of such trade. Such a power would be "an injury and wrong which [would] violate the right of another."[29]

The First Bank was promoted both as a private commercial bank and as a public (or national) bank, but not as a central bank. It would serve as a fiscal agent to the Treasury; it would issue a uniform national paper currency based on commercial credit; and it would furnish credit to the government, perhaps soaking up long-term government debt as a "permanent" investment. It definitely would not increase or decrease its issues of paper money as a means of stabilizing trade. It passed both houses of Congress by two-to-one majorities in 1791 and was incorporated much along the lines of Hamilton's original plan.

The impression from the scanty evidence on the operations of the First Bank compiled by John Thom Holdsworth is that it used its public position discreetly. The dividends it paid were somewhat more modest than those of competing commercial banks, and the market value of its stock showed at best no appreciation even before its recharter became an issue. Meanwhile, the market values of its competitors' stock increased considerably. The bank and its branches had over half of total bank-held specie ($5 million of a total of about $10 million) in 1811. This amount gave it a specie reserve that was 37 percent of its outstanding demand obligations and almost 50 percent of its capital and surplus.[30] It might therefore have generated considerably more credit and demand obligations than it actually did.

The First Bank in its public aspect was both a creditor and a debtor of the government, a creditor because it held government debt and a debtor because it held government deposits. Gradually its government deposits became much greater than its government debt. In fact, government debt outstanding was reduced by about 50 percent between 1804 and 1812, while the First Bank's holdings of federal debt dropped from $6.20 million to $2.23 million. This change reduced in large measure the function of the bank as a sustainer of government credit.

The final comment of the study by Holdsworth was that the bank had been managed with extreme caution—too much so "for its full usefulness to the business community and its returns to the stockholders."[31] At the same time other factors prevented the bank from extending maximum credit. First, its position as a public bank required it to hold a fairly high fraction of specie reserves in anticipation of demands for these funds by the government. Second, aggressive lending operations by the bank would have emphasized its enviable position as a receptacle for public deposits. A growing volume of private bank competition in the decade 1800-1810 made this inhibition more pertinent.

The First Bank's relationship to the growing number of commercial banks became invidious despite careful efforts by the bank's managers to restrain its activities. Both the Bank of England and the First Bank had so much private business, observed Bray Hammond, that their "public function was to many persons quite unapparent except as usurpation and privilege."[32]

The relatively high reserve ratio maintained by the First Bank, as well as the sheer dollar volume of its reserves, suggests the possibility of its development as a central bank, albeit with limited powers. It felt constrained from operating purely for profit, and its very size meant that it willy-nilly would have a significant influence on the volume of bank credit. For such an institution to have been in this strategic position and then to have adopted an attitude of "no policy" would have denied the utility of human management. It would have denied the ability of human intervention to make a good thing work better.

The First Bank's central banking functions became manifest through its currency transactions with other banks. If it felt that credit restraint was called for, it would present the notes of other banks for redemption in specie. If it felt that credit ease was in order, it expanded its own credit availability to businesses and to other banks and generally treated the notes of other banks with "forebearance." It was able to manage such effects because much money went through its offices in fulfillment of its fiscal aids to the government and because it kept a reserve balance large enough to maneuver in this way. It may not have seemed much more than a primus inter pares to the state banks; but it must have looked much more primus than pares when it was able to curtail the credit activities of these banks by acquiring the public deposits they might have had.

The First Bank was first recognized as an emerging central bank by the directors. Their "memorial" to the Senate in 1810 arguing for recharter clearly implied that the bank had acted as a central bank and that its actions were beneficial. The bank, they said, had been a "general guardian of commercial credit, and by preventing the balance of trade in the different States from producing a deficiency of money in any, has obviated the mischiefs which would have been thereby produced. It has fostered and protected the banking institutions of the States, and has aided them when unexpectedly pressed."[33]

Another memorial to the Senate from the Philadelphia Chamber of Commerce imputed a similar desirable central banking effect to the First Bank's operations by the unavoidably "great and constant accumulation of paper of other banks in its vaults." During the banking crisis of 1810, the memorial continued, the bank had "diffused its accommodations to the greatest extent."[34]

Henry Clay in the Senate also demonstrated awareness of the bank's central banking potential, but he believed that such power demanded restraint rather than license. The bank, he argued, had been chartered to assist the Treasury in its fiscal functions and should have done nothing more. "It is mockery," he exclaimed heatedly, "worse than usurpation, to establish [the bank] for a lawful object, and then extend to it other objects which are not lawful . . . You say to this organization, we cannot authorize you to discount—to emit paper—to regulate commerce, etc. No! Our book has no precedents of that kind. But then we can authorize you to collect the revenue, and, while occupied with that, you may do whatever else you please!"[35]

Clay's statement provides a sharp contrast between the Federalist thought for which he was such an astute spokesman and the Democratic attitude as manifested by Secretaries of the Treasury Albert Gallatin and William Crawford.[36] Gallatin advocated the bank's continued existence and urged renewal of its charter for the usual fiscal reasons in 1809, but he was forced to phrase his brief for the bank's usefulness in sustaining the government's credit in the past perfect tense: "The bank had heretofore been eminently useful in making the advances which . . . were necessary . . . And a similar disposition has been repeatedly evinced whenever the aspect of public affairs has rendered it proper to ascertain whether new loans might, if wanted, be obtained."[37] Otherwise, it was a good bank. It had kept the public moneys safely, it had transferred government payments efficiently, and it had aided in collection of the revenues. In 1810, Gallatin noted, the bank had supplied short-term funds to the government, thus avoiding the necessity of an increase in "permanent" debt outstanding.[38]

Unlike Clay, Gallatin at this time evinced no recognition of any regulatory monetary powers in the First Bank. He saw only its ancillary and subordinate role to Treasury operations. Later Clay and his party would embrace the central bank as a desirable and utilitarian organization; while the Democrats, on finding that a central bank was loose in the land, would conduct a campaign of extermination.

The First Bank, by reason of an organization that included branches and by reason of its legal relationship to the government, was undoubtedly a more enthusiastic supporter of government credit than the state banks would have been. This factor was emphasized in a letter from Gallatin to Crawford, who was then chairman of the Senate Committee on Finance. The state banks could manage the government's funds, Gallatin said, "without any insuperable difficulty." But the First Bank was generally safer since it was responsible for all the deposits in its separate branches.[39]

Crawford took the case for renewal of the bank's charter to the Senate. He urged Gallatin's authority, even though he knew that Gallatin was unpopular with many senators. He also stressed the bank's aid in the fiscal operations of the government; and he pointed out that the opposition to renewal of the charter came from state legislatures. These bodies wanted the First Bank compromised so that the state banks, in which the states themselves had extensive stock holdings, would profit by the deposit of federal government moneys.[40]

Crawford was correct, but other nonfiscal and nonmonetary factors were also important. The continuing question of the bank's constitutionality and the alleged dominance of British stockholders contributed to the indecisive one-vote margin by which the bill for renewal of the bank's charter was laid on the table "indefinitely"—forever.[41]

2. Treasury Policy, 1811-1820

> The power of the federal Government to institute and regulate [the monetary system] must . . . be deemed . . . an exclusive power.
> (*American State Papers Finance*, 1815)

One of the most persistent myths of monetary policy is that a central (or quasi-central) bank provides stability and order to a financial system in a period of stress or "emergency" and that without a central bank the system disintegrates into chaos. The prime example for this contention in the United States is the series of financial events that occurred in the period 1811-1820. The year 1811 marked the end of the First Bank of the United States; the interval 1812-1815 included the years of the War of 1812; 1816-1818 saw the Second Bank become operational; the final years of this period, 1818-1820, were marked by a severe crisis or "panic" and subsequent recovery.

The myth that has come to govern analysis of the monetary-fiscal happenings in the United States between 1811 and 1820 is usually told along the following lines. The First Bank of the United States was created in 1791 with a charter permitting it to operate for twenty years. This institution early showed its propensities as a central bank, most particularly by controlling the flow of state bank notes that passed through its offices on their way to being redeemed or "cleared" in specie by the state banks.[1] Unfortunately, shortsighted policy by national leaders in 1810-11 allowed the First Bank to expire just as a national emergency developed. When war actually occurred between England and the United States in June 1812, the federal government did not have the services of a central bank. Consequently, fiscal and monetary policies were conducted on an ad hoc basis. The inordinate demands of the war caused government expenditures to increase substantially, while ordinary revenues declined. The resulting fiscal deficits put a heavy administrative burden on the Treasury Department.

Having no First Bank to assist it, the Treasury financed its expenditures as best it could through the state banks. The number of state banks mushroomed. Without the central banking restraint of the First Bank, "the state banks would neither pay specie nor accept each other's notes at par, ... and hence, the government was forced to receive its revenues in state-bank paper and treasury notes of all degrees of depreciation."[2] Inflation developed from the proliferation of banks and the concurrent expansion of bank credit. After the war ended, the government instituted a new central bank, the Second Bank of the United States. This new bank, in cooperation with the Treasury Department and by skillful technique or the art of central banking, was able to induce the state banks to resume specie payments, and ultimately it was able to provide a uniform and sound currency for the economy.[3]

This traditional analysis includes at least the following errors of judgment or omissions of pertinent details:

(1) an almost complete failure to notice or account for the inflationary issues of treasury notes during the period 1812-1817; (2) a similar lack of attention to the influence that the retirement of these same notes had on the recession of 1819 and on the resumption of specie payments; (3) the incorrect or highly questionable allegation that the presence of a central bank would have prevented either the proliferation of state banks or the inflation; (4) the idea that mere multiplication of banks promotes or causes inflation.

When the War of 1812 began, just one year after the end of operations by the First Bank, the increase in the federal government's expenditures to wage the war generated a fiscal deficit that Congress attempted to meet by authorizing sales of government securities. The loan was taken up by the public and banks so slowly, however, that the government resorted to an issue of treasury notes.

Treasury notes were endowed with a combination of characteristics that permitted them to be issued as nonmoney by the government, but also allowed them to be regarded as money by the people who held them. They bore interest—in the case of the 1812 issue 5 2/5 percent per year—so they were interest-earning assets to the public. They were also short-term, that is, redeemable in one year; but they could be used to pay all duties, taxes, or debts of the United States until redeemed.[4] Thus they were legal tender for all government transactions and quasi-legal tender in all private transactions. They could be used as hand-to-hand currency, although the denominations in which they were issued (none under $100) meant that few would serve in this capacity. They could also be held as interest-earning assets, but they were most useful as bank reserves. What could be more attractive to a bank than reserve assets that were legal tender and yet returned interest income as a part of the bank's investment portfolio?

The first issue of $5 million in treasury notes was authorized in June 1812. The notes were supposed to be redeemable in specie one year after their date of issue; but many of them circulated or were held as bank reserves long after they were due, that is, long after interest accruals had stopped. The total issues authorized and the amounts outstanding during the period 1813-1817 are shown in table 2.1.

Specie in the banking system during this same period amounted to between $5 million and $10 million. Table 2.2 shows specie and the other major assets and liabilities of reporting incorporated banks in the United States, as compiled by J. Van Fenstermaker. While this table covers only part of the banking system, it includes most of the specie-paying (New England) banks. It does not include treasury notes in either the specie or notes columns so far as can be determined. Thus if the specie entries are good approximations to the total specie actually in the banks, the outstanding volumes of treasury notes were 27 percent of the total specie

TABLE 2.1 Authorizations and outstanding issues of treasury notes, 1812-1817.

Authorized by act of	Total issued ($ millions)	Cumulative total of issues outstanding ($ millions)	As of or near
June 20, 1812	5.00	2.84	Jan. 1, 1813
Feb. 25, 1813	5.00	4.91	Jan. 1, 1814
Mar. 4, 1814	10.00	8.00[1]	Sept. 30, 1814
Dec. 26, 1814	8.23	10.65	Jan. 1, 1815
Feb. 24, 1815			
($100 notes)	4.42		
(Small notes)	3.39	15.46	Jan. 1, 1816
		8.73	Aug. 1, 1816
		0.64	Sept. 30, 1817

Source: *ASPF*, 3, pp. 23, 32, 70, 79, 103, 136, 229.
1. Approximate value.

TABLE 2.2. Principal assets, liabilities, and number of reporting incorporated banks in the United States, and total treasury notes outstanding, 1809-1818 (dollar values in millions).

Date[1] (June-Dec.)	Chartered banks	Reporting banks No.	Reporting banks %	Loans and discounts ($)	Specie ($)	Total bank notes in circulation ($)	Individual deposits ($)	Total notes and deposits ($)	Treasury notes outstanding ($)
1809	92	31	34	12.63	1.99	3.80	2.91	6.71	—
1810	102	30	29	14.69	2.49	5.58	4.22	9.80	—
1811	117	30	26	16.22	2.57	5.68	5.27	10.95	—
1812	143	32	22	17.94	5.70	6.32	7.43	13.75	2.84
1813	147	39	27	21.65	7.72	7.23	10.44	17.67	4.91
1814	202	63	31	36.74	9.29	13.69	15.76	29.45	10.65
1815	212	98	46	44.07	5.40	19.91	11.67	31.58	15.46
1816	232	91	39	40.46	4.74	17.22	9.14	26.36	8.73
1817	262	100	38	32.76	4.79	13.31	9.66	22.97	0.64
1818	338	147	44	48.24	5.47	18.07	9.65	27.72	—

Source: J. Van Fenstermaker, *A Statistical Summary of the Commercial Banks Incorporated in the United States prior to 1819*, (Kent, Ohio: Bureau of Economics and Business Research, Kent State University, (1965), p. 5.

Note: Van Fenstermaker's statistics on the banking system seem to be as good as are obtainable. However, the number and percentage of *reporting* banks more than tripled between 1812 and 1817, probably because of improvements in communications, growth in the number of banks, and the use of commercial banks as government depositories. Therefore the growth in the values cited, especially in the specie item, is biased upward. Many of the banks included in this table enjoyed specie inflows from other banks in the economy (because of interregional balance of payments surpluses) and did not suspend specie payments.

1. Reports from banks were not available at a point in time, such as June 30 or December 31. For expediency's sake, the time for each year's data had to be an interval, and the six-month period of June to December was chosen by Van Fenstermaker. The column showing treasury notes outstanding (taken from table 2.1) is synchronized with the bank data as closely as possible, discontinuous data and the judgment of the author permitting.

and treasury notes (that is, of all bank reserves) by 1813 and 75 percent by 1816. Even with large errors in the available data, treasury notes had to be a significant fraction of total bank reserves. This contention is also suggested by John Jay Knox's investigation and his remark, "The banks would give the Government credit for [the notes] and in return the Government could draw gold and silver from the banks."[5]

Secretary of the Treasury G. W. Campbell in his report for 1814 observed that of approximately $8 million of treasury notes in circulation at that time, only about $6 million could be circulated "without embarrassment" if past monetary experience was any guide.[6] Campbell made this judgment on the basis of the amount of bank currency being supplied before the issues of treasury notes and on the assumption that an infusion of one type of money—treasury notes in this case—would necessitate the expulsion of another kind, such as specie.

The economy was indeed embarrassed. Specie payments had been suspended by all banks except those in New England, so "the circulating medium of the country . . . [was] placed upon a new and uncertain footing." Campbell looked to Congress for a solution to this problem, all the while seemingly oblivious to the possibility that the treasury notes were the fundamental cause of the currency "redundancy."[7]

The usual account of the inflation of 1814-1817 stresses as a primary cause the large number of banks that came into existence with the demise of the First Bank. As table 2.2 shows, the annual rate of growth in the number of banks was highly variable after 1811. The rate of growth was negligible in 1812-13 when no public bank existed, and one of the greatest rates of growth occurred during 1817-18 after the Second Bank was in operation. Thus the mere existence of a United States bank could not have exerted a fundamental effect on the number of state banks.

A more technical criticism of this thesis is that the mere *number* of banks is virtually unrelated to inflation. Claiming that they are related is analogous to asserting that the distance a vehicle travels depends on the number of wheels it has rather than on the amount of fuel propelling it. Inflation in all known and measurable cases has resulted from significant increases in the quantity of money. During the period 1814-1817 the large increase in the quantity of money was activated by the creation and circulation of treasury notes. These note reserves were the fuel that moved the vehicle; the number of banks was both incidental and irrelevant to the inflation that developed. The existence of a public bank made little difference, if the experience of the British economy under a Bank of England during 1797-1820 and the experience of the United States economy under the Federal Reserve system in the twentieth century are valid evidence to the contrary.

The myth that the government was innocent of the inflation and corresponding suspension of specie payments by the banking system was continued by Secretary of the Treasury A. J. Dallas. In his report for 1815 Dallas noted that the banks south and west of New England had ceased specie payments. "In this act," he declared, "the Government of the United States had no participation." Not only are the state banks responsible for inflation and the suspension of specie payments, but it is with them that "the measures for restoring the national currency of gold and silver must originate." He expressed the hope "that the issue of bank paper [would] soon be reduced to its just share in the circulating medium of the country." The Treasury "from necessity" had been accepting bank paper, "but the period approaches, when it will probably become a duty to exact the payment [of government dues] either in Treasury notes, or in gold and silver coin, the lawful money of the United States."[8]

The use of treasury notes primarily as bank reserves made their effect on prices even more pronounced than their use as hand-to-hand currency. As banks increased their holdings of treasury notes, their own note issues could increase by multiples of the treasury notes obtained. Bank notes were thus used as hand-to-hand currency, and the treasury notes were used mainly as bank reserves in lieu of specie.[9] (See figure 2.1.)

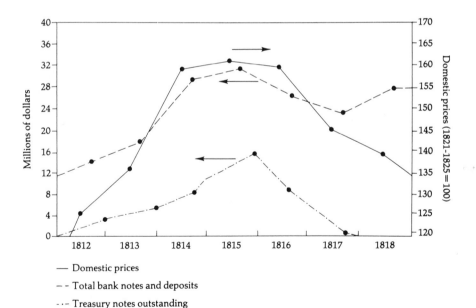

— Domestic prices

– – Total bank notes and deposits

- · – Treasury notes outstanding

FIGURE 2.1. Total bank notes and deposits, treasury notes outstanding, and prices, 1812-1818. Domestic commodity prices are from *Historical Statistics*, Series E69, p. 119 (Bezanson). For bank notes and deposits and treasury notes, see table 2.2.

The monetary effects on the economy were just what should have been expected. Prices rose as the quantity of money increased. The market prices of gold and silver as commodities tended to do likewise. But since the mint prices of gold and silver were fixed by statute, their mint values tended to be cheaper than their market prices. The consequence was that specie moved where the price-specie flow mechanism directed it, that is, where paper money was not inflated. Besides flowing to foreign countries, much of the specie went to New England. The banks there, as Secretary of the Treasury Crawford later observed, were "fettered by the stipulations of their charters . . . Their issues of notes have been very limited, and the necessities [sic] for a circulating medium have been principally supplied by Treasury notes . . . Government revenue . . . has been, almost entirely, collected in Treasury notes."[10] Unlike the bank notes of other regions, the bank notes of most New England banks were at par in specie and therefore at a *premium* over treasury notes.

By 1816, the Treasury Department kept as many as four accounts with each depository bank: (1) cash, meaning local currency; (2) notes issued by other banks and held as a credit to the Treasury, but not at par with local currency; (3) treasury notes that bore interest; and (4) treasury notes that did not bear interest.[11] The Treasury, reported Crawford in 1816, was obliged to accept all bank note currency. A requisition for coin payments would generate distress in private business and result in general liquidation and bank failures,[12] but resumption had to take place. The questions then were, How would the government initiate it, and how could it be carried out so that distress to the private economy was minimized?

The general drift of governmental policy had been established by Secretary Dallas, Crawford's predecessor, when he declared that the state banks would have to reduce their outstanding amounts of paper money, "but the interposition of Government will still be required to secure a successful result."[13] The possible "interposition" of the government Dallas had in mind was the creation of another bank of the United States that might facilitate resumption by absorbing some of the outstanding national debt in its capital structure.

In his brief for a new United States bank in 1815, Dallas felt obliged to discuss the monetary situation generally. Notes of the First Bank, he stated, had been declared receivable by law for all debts due the government. "Treasury notes," he continued, "which have been since issued for the services of the late war, have been endowed with the same quality."[14] Dallas found a defense for issuing treasury notes in the "adequacy" of the "motive" that prompted them. The government's motive had been its incurrence of fiscal deficits, payments for which could be anticipated from future revenues. The war over, fiscal budgets would be balanced and no government "motive" for issuing paper money would remain.[15] A national bank, however, could assume the note-issuing function. Since its notes would be partial legal tender in the same fashion as treasury notes, they would be received uniformly everywhere; and since the bank would be chartered by act of Congress, "the sovereign authority of Congress relative to the coin and currency of the United States" would be preserved.[16]

Unfortunately, the irresponsible state banks posed a problem to the stability and soundness of the system. The government had to accept the paper currency that these banks had so capriciously created. To do otherwise, wrote Crawford a year or so later, would "visit the sins [sic] of the banks upon the great mass of unoffending citizens."[17] In virtually the same language as Dallas he then declared: "To restore the national currency of gold and silver it is essential that the quantity of bank paper in circulation should be reduced . . . By reducing the amount of bank paper its value must be proportionably increased."[18]

The national bank would further this process. Since it would open its doors on a specie-paying basis, it would not need to resume, only to commence. The state banks would have to cooperate by restraining their issues, but such cooperation would be rewarded. "It will be proper to apprize them," Dallas said pointedly, "that, after a specified day, the notes of such banks as have not resumed their payments in the current coin will not be received in payments, either to the Government or to the national bank." At the same time, he suggested some compensation for their cooperation. "It will be peculiarly incumbent upon the national bank, as well as the Treasury," he said, "to conciliate the state banks; to confide to them, liberally, a participation in the deposits of public revenue, and to encourage them in every reasonable effort to resume the payment of their notes in coin."[19]

Dallas's views were presumably official. The national bank he envisaged would function as an auxiliary of treasury policy. It would be the shepherd in the field keeping the flock both disciplined and nourished. It would be "responsible" to Congress, but also "independent" of Congress. Dallas specifically denied the possibility of governmental interference. "Whatever accommodation the Treasury may have occasion to ask from the bank can only be asked under the license of law; and whatever accommodation shall be obtained must be obtained from the voluntary assent of the directors acting under the responsibility of their trust."[20]

Five years earlier David Ricardo had observed a Bank of England operating in the mode anticipated for the Bank of the United States. His perceptive comment on the relationship of a central bank to its govern-

ment stands as a caution for all time. "It may be questioned," he remarked, "whether a bank lending many millions more to Government
than its capital and savings can be called independent of that Government."[21]

The new bank bill went through Congress early in 1816 and was approved by President Madison on April 10. The first president of the bank
was William Jones, a pedestrian politician who had previously held cabinet posts in a temporary capacity. Almost simultaneously Secretary Dallas was succeeded in office by Crawford, a prestigious politician who had
been chairman of the Senate Finance Committee and who would have
been president of the United States in 1824 except for a sudden and debili-
tating illness.

The long series of communications between Crawford and Jones re-
flects both the order of the monetary decision-making process and the
contemporary official concept of the Second Bank. Crawford was clearly
the dominant master and Jones the obsequious man in this exchange.

A popular prejudice of the times was that if *all* the banks and the government simply agreed to resume specie payments at the same time, ipso
facto resumption would be accomplished. This optimistic belief was
based on the correct presumption that all money prices and wages are
merely nominal. It was also based on the faulty inference that all prices
and wages can be cried up or cried down by popular voice if the voice is
unanimous, without regard to the level of the current cost-price structure
as determined by an existing stock of money. While unanimity is always
impossible to obtain in practice, the real flaw in this reasoning was that
many interest-bearing fixed-dollar claims and money wages had been
contracted for later payment on the then-current value of money. Any
decline in the general price level, therefore, was bound to hurt debtors
and residual-income claimants and to enrich creditors. It would also enhance both the value and the utility of the money stock beyond what
people wanted them to be. Therefore price level adjustment by decree, or
jawbone price control as it is now called, simply could not and would not
take place. It was and is King Canute railing at the waves.

The commercial banks were described by Jones in 1817 as being "not
only solvent but rich in surplus funds and resources."[22] The implication
was that they could resume specie payments if only they wished to do so.
Secretary Crawford, in contrast, recognized a fundamental interrelation-
ship between the outstanding stock of treasury notes, the "overissues" of
state bank notes, and the obstacles these moneys posed to a genuine
policy of resumption. To effect resumption, he promised Jones, the government would withhold "from circulation as much of their paper now in
the Treasury . . . as the demands upon the Treasury during the ensuing
year will permit . . . As the sum which it will be in the power of the Government to retain in the Treasury will be considerable, it may present a

sufficient inducement [to the state banks] to change their determination not to resume specie payments before the first day of July next [1817]."[23]

A circular to all the depository banks was issued by Crawford on December 20, 1816. The essence of this announcement was that the Bank of the United States would commence operations on January 1, 1817, but that the public funds would not be transferred to it if the state banks would agree to resume specie payments on February 20, 1817, in conjunction with the Second Bank's "commencement." If the banks were agreeable, treasury balances with them would be reduced only gradually to pay public dues. The bank, Crawford reassured the state banks, must be "friendly" to them: "The deep interest which the Treasury has in the support of bank credit . . . would . . . be sufficient to protect [the state banks] against an illiberal policy on [the] part [of the Bank of the United States]."[24]

In June 1817 Crawford sent out another circular about treasury notes to all depository banks, urging that all such notes be canceled and returned to the Treasury. As late as November 1817 substantial amounts of notes were still outstanding despite Crawford's pleas and reports to the contrary.[25]

Table 2.3 shows the monetary-fiscal flows experienced by the Treasury

TABLE 2.3. Federal fiscal expenditures and receipts and cash balance position of the treasury, 1812-1821 (expenditures and receipts in millions of dollars per year; cash balance in millions of dollars.)

Calendar year	Ordinary receipts[1]	Ordinary expenditures[1]	Treasury cash balance (near Jan. 1)		
			Treasury notes	Bank notes	Total
1812	9.80	20.28	—	3.95[2]	3.95
1813	14.34	31.68	—	2.36[2]	2.36
1814	11.18	34.72	—	5.20	5.20
1815	15.73	32.71	—	1.53	1.53
1816	47.69	30.59	6.36	6.75	13.11
1817	33.10	21.84	10.67	11.30	21.97
1818	21.59	19.83	8.81	6.18	14.99
1819	24.60	21.46	—	1.45	1.45
1820	17.88	18.26	—	2.08	2.08
1821	14.57	15.81	—	1.20	1.20

Sources: *Historical Statistics,* Series Y-259 and Y-350, pp. 712 and 719, for fiscal receipts and expenditures. *Treasury Reports* for the years indicated, *ASPF* 2 and 3, for cash balances.
1. Does not include debt flotations or reductions.
2. Near October 1 of year indicated.

in this period and the Treasury's cash balance at the beginning of each year. During the war, up to the beginning of 1815, expenditures outran receipts by two or three to one. Issues of treasury notes made up for some of this deficit. Peacetime conditions dramatically reversed this pattern. As receipts soared past expenditures in 1816, the Treasury accumulated a large balance of bank notes and treasury notes. The treasury notes still in circulation (largely in banks) were ordered returned to the Treasury, and the federal government's balances in depository banks were correspondingly debited.

The retirement of treasury notes was both a necessary and a sufficient condition to force the contraction of bank credit and of bank note currency and to provoke a general deflation. Prices started declining in 1818, after having been stable for two years, and fell 30 percent in the next three years.[26]

The new Bank of the United States could do nothing about the quantity of treasury notes in existence. The Treasury Department had sole responsibility for their issue and retirement. In an attempt to get state bank agreement on resumption in early 1817, the new bank agreed (1) to accept responsibility to the government for the public deposits held by the state banks, but to refrain from demanding redemption of these deposits from the state banks until July 1, 1817, and (2) to discount $6 million of paper for either individuals or banks before any other balances against state banks were called for.[27]

The letters of William Jones, the president of the bank, to Secretary Crawford reveal Jones's principal tenets: (1) The bank should be operated profitably for its stockholders (including the government). (2) It should set a good example by paying specie on demand for its notes. (3) It would have to make concessions to the state banks to prevent invidious feelings on their part. Jones clearly did not realize that the structure of bank credit and the cost-price framework would have to suffer a general contraction for resumption to be genuine, universal, and permanent. Under his direction the bank acted as if it were a large bank constrained to indulge the state banks, as the Treasury Department had implied it should. When the Treasury pinched the money supply by wholesale retirements of treasury notes in 1816-17, the bank compensated in part for Treasury austerity by expanding credit in accordance with concessions it had made to the state banks to encourage their resumption of specie payments, apparently without realizing that it could not contradict treasury policy. On balance the bank absorbed notes of state banks on government account, *agreeing not to demand specie for the notes from the state banks.* It then paid out its own notes convertible into specie.[28] This process could not go on indefinitely, and the inevitable shakedown was going to be severe.

Crawford was the entrepreneur-architect of the deflation and of subsequent resumption. He understood what had to be done; he had the power to do it; and he had enough bureaucratic hypocrisy to carry out what was bound to be an austere and unpleasant policy. He somewhat prematurely congratulated himself and the bank for the shaky resumption that was in effect during 1817. The bank had assisted in this process, Crawford told its directors in a letter, despite resistance from the state banks, who felt that "the circulation of their paper is contracted within narrower limits than heretofore." This complaint was natural, he allowed, but the bank need have nothing to fear from the state banks so long as it continued to make facilities available "to the commercial class which it has amply furnished from the commencement of its operation."[29]

If 1817 was the preparation for monetary fasting and cleansing, 1818 was penitence. One manifestation of the coming recession was the state banks' hesitation to pay specie when requested by the Bank of the United States. This development raised the question of whether the bank or the Treasury was responsible for the redeemability of notes received by the depository banks to the credit of the government. Jones complained to Crawford that the bank was paying out specie on demand for its notes, "whilst the banks, our debtors, plead inability, require unreasonable indulgence, or treat our reiterated claims and expostulations with settled indifference."[30] The Treasury, Jones continued in another letter to Crawford, had made "suggestions of forebearance" to the Second Bank on the collections of state bank notes. The bank, however, "is bound to receive and transfer but not collect the public money. A state bank note is nothing more than a bill at sight, payable to the bearer at the place of location; it is not money. Many banks have recently failed; many more will certainly fail." Many "specie banks (so called)," he noted bitterly, were unwilling or unable to liquidate their debts to the bank, or even to prevent their increase. He concluded with a final despairing (and revealing) complaint. The public money was to have been deposited with the bank and its branches. However, the unexpended public money in the offices of the Treasury had not been so deposited. "If these deposits were faithfully made and kept in the bank and its branches it would have a salutary effect. They are now made to operate directly to the prejudice of this institution."[31]

Well might Jones say so. Not only had the public moneys in the form of treasury notes been withheld and retired, but the policy was contrived, purposeful, and deliberate. The Treasury Department was indeed the central bank.

Crawford answered his subordinate with contemptuous brusqueness. On Jones's "intimation that the Government has prepared a crisis by the legitimate employment of the public money in payment of the public debt," he wrote, "comment is considered unnecessary." (He nevertheless commented, albeit briefly.) The interests of the Second Bank and of the state banks had to be weighed against the interests of the community. Treasury notes were part of the public debt. Their retirement was likewise retirement of that debt and was thus in the interest of the community. This advantage had to be balanced against the beneficial effects the Bank and banks would experience if the notes were redeposited in banks and used as reserves.[32] With these dicta, he dismissed the case.

Retirement of treasury notes was the equivalent of a contemporary central bank open-market sale that erases bank reserves. In truth, it was the kind of harsh action that had to be taken if resumption was to be accomplished. The alternative was to maintain price level stability at the inflated plateau then current. Bankers who were unable to resume specie payments would have preferred treasury support of bank credit. In this case, however, the maintenance of the gold standard system at the pre-war parity was considered worth some sacrifices, especially if the sacrifices were borne by banks that had "overtraded" and "speculated" in the first place.

Jones's account of the bank's problems demonstrated the frictions involved in the resumption process. The Treasury used the bank's credit to obfuscate its basic policy of contracting the money supply. This role made the bank the target for complaints by those who were most seriously hurt, namely, banks that issued bank notes and people who used bank notes. The bank's directors were no better able to tolerate this pressure than anyone else. Their attempted solution was to accept media of exchange that might or might not be the equivalent of specie; for what constituted a specie equivalent was a matter of judgment.

The price level decline of 1818-1820 that resulted in full-scale resumption was accompanied by the usual symptoms of failing banks and business hardships. Crawford may have had the only overall view of what was actually going on. The pressure now on the banks, he stated in his report for 1818, resulted from "the excessive issues of the banks during the suspension of specie payments, and the great exportation of the precious metals to the East Indies during the present year." The banks then found that they were forced "to contract their discounts for the purpose of withdrawing from circulation a large proportion of their notes. This operation, so oppressive to their debtors, but indispensably necessary to the existence of specie payments, must be continued until gold and silver shall form a just proportion of the circulating medium." If the depression became too severe, Crawford hedged, the Treasury might again be forced to issue treasury notes![33]

The dramatic fall in the price level and in business activity provoked a congressional committee to ask for a report from Secretary Crawford on the relation of the Bank of the United States and other banks to the currency. Crawford's reply to this inquiry absolved the Bank of the United States of any responsibility for the inflation or subsequent depression. The bank, stated Crawford, was "a passive agent in the hands of the Government [read, Treasury]."[34]

The last section of the congressional inquiry seemed to question the necessity of a specie standard. It asked Crawford to "suggest such measures as, in his opinion, may be expedient to procure a circulating medium, in place of specie, adapted to the exigencies of the country, and within the power of the Government."[35] That such a request could be made at all is indeed surprising in view of the sanctimony with which the ideal of a specie standard had come to be regarded. Early legislators may have been more experimental than reputed!

Crawford replied forthrightly that such a question would be only academic "if the power of Congress over the currency [were] not absolutely sovereign . . . The general prosperity [welfare] will not be advanced by demonstrating that there is no intrinsic obstacle to the substitution of a paper for a metallic currency, if the power to adopt the substitute has been withheld from the Federal Government."[36] In short, Congress's very act of inquiring implied that the constitutional power, at least, was available for the development of a paper currency system. Crawford had declared unequivocally under other circumstances that "[t]he power of the Government over the currency [must] be absolutely sovereign."[37] The primary obstacle to the establishment of a paper currency, in his opinion, was neither the lack of right nor the lack of power, but "the danger of the instability [inconsistency?] and want of integrity and intelligence of the Government." Division of powers between federal and state governments also allowed for the possibility of "collisions" in jurisdictional controls over the monetary system. On these grounds Crawford rested his case against a paper money issued by the government. He was not opposed to a paper currency issued by banks. In fact he advocated such a system. In the mode of most "mixed-currency" spokesmen, he recommended that the paper currency be issued by commercial banks so that it would be coordinated with the growth of trade. The quantity could be constrained, he felt, by requiring that the paper money be convertible into specie on demand.[38]

"Resumption was an achievement and the Secretary's own," Bray Hammond has written. "Central banking policy was more intelligently developed in the Treasury than in the central bank itself."[39] Hammond's appraisal contains both explicit truth and implicit error. Crawford was indeed the central banker who promoted deflation-resumption after the treasury note issues of his predecessors had provoked inflation-suspension. But the Second Bank of the United States was not yet the central bank that it would become under the leadership of Nicholas Biddle. In this early era the bank proved to be nothing more than a convenient buffer for the unpalatable but "necessary" policies initiated by the Treasury Department.

3. Central Banking Growth of the Second Bank

> That the [Second] bank adds facilities to trade and commerce generally, and, to a certain extent, regulates the course of exchange, will not be questioned: but does that justify Congress in erecting a broker's shop to do what is the business of individual enterprise, and the natural channel of trade itself? (McDuffie Report, House of Representatives, 1830)

Scholars have almost universally neglected the emergence of many central banking institutions and concepts, but they have more than made up for this oversight in their specific studies on the Second Bank of the United States. Books and articles on both this institution and its most illustrious president, Nicholas Biddle, abound—to the extent, in fact, that little can be added. The obvious case for research on such a glamorous institution has cast a penumbra around other historical monetary areas worthy of study. The Second Bank, though short-lived, became one of the most notable examples of incipient central banking during the nineteenth century.

Bray Hammond has argued that the function of the early American commercial banking system was to furnish the economy with the credit it "needed" to grow, while the central bank's primary role was to stabilize the banking system. Hammond's general thesis is that the Second Bank, and to some extent the First Bank, was *intended* by its more sophisticated sponsors to stabilize the unrestrained state banking system; that under Nicholas Biddle in the 1820s the Second Bank fulfilled this role; but that its potential usefulness was cut short in the 1830s by the ignorant and acquisitive segment of society led by the Jackson administration. Enlightened central banking thought and action in the United States, Hammond concludes, were thus stifled until the organization of the Federal Reserve system in 1913.[1] (W. B. Smith shares this view in his book on the Second Bank.[2])

Though based on extensive and competent research, none of the books on the Second Bank confirms the thesis that this institution was created in the image of a central bank. Like the First Bank, the Second was chartered for the overt and pragmatic function of housing the interest-bearing debt created by the federal government during the War of 1812. After the war ended, the bank was considered a fiscal auxiliary to the Treasury Department; the kind of monetary intervention that a central bank might introduce was dismissed as either undesirable or unconstitutional.[3] When central banking opportunities presented themselves in the early 1820s, for example, the Second Bank was given no license to undertake them. The Treasury's debt retirement policy was such an opportunity. In his report for 1823 Secretary Crawford recommended that Congress authorize the repurchase of a portion of the public debt at a "fair" price (above the par value) with the fiscal surplus of $8.61 million that had accrued to the government that year. He suggested that the commissioners of the sinking fund be appointed as what is now called an "open-market committee" to carry out the repurchase.[4] The bill to repurchase passed routinely, but the Second Bank was not even mentioned. In his report for 1824, Crawford offhandedly remarked that the bank was a useful instrument for assisting in debt flotations and reductions.[5]

Up to this point Secretary Crawford had been directing all the monetary and fiscal policies of the government. Ill health, however, caused him to forego further administrative or political activities. At approximately the same time Nicholas Biddle succeeded Langdon Cheves as president of the Second Bank. During the four years that Cheves had been president, the bank had been a part of and a focal point for the monetary contraction that had resulted in resumption of specie payments. Cheves had thought of the bank as "small" and decentralized. He felt that each branch should be largely autonomous and responsible in specie for only its own notes.[6] He was apparently well read in the economic literature of the time; and the principles of the discipline would indeed have deterred him from allowing the Second Bank any regulatory role. He clearly did not regard it as a central bank. The specie standard had just been reaffirmed by resumption of specie payments, and it—not the bank—was the recognized regulator of the money supply.

Biddle had become a director of the bank in 1819, shortly before Cheves was appointed president. By the time he himself became president in 1823, the Second Bank had been refortified with specie reserves through its public depository role for the government and the severe reduction of its loans and discounts. Not only was its reserve ratio a high 37 percent, but it had about one-half of total bank-held specie. It was also the exclusive collector and depository of government revenues, and its notes were legal tender for all payments to and by the government. This last provision meant that its outstanding notes had the same investiture as the treasury notes issued between 1812 and 1815 and those issued in several other periods before 1860. (See table 3.1)

The 1813-1817 issue of treasury notes was regarded as a distasteful and temporary emergency measure of questioned constitutionality. These notes were at least issued by an agency of the government under congressional authorization, whereas the notes of the Second Bank, were issued

TABLE 3.1. Selected assets and liabilities, and reserve ratios of the Second Bank of the United States, 1817-1840 (millions of dollars).

Year	Loans and dis-counts	Notes of state banks held by Second Bank	Specie	Circula-tion[1]	Deposits[2]	Total circula-tion and deposits	Reserve ratios (%)[3]
1817	3.49	0.59	1.72	1.91	11.23	13.14	13.1
1818	41.18	1.84	2.52	8.34	12.28	20.62	12.2
1819	35.77	1.88	2.67	6.56	5.79	12.35	21.5
1820	31.40	1.44	3.39	3.59	6.57	10.16	33.4
1821	30.91	0.68	7.64	4.57	7.89	12.46	61.3
1822	28.06	0.92	4.76	5.58	8.08	13.66	34.9
1823	30.74	0.77	4.43	4.36	7.62	11.98	37.0
1824	33.43	0.71	5.81	4.65	13.70	18.35	31.7
1825	31.81	1.06	6.75	6.07	12.03	18.10	37.3
1826	33.42	1.11	3.96	9.48	11.21	20.69	19.1
1827	30.94	1.07	6.46	8.55	14.32	22.87	31.1
1828	33.68	1.45	6.17	9.86	14.50	24.36	25.3
1829	39.22	1.29	6.10	11.90	17.06	28.96	21.0
1830	40.66	1.47	7.61	12.92	16.05	28.97	26.3
1831	44.03	1.50	10.81	16.25	17.30	33.55	32.2
1832	66.29	2.17	7.04	21.36	22.76	44.12	15.9
1833	61.70	2.29	8.95	17.52	20.35	37.87	23.6
1834	54.91	1.98	10.04	19.21	10.84	30.05	32.9
1835	51.81	1.51	15.71	17.34	11.76	29.10	54.0
1836	59.23	1.74	8.42	23.08	5.06	28.14	29.9
1837	57.39	1.21	2.64	11.45	2.33	13.78	19.1
1838	45.26	0.87	3.77	6.77	2.62	9.39	40.2
1839	41.62	1.79	4.15	5.98	6.78	12.76	32.5
1840	36.84	1.38	1.47	6.70	3.34	10.04	14.6

Source: *Historical Statistics*, Series N, p. 261.

1. Circulation is the sum of the bank's own notes in circulation.

2. Deposits are the sum of both private and government deposits.

3. The reserve ratios given are computed by dividing the sum of circulation and deposits into specie.

by a primarily private corporation, with virtually no legal constraints on their issue or on the length of their existence. Yet the notes of the Second Bank have been eulogized as the basis of a sound and uniform currency, while the treasury notes have been swept under the rug as disreputable and spurious. In both cases outright unconstitutionality was avoided by making the notes legal tender only for payments to and by the government. But this limitation was specious; anything the government had to accept and that had to be accepted by government creditors was bound to be accepted by everyone else.

The Second Bank, by virtue of its most favored position in the financial fabric, could discreetly assume certain central banking functions. It was a public bank; it was also a commercial bank. It had financial communications with the state banks, both because of its own commercial nature and because it was *the* government depository. Its only constraint, self-imposed, was maintenance of a reserve ratio slightly greater than that deemed sound for ordinary commercial banks. One would have to be either obtuse or modest in the assumption of power not to recognize and cultivate the central banking potential of such an institution, even if such power was ultimately subordinate to the discipline of a specie standard. Langdon Cheves was probably not obtuse, but he probably was unassuming. Nicholas Biddle was neither. He soon recognized the bank's forceful position; but the argument that he came to the presidency with such a preconception is untenable.[7] Undoubtedly he cultivated central banking ideas and policies in the later 1820s, but they were a pragmatic realization of the bank's position and not the result of a previously determined central banking philosophy. Hammond quotes Albert Gallatin's remark in 1831 that the bank "operates as a screw" and "was for that very purpose . . . established,"[8] but this concept of the bank was wishful thinking and historically inaccurate. Not only was it absent from the charters of the First and Second Banks; it was not even imputed to them by anyone—particularly secretaries of the Treasury, including Gallatin—before about 1828.

The report of the secretary of the Treasury for 1828, however, expresses lengthy approbation over the operations of the Second Bank. The bank and the John Quincy Adams administration were, to use a contemporary expression, in accord; and Richard Rush, Adams's Treasury secretary, praised the bank highly. He cited first the bank's utility as a helpmate to the Treasury: "This capacity in the treasury to apply the public funds at the proper moment, in every part of a country of such wide extent, has been essentially augmented by the Bank of the United States." It aided in the collection of public moneys, and in so doing,

> it receives the paper of the State banks paid on public account, . . . and, by placing it to the credit of the United States as cash, renders

it available wherever the public service may require. By this course, a course not enjoined by its charter, it widens the field of business and its usefulness to the State Banks. [It also secures stability of property to the community] . . . by confining within prudent limits its issues of paper . . . Sometimes (judiciously varying its course) it enlarges its issues to relieve scarcity, as under the disastrous speculations of 1825.[9]

The state banks had been suitably restrained, thus demonstrating that "a national bank is the instrument alone by which Congress can effectively regulate the currency of the nation."[10]

This report reveals several beliefs that Rush held. First, he saw the Second Bank as a public bank and as a commercial bank, but also as a central bank. Second, while he deemed its policies benign, he acknowledged that its central bank activities were not provided by its charter. Third, he implied that Congress created the bank to regulate the currency while contradictorily stating that "this course [was] not enjoined by its charter." This sequence of ideas is surely ex post facto justification of an institution that seemed to work. But it also indicates that the central banking concept had emerged—a genesis resulting from the strategic position of the bank in the monetary system and from the entrepreneurship of Nicholas Biddle.

In an unpublished manuscript, Jacob Meerman has concluded that Biddle "developed a system of control over the state banks, a system of keeping them within their means," and that this control was his own innovation. Meerman cites Biddle's assertion that if the Second Bank withdrew this control, within three months "there [would] be no general specie payments throughout the union."[11] Time proved this claim false, but it emphasizes the self-conscious importance Biddle attached to his own central banking operations.

The alleged necessity for some agency such as the Second Bank to contain state bank credit was part of the myth that state bank credit had expanded capriciously during the War of 1812, an expansion that actually resulted from government issues of treasury notes. As long as the state banks had to obey the requisites of specie convertibility, they could not overexpand to any great extent. Too zealous an extension of credit would lead to exports of specie and in turn to an intense reappraisal of bank portfolios by commercial bank managers.

Several questions could be raised concerning the adequacy of this process. For example, would the ordinary commercial banker realize soon enough the boundaries of credit expansion he might safely approach in his self-interested desire for maximizing returns? If not, he would very soon be an ex-banker. Still, why not have a central bank working within the confines of the specie standard to limit commercial bank expansion before specie reserves became too fragile to support the expanding volume of bank credit? Such an arrangement might well be an improvement; but it might also be disastrous if the central banker, whose judgment determined tightness and ease of bank credit, made a mistake.[12] To some extent, this unhappy possibility could be avoided by congressional prescription for the central bank; but Congress has ever been reluctant to give such direction, and central bankers have long discouraged it.

The Second Bank under Biddle's presidency undertook policies "with a consciousness of quasi-governmental responsibility and of the need to subordinate profit and private interest to that responsibility." Biddle's primary signal for action was the state of the foreign exchanges. A tendency for the exchange to fall "against" the United States brought out a more rigorous policy by the bank in collecting specie on state bank notes and deposits and greater restraint in its own discounting. In addition, the bank would counter the effects of an adverse trade balance by means of its open credits with Baring Brothers, its London correspondent, "allowing banks time to diminish their issues without ruin to their customers."[13]

All these accounts of Biddle's countercyclical policies emphasize again the primacy of the metallic standard in determining the stock of money. Biddle and the Second Bank simply facilitated the process of change by a timely awareness and evaluation of the foreign exchanges. Perhaps they kept the changes less radical than they otherwise might have been, but they could not (and did not try to) thwart the effects of a specie standard adjustment the way central banks can today. The analogy of the Second Bank as a balance wheel is faulty; it was more a shock absorber when it operated according to the Biddle blueprint.[14]

The bank, of course, was a fiscal agent for the Treasury, a function consistent with the notion of a public or national bank. It was a legitimate duty for such a public institution, although one that a mere administrative extension of the Treasury itself could have accommodated.[15] But its most significant effect was that it gave the bank an entree to monetary policy, as Henry Clay had observed earlier. If the bank was collecting money for the Treasury, it was a depository for the money; and if it was a depository, it had sizable amounts of money flowing through it; and if it had all that money within its reach, it had every opportunity under the "right" kind of leadership to manipulate that stock, in ways either good or evil. Under Nicholas Biddle the ways were mostly good, even though limited by meeting specie requirements. But as Clay had concluded with respect to the First Bank, the right to undertake intervention in the money market, for good or for evil, had not been delegated to it.

With the election of Andrew Jackson as president of the United States in 1828, the question of the bank's existence became problematical. Rush's extensive and favorable report on the bank in December 1828 was no doubt inspired by Jackson's election in November.[16] Knowing he was part of a lame-duck administration, Rush wished to put forth some favorable testimony for the institution while he still had the chance.

The bank had been in existence for twelve years and therefore had eight years left to operate on its current charter. In his inaugural message in 1829 Jackson gave the first implication of trouble by stating that the question of recharter should be considered soon, since the constitutionality of the bank and its utility in providing a uniform and sound currency were "well questioned by a large portion of our fellow citizens."[17]

The president's charges were referred to congressional committees for investigation and report. The House Committee of Ways and Means, to whom this duty fell, analyzed and discussed at length the issues raised by Jackson. In so doing, it revealed the quality of central banking at that time and the extent to which the central banking concept had developed.[18]

The particular questions the committee faced were: (1) Has Congress the constitutional power to incorporate such a bank? (2) Is it expedient to establish and maintain such an institution? (3) Is it expedient to establish an alternative national bank, founded on the credit and revenues of the federal government—that is, a government-owned and -operated agency?

The probank majority of the committee, headed by George McDuffie of South Carolina, stated that the constitutionality of the bank was in accordance with the grant of power to Congress "to coin money and regulate the value thereof." *Coin* could not be conceived narrowly, the majority argued, as it was synonymous at the writing of the Constitution with *currency.* "It was then generally believed that bank notes could only be maintained in circulation by being true representatives of the precious metals. The word 'coin,' therefore, must be regarded as a particular term, standing as the representative of a general idea." Congress's power to regulate the value of money, they continued, was in the same clause as its power to specify uniform weights and measures. "The one was designed to ensure a uniform measure of value, as the other was designed to ensure a uniform measure of quantity."[19]

The authorization for the First Bank had been found in the power of Congress to levy and collect taxes, a duty for which the First Bank was made an auxiliary. By 1830 the primary function of the Second Bank had been promoted to regulating the value of money. The committee saw no embarrassment in this convenient and opportunistic shift of constitutional justification for the existence of the bank. The majority, moreover, had accurate and sophisticated knowledge of the value of money. They did *not* say that it was a specified weight of some precious metal; this too literal definition had already been disallowed by their generic interpretation of the word *coin.* In discussing the inflation of 1815-1817, they stated: "No proposition is better established than that the value of money, whether it consists of specie or paper, is depreciated in exact proportion to the increase in its quantity, in any given state of the demand for it . . . A rise in the price of commodities [equals] depreciation in the value of money." John Stuart Mill did not state the case much differently or much better in his *Principles* published eighteen years later. "Money," they concluded in their summary of theory, "is nothing more nor less than the measure by which the relative value of all articles of merchandise is ascertained."[20]

The question of a metallic versus a mixed currency was precluded, they argued, "by the existing state of things"; that is, by the fact that the currency was mixed. The real normative issue was between a paper currency of uniform value and a paper currency subject to a fluctuating value. The Second Bank, they suggested, was admirably equipped to provide the former alternative and had been doing so.[21] In fact, by saving the cost of transporting as much specie as would have been necessary without it, the bank "*has actually furnished a circulating medium more uniform than specie.*"[22]

Neither this committee nor any other defined a uniform currency. Two interpretations are possible. First, the currency could be uniform in size, shape, and value and redeemable at par "in every part of the Union," meaning redeemable in specie at the same rate of exchange at any location. The Second Bank in exchanging its own notes at par tended to promote this kind of uniformity. To the extent that it did, it was subsidizing the collection and clearing of notes and deposits. Although it may not have charged explicitly for this service, the costs of clearing were real and had to be borne by some part of the bank's operations. Bill brokers performed this function at an explicit cost and brought Shylock calumnies on themselves. Naturally public sentiment would favor an institution that did it "without cost," even though the costs were hidden in general expenses.

Second, the currency could be uniform in purchasing power over time, regardless of its exchange value from place to place at any given time. The majority, recognizing the merit of such a characteristic, implied that the bank had been instrumental in furthering it.

This second notion, however, exaggerated the scope of the bank's operations. The bank could have dramatic short-run effects, but it could not counteract flows of specie for more than a limited time. Its own gold reserves would determine just how long that time would be, and many of the bank's policies had been simply to anticipate specie flows and provide for them as comfortably as possible.

The last part of the majority report raised the issue of control by a central bank. It even used the term *central bank*, but conceived of it as completely government-owned and monolithic in contrast to the hybrid commercial-national bank with branches then under consideration. "A great central bank established at the seat of the Government without branches" would provide a uniform currency, they stated, but "the promise to pay specie for its notes would almost be purely nominal." Their opinion was that the notes would circulate so far from the "seat of the Government" that they would never be redeemed but would continue being exchanged. They did not find such a currency illegal; however, "the notes of a central Government bank . . . would be subject to depreciation from a cause which constitutes a conclusive objection to such an institution. *There would be nothing to limit excessive issues, but the discretion and prudence of the Government or of the direction.*" The implication was that government prudence and discretion would be neither prudent nor discreet. Political considerations would rule in locating branches; and patronage powers would promote evil, especially since the central bank would be a bank of discount and deposit, with the government a "great money lender."[23]

The Bank of the United States, by contrast, was a superior organization to the "central Government bank" or to a treasury department because all relations between the bank and the government were "fixed by the law, and nothing is left to arbitrary discretion." It was, primarily, a privately owned company. Even so, "the interest of stockholders . . . is quite a subordinate consideration. The maintenance of a uniform currency, and the facilities afforded for collection, transferring, and disbursing the public revenue, are the great and paramount objects to be accomplished by such an institution."[24]

The Second Bank's charter from the federal government gave it license to act as a commercial bank and to help in the fiscal affairs of the government, and in these respects "nothing was left to arbitrary discretion." But the maintenance of a sound and uniform currency, however defined, was not prescribed by any statute and, to the extent that it was practicable, was left very much to the discretion of the bank's executive. The majority of the committee had spelled out all the characteristics of a central bank and had argued convincingly that the Second Bank fitted the mold. They had only *alleged* that the mold had originally been conceived in the law chartering the bank. They now had to recommend that the new charter fit the structure that had emerged. Intuitively they sensed this disparity, this lack of integrity between the role the bank had been born to and the functions it had assumed. Their conclusions were accordingly subdued. They did not recommend centralized discretionary control over the money market, the exchanges, the commercial banking system, or any other areas peculiar and unique to central banking. They saw the bank furnishing a uniform paper currency and assisting the Treasury, but these jobs were ancillary to the principal central banking function of regulating the money supply and could have been performed by a number of institutions. Probably McDuffie and the other members of the majority sensed that a bank bill embodying too many overt central banking features would have no chance of getting past Jackson or of getting the two-thirds vote in Congress necessary to override the presidential veto.

The minority portion of the same committee consisted of two members, Mark Alexander of Virginia and Naithan Gaiter of Kentucky. They faced the central banking character of the Second Bank and objected. The bank, they said, "cannot be necessary . . . to regulate trade and commerce, which if left to individual enterprise, will regulate itself without such agency, under the rules which have been prescribed by law."[25] They allowed that the bank had a regulatory effect on "trade and commerce," but they apparently did not distinguish between regulating commerce and regulating the monetary framework within which commerce took place, a distinction as fundamental as the conceptual difference between money and all other things. Furthermore, a philosophy of government that would control the value of the medium of exchange may be just as liberal (libertarian) as one that would hang the value on a metallic standard. The value of the circulating medium can be sustained by controlling its quantity without resorting to ubiquitous political intervention in other sectors of the economy.

The minority did not allow the majority opinion on the constitutional license for the bank to slip by without comment. The bank, they argued, could not have been formed under the clause that gave Congress power to coin money and regulate its value because this provision applied to metallic money: "It is not the *paper currency* which Congress is entrusted with the power of regulating."[26] This argument was weak and must be considered a loser to that of the majority. If paper money had replaced coin, as it had, then taking these words literally would have greatly vitiated Congress's power over the monetary system. This literal interpretation could also be viewed as contrary to the life, liberty, and property doctrine of that document. An appreciating or depreciating unit of account necessarily implies unjustified changes in real property rights.

Although they lost on this constitutional point, the minority correctly criticized the inconsistency between the two constitutional points on which proponents had based their arguments for the First and Second Banks. They cited Henry Clay's caustic statement on the constitutional rationale for the bank in 1811: "This vagrant power to erect a bank . . . has at length been located by the gentleman from Georgia [Mr. Crawford] on that provision to lay and collect taxes."[27] This incisive criticism again emphasizes that central banking was not intended in the original construction of the two banks. The convenient shift to "coin money and regulate the value thereof" from "to lay and collect taxes" was ex post facto acknowledgment that monetary regulation had not been born but made.

Another of their arguments had merit. They denied that the Second Bank had been instrumental in restoring the currency to specie convertibility after the War of 1812. The secretary of the Treasury had been instructed by both houses of Congress not to receive any notes except those of specie-paying banks. And it was the Treasury, they continued, that brought about the desired result before the Second Bank was in operation. The secretary, by accepting convertible notes and refusing inconvertible ones, "could prove as salutary a check against excessive issues as any supposed agency of the bank, and is the only rightful control which the Government should exercise over such local institutions of the States." Only the investiture of Bank of the United States notes with limited legal tender status, they said, gave these notes their universal acceptability.[28]

As the bill to recharter the Second Bank became current in early 1832, yet another committee was formed in response to Jackson's later allegation that the bank had violated provisions of its charter. This time the new committee was made up of seven members and was controlled by the antibank forces. Its chairman was Augustin Clayton of Georgia. George McDuffie, chairman of the former committee, was a member of the probank minority as was John Quincy Adams. The committee was appointed in the middle of March 1832 and was supposed to report its findings by the end of April, six weeks later.[29]

The antibank majority report is notable for its damnation by allegation and innuendo and for its ignorance of routine monetary affairs. It criticized the open-market sales of government securities conducted by the bank in 1825, but only on the grounds that the government might better have realized the profits itself. More significant, in the committee's opinion, was the bank's action in the business depression that developed in late 1831. At the same time that the bank let its specie be drained off, it increased its note and deposit obligations. This true central banking operation was criticized by the committee on the grounds that such additional issues of notes caused specie to flow out of the country to Europe, "and but for a decline in the price of specie in Europe, it would still continue to be exported . . . No measure can be invented to restore a sound currency," the committee concluded, "but a withdrawal of a large portion of notes in circulation, by the bank, which will compel other banks to do the same."[30] Thus they recognized that the bank was ultimately unable to stop specie outflows and that its note issues actually provoked such outflows. The committee prescribed the contraction of notes (with a falling price level implicitly recognized, certainly) and the conservation of specie. Whether they realized the hardship such a policy would have imposed on the economy is not indicated.

The probank minority of the investigating committee excused the open-market sales by the bank in 1825 as a defensive measure that protected the reserves of the bank. They argued further that the bank in protecting itself from "the extraordinary pressure upon the money market . . . averted from this country the calamity of a general failure of the banks."[31] This argument again suggests a public bank rather than a central bank. The bank sold its securities in order to protect itself; as a central bank it would have bought securities to enhance the reserves of the other banks, thus parlaying its excess specie reserves as effectively as possible among the satellite banks. The bank's policy in 1825, except for its correct anticipation of a shift in the balance of payments, hardly rates as a central banking operation as that term is generally understood today.

The minority report also pointed out that the bank's discounts had remained stable from 1829 to 1831, so the unfavorable balance of trade that developed had its causes in the internal economies of European export countries. The bank had subsequently extended its discounts "to relieve the community from the temporary pressure to which it was thus exposed."[32] Clearly the bank did act as a central bank at this point, and its balance sheet substantiates such an inference (see table 3.2). Not only did note and deposit liabilities increase slightly while reserves fell, but forbearance was shown in presenting notes of other banks for redemption.

The minority upbraided the majority's inconsistency for complaining that the bank was too liberal in its discounts while lamenting that it was too restrained in extending its relief. "The very complaint urged by [the majority] of the committee against the bank is, that it has been too liberal

TABLE 3.2. Principal items in the balance sheet of the Bank of the United States (millions of dollars).

Date	Specie	Notes of other banks	Loans	Circulation (notes out)	Deposits
Sept. 1, 1831	11.55	2.08	35.81	22.40	15.88
April 1, 1832	6.80	2.84	42.12	23.72	17.06

Source: U.S. Congress, 22nd Cong., 1st sess., *Reports of Committees, House Report No. 460*, pp. 330-331.

in its discounts; . . . and yet it is here set down as a subject of lamentation, that the bank is not able to *extend* this relief still further!"[33]

The bank clearly acted like a central bank in 1831. The majority of the investigating committee at times saw it as such and at other times thought of it as nothing more than a corporation receiving unwarranted favors. In either case it condemned the bank, and the impression from the report is that the decision to find the bank guilty was prejudged.

The minority report was much more sophisticated and incisive, not to mention objective. Similar to the McDuffie report of two years earlier, it emphasized the regulatory and benevolent power of the bank in guiding the monetary system. Despite its more objective investigation of the facts and its considerate analysis of testimony, it was in the predicament of having to support the central banking activities of the bank by referring to "provisions" of the charter that were not there. The minority report continually alleged that they were there, just as Nicholas Biddle had done in his testimony. They had to admit that the bank had power; and power was hard to defend, especially when it was not circumscribed by rules. "Power for good," wrote John Quincy Adams in his part of the report, "is power for evil, even in the hands of Omnipotence." In discussing bank policy when overtrading took place, he remarked that "it was difficult to determine" the means and ends of policy, and "the soundest discretion may come to different results in different men." Put these judgments together, and the neophytic central bank and its director come out as authoritarian and despotic. Never mind that the policies of the despot were benevolent; with such unbridled power, probabilities were not certainties that benevolent results would continue. Coincidentally, and as if to confirm the worst possible fears of the bank's enemies, Biddle stated: "There are very few banks which might not have been destroyed by an exertion of the [Second] bank."[34] He meant that the bank had been gentle; but his antagonists heard only "destroyed."

Biddle had his opportunity to defend the bank when the majority of the committee presented him with a volume of complicated and detailed questions meant to embarrass him by their implications and ambiguities. The questions were conceived by Churchill C. Cambreleng of New York, a leading Jacksonian and antibank man, and they amounted to a comprehensive examination on central bank policy. Biddle had already been indicted as far as the majority was concerned, and they therefore did not wait for his answers. They recorded meanly that Biddle had "not been able, from the press of his other indispensable duties, to answer" the questions.[35] The minority group, however, delayed its report long enough to allow Biddle to respond.

Biddle's answers to Cambreleng's questions were sophisticated and polished, but by no means internally consistent. He underplayed the extent of bank policy—for example, the policy during 1831-32. The attitude of the bank then, he said, was "to deal with the utmost gentleness to the commercial community, . . . to stand quietly by, and assist, if necessary, the operations of nature, and the laws of trade, which can always correct their own transient excesses."[36]

This passage suggests obsequiousness and restraint. In the next paragraph, however, the tone of Biddle's remarks implies an exertion of power, and a power legally vested in the bank. In assuming the role of a central bank, he said, "the bank deemed itself only acting as it was designed to act by the Congress which created it, and [only] placing itself in its true national attitude to the Government and the country."[37] Like others before and since who have vested the two banks of the United States with statutory powers from Congress, Biddle cited no evidence to show that the allegation was well-founded.

The bank in Biddle's opinion was in little danger of overissuing paper currency. The issue of new currency was beneficial if the "trade and business of the country require it." And "if they do not require it, the evil will soon correct itself, because it will be converted into coin." While discussing the demand for and supply of money, he repeated that he saw "no connection whatever between the bank and the demand for money, except that the bank has supplied the demand . . . Now, if there was a demand for money, and the bank had the means for supplying it, why should it not? The object of its creation was precisely that [sic] . . . It seems a singular objection to a bank, that, finding a demand for money, and having the means of supplying it, it did supply it."[38]

Whatever Biddle and the other probank people declared, the bank was *not* created to supply money as a policy matter; if anything, it was created to maintain the market for government securities. Especially revealing in this passage is the use of "a" in front of "bank." "A" commercial bank might well furnish money "when there was a demand for it"; a central bank—the Second Bank—might do just the reverse, in order to moderate developing fluctuations in business activity. The commercial bank-central bank roles that the bank had come to play were again muddled, and the hybrid nature of the institution was again underscored.

Biddle's answers to the questioned relationship between the United States bank and the state banks were ambiguous. Does not an increase in Bank of the United States notes increase local currency? one question asked. No, he answered. Circulation of the bank "supersedes, in many cases, the local circulation, as it was designed to do, and no inference can be drawn" on what the net effects might be.[39]

This question and the frank answer to it could not make many friends for the bank. The antibank forces had already shown that the bank was *not* so designed. And if bank currency superseded local currency, was not the bank a potential engine of inflation and with unbounded powers? Was it not squeezing out the local banks? The antibank faction clearly thought so.

"Does not a national bank . . . excite over-trading among local banks as well as among merchants?" another question asked. "Not necessarily," answered Biddle. "Its natural tendency would be to control them, and thus prevent, rather than excite excessive issues." His general theme was to cast the bank as a stern but friendly shepherd: The Bank of the United States did not "encroach on [the state banks'] freedom." It only kept them strictly responsible for their issues. It "is the enemy of none, but the common friend of all."[40]

The House passed the bill to recharter the Second Bank in the early summer of 1832 by a vote of 107 to 85, and the Senate by 28 to 20. Jackson vetoed the bill on July 11 and returned it to the Senate with his objections.

His arguments for vetoing the bill ostensibly hinged on three factors: First, the unrestrained power of the bank: "The President of the Bank," his veto message read, "has told us that most of the State banks exist by its forbearance."[41] Second, the constitutionality with respect to the "necessary and proper" power of Congress in carrying out governmental functions: "The public debt . . . has been nearly paid off." Therefore the greater capital of the Second Bank (as compared to the First Bank) was not *necessary*. It can exist only "for private purposes [profits]," in which case governmental sponsorship was improper. Third, a denial that Congress had the right to delegate its powers: "It is maintained by some that the bank is a means of executing the constitutional power 'to coin money and regulate the value thereof.' " But the mint was the institution that coined money, and "Congress . . . passed laws to regulate the value thereof." In any event, this power could not be delegated; "it was conferred to be exercised by [Congress], and not to be transferred to a corporation."[42] This state of things, Jackson decided, was unconstitutional and not to be prolonged. On this case he registered his veto.

In all fairness it is not a bad case. The bank had extended its powers without license; it did not operate as it had been conceived to operate; its activities were not prescribed by congressional statute. It may have operated benignly in the past, but it would not necessarily do so in the future. Its only constraint was the necessity of converting its demand obligations into specie when requested to do so. While an ultimate obligation, such a constraint still permitted variable amounts of discretionary monetary policy that could have extended the scope of the bank's operations to the point where the bank superseded the gold standard. The Federal Reserve system in the twentieth century provides an example of a central bank that followed this pattern.

4. Decline of the Second Bank and Rise of the Treasury

When you give power to a Secretary of the Treasury (we know of what stuff they are made of) to transfer at pleasure the deposits of the revenue to such banks as may court his favor, you are adding to the President of the United States, whose creature he is, and that by the legislation of this House, a most tremendous and gigantic power. (William F. Gordon, House of Representatives, 10 February 1835)

One of the major issues in the 1832 election between the federalist Whig Henry Clay and the agrarian Democrat Andrew Jackson was the rechartering of the Second Bank of the United States. Jackson's victory was considered a vote of confidence on his veto of the bank bill. Other evidence suggests that this conclusion is unwarranted. Several issues besides rechartering were of major importance—internal improvements of roads and canals by the federal government, and the tariff, to mention just two. Jackson's personal charm and his glamorous military career considerably enhanced his power to get votes. Finally, if the bank issue had been at the root of Jackson's victory, the complexion of Congress would have changed to suit the same consensus. But Congress did not change appreciably; the majorities in favor of the Second Bank in 1832 remained majorities in the next session.

During the early years of the campaign against the bank, Jackson's Secretary of the Treasury, Louis McLane, joined with a few other administration confidants in tactful but unsuccessful attempts to persuade Jackson that a national bank would be desirable.[1] After his election and second inauguration Jackson and his antibank lieutenants felt that some overt act of hostility to the bank was called for. The tactic they chose was removal of the government's deposits from the Second Bank and its branches. Secretary McLane, within whose office any such action had to originate, resisted. Jackson then shuffled his cabinet, switching McLane to secretary of state and bringing in a relatively unknown newcomer, William J. Duane, as secretary of the treasury. Duane was neither a legislator nor a jurist. His only previous experience in public office had been in the Pennsylvania House of Representatives; but he was known to be antibank, and he had an aura of respectability that Jackson may have needed to give a less buccaneering tone to his administration.[2]

Duane proved to be opposed to all banks, not just the Bank of the United States. He refused to order the removal of the deposits when given this directive by Jackson, because he felt that the government's deposits were safer in the Second Bank than in state banks of questionable status.[3] He was summarily dismissed for his obstinacy. Jackson then appointed Roger B. Taney as secretary and had him affix his signature to a predated order for the removal of the deposits.[4]

Taney defended this action in a letter to the House of Representatives. According to the charter of the Second Bank, he wrote, the public deposits were to be kept in the Second Bank "unless otherwise directed by the Secretary." He also noted that Secretary of the Treasury Crawford had mentioned this same provision in a letter to the president of the Mechanics' Bank of New York in 1817. In that letter he had stated that the secretary "will always be disposed to support the credit of the State banks, and will invariably direct transfers from the deposits of the public money in aid of their legitimate exertions to maintain their credit."[5]

When Congress resumed after this incident, an unprecedented uproar began. The Whigs were especially critical. They held that the secretary's duty to report to Congress, particularly when a movement of the public funds was involved, implied that Congress could judge and even overrule such action.[6] The removal of the deposits had not only denied this control to Congress, but had seemingly opened up unlimited discretionary power for the use of the executive branch in the future. Senator Southard voiced the sentiment of the majority when he said that the secretary might decide at his pleasure which state banks should be depositories, when transfers from bank to bank should take place, and what security, if any, should be required of the banks. "All this he may do for causes entirely unconnected with the business of the Treasury, and in no way concerning the public interest . . . This state of things is prescribed by his discretion. And the man who presumes thus to act tells Congress that his acts are under the control of the President . . . If there has been a larger or more dangerous stretch of executive power and influence, I have not discovered it."[7]

Most of the critics of Jacksonian policy, and they composed a majority of Congress, wanted the Second Bank to continue because it had been acting as a central bank as well as a fiscal agent to the government. At issue were the powers of the executive branch assumed by Jackson and his close advisers, not the power of the Treasury Department in particular; the controversy over the Treasury Department was simply the focal point of the conflict.

The Whig view of the secretary's office was given by Henry Clay: The office was "altogether financial and administrative. He [the secretary] has no legislative powers; and Congress neither has nor could delegate any to him." Clay did not explain how Congress could delegate such powers to a private, commercial, "national" bank—the Second Bank of the United States. The report of the Committee on Finance, chaired at this time by Daniel Webster, was equally critical. "It is no part of his [the secretary's] duty," it stated, "either to contract or expand the circulation of bank paper." A more tolerant view was voiced by Horace Binney, a close friend of Biddle's and a sophisticated supporter of the Second Bank. Although he held no brief for the Treasury Department, he observed: "The direction which is to govern the Secretary is left, by the terms of the act [creating the office], to be settled according to the character of the function to be exercised."[8]

The Jacksonians tried to give the impression that their actions and arguments were simply reflections of a great "popular" movement, but this movement was not mirrored in Congress. Clay's resolutions that Jackson had acted unconstitutionally in removing Duane and that Taney's reasons for the removal of the deposits were unsatisfactory and insufficient passed by an overwhelming majority in the Senate, while similar resolutions lost in the House by only a small margin. Nor was this popular movement reflected in public sentiment. Countless memorials to Congress from all over the country overwhelmingly "prayed" for the restoration of the deposits and recharter of the Second Bank.[9]

Taney, Benton, and the other doctrinaire Jacksonians had been quick to condemn the monetary policy activities of the Second Bank, but they soon learned that the fiscal requirements of the Treasury could not operate in a monetary vacuum. At first the Jacksonians had argued that the state banks were just as much a menace to the economy as the Second Bank. But the routine fiscal cash flows through the Treasury Department forced the administration to accept and use these banks.

Secretary Taney rationalized toleration of the state banks by alleging that their abolition would seriously interfere with states' rights and by claiming that banks of credit were relatively innocuous, and that only the suppression of state bank notes was necessary.[10] He did not specify how commercial banks might generate credit without issuing notes.

Taney's official statements show that he was self-consciously aware of his policy position. In his letter to Congress on the removal of the deposits, he said that the safety of the deposits was only "a part of the considerations by which his judgment must be guided. The general interest and convenience of the people must [also] regulate his conduct." Similarly, his letter of instruction to the state banks selected as depositories is loaded with policy implications. He wrote: "The deposits of the public money will enable you to afford increased facilities to commerce, and to extend your accommodation to individuals. And as the duties [tariffs] which are payable to the Government arise from the business and enterprise of the merchants engaged in foreign trade, it is but reasonable that they should be preferred, in the additional accommodation which the public deposits will enable your institution to give."[11]

Not only did Taney exhort the banks to expand credit with their public deposits, but he also exercised a marked qualitative credit control by urging them to give preferential treatment to merchants in foreign trade. One had to be an obtuse banker indeed not to get the drift of this remark.

The recession developing in the economy in the spring of 1834 was the second problem to confront the Jackson administration. Fortunately for the Jacksonians, one measure that could be quickly legislated had the dignity of approval from unbiased authorities, had the support of many antiadministration congressmen, and was compatible with the thesis of hard money. This measure was devaluation of the gold dollar, known in the statutes as the Gold Coin Act.

On April 15, 1834, Taney wrote a letter to James Polk, chairman of the House Ways and Means Committee, in which he gave current administration views toward devaluation: "The first step towards a sound condition of the currency, is to reform the coinage of gold . . . As this general paper currency [notes of the Bank of the United States] is gradually retiring from circulation, the gold should be prepared to take its place." Benton made several speeches to the same effect in the Senate and added that devaluation would end the necessity for *any* paper money. He further noted that four previous secretaries of the Treasury (Gallatin, Dallas, Crawford, and Ingham) had recommended "correction of the error" in fixing the bimetallic ratio at 15 to 1.[12]

The anti-Jackson contingent in Congress had little choice but to go along with the proposal. Gold was undervalued at the mint, certainly so relative to the ratios then prevailing in other countries with respect to silver. The Whigs were as aware as the Democrats of the developing business recession and had to forget (remember!) politics long enough to pass an antideflationary measure. No one in Congress who approved of increasing the silver-gold ratio from 15 to 1 to 16 to 1 would have accomplished the change by increasing the silver content of the silver dollar.[13] The measure passed 145 to 36 in the House and 35 to 7 in the Senate. It devalued the gold dollar by about 6 percent.

From October 1, 1833, to November 1, 1835, net imports of specie to the United States were $27 million.[14] Secretary Taney estimated that $8 million of this amount flowed in between January and May of 1834.[15] In response to the continuing increase in the stock of specie, the stock of money (currency plus bank deposits) increased by approximately 42 percent between 1834 and 1837, while the price level rose a corresponding 36 percent.[16]

Just about the time the Gold Coin Act passed, the Senate refused to confirm Taney's nomination as secretary, thus registering formal disapproval of Jackson's tactics. In Taney's place, Jackson nominated Levi Woodbury, who was duly confirmed. Woodbury, who had been attorney general, was one of the few cabinet members to have approved the removal of the deposits the previous year. He remained in the office of secretary of the Treasury through Van Buren's administration, then returned to the Senate, and finally became a justice of the Supreme Court.

By the time Woodbury took office only a few doctrinaire hard-money men still talked of a completely metallic currency and abolition of the state banking system. The public deposits were not hard money, and their placement in the state banks required the discretion of the secretary of the Treasury. When the magnitude of this responsibility came to the attention of Congress, the feelings of many were voiced by John Robertson in the House when he inquired incredulously: "Who is to conduct all this complex machinery [of deposit banks]. A Secretary of the Treasury: the incumbent of an office filled once in four years; perhaps . . . four times in one year. This officer [is] to become . . . the head of what might be called the confederated banks of North America?"[17] Senator Southard then observed that if the administration did not exterminate the state banks but used them, "either the Government must itself become responsible for these banks, or the banks themselves must become responsible for each other."[18]

All parties agreed that the deposit banks had to be regulated, and in the session of Congress that opened in December of 1834, the legislation designed to prescribe such regulation was begun. This bill was especially interesting because it incorporated for the first time in the banking history of the United States a minimum legal reserve requirement against all demand liabilities. This provision, inserted by an amendment initiated by Daniel Webster, directed deposit banks to hold at least 20 percent of all deposits and notes in specie. Benton called for even tighter requirements and amended the ratio to 25 percent. His amendment lost by a vote of only 17 to 19, while Webster's original amendment carried by 27 to 6. In the House, Horace Binney made the same amendment (20 percent) to the bill as it came out of committee. The House also carried the measure, but by a vote of only 109 to 99.[19]

The reserve requirement bill was a sophisticated measure. It reflected the general antipathy of Congress to discretionary executive control. It was a product of knowledgeable Whig leaders and hard-money Democrats. The reserve requirements it imposed on the deposit banks at this time would have tended to restrain the state banking system and might have moderated the inflation that took place within the next few years. The stronger reserve position it required of the deposit banks would have enabled them to administer the federal government's surplus distribution to the states with much less disruption to the monetary system than actually occurred.

A week after the reserve requirement measure had passed both houses, it was brought up for reconsideration in the House of Representatives on the motion of James Polk. He argued that the deposit banks would have to be specie-paying in any case and that the specie requirement was therefore redundant. Clearing the notes of country banks took so long, he continued, that no bank could meet the requirement if an inordinate demand were put on it as an agency of the government—as would happen in the sales of public lands. He implied that the requirement was a political effort, passed only as a means of sabotaging the new deposit bank system and forcing the revival of a national bank.[20]

Polk succeeded in getting the bill buried for the remainder of the session, but it was brought up again in the Senate during 1836 with the provisions for the distribution of the government's fiscal surplus tacked on at the end. After much debate—confused and confusing because two bills were now combined into one—Calhoun moved to strike the reserve requirement, arguing that it would operate "oppressively." His sentiments were echoed by many, including Webster, who said that he did not think the provision was of much value and that he had proposed it only to keep specie in the country.[21]

After the Senate agreed to delete the reserve requirement, Senator Silas Wright of New York offered the substitute that finally became section 8 of the distribution bill. It stated that each of the selected depository banks "keep in its vaults such an amount of specie as shall be required by the Secretary of the Treasury, and shall be in his opinion, necessary to render the said bank a safe depository of the public moneys."[22]

Only Benton resisted. He objected both to the absence of a specific reserve requirement and to the discretion left to the secretary of the Treasury. Some of the deposit banks were "far in arrear," and "as a whole, they are far behind the point of specie responsibility at which the Bank of the United States stood at the time of the removal of the deposits."[23]

The action on the specie reserve requirement is strong evidence that Congress was functionally unable to prescribe or to conduct monetary policy. Having initiated legislation for the express purpose of limiting the discretion of the secretary of the Treasury in monetary affairs, Congress terminated action with a bill that made de jure the exact powers they had originally intended to limit! Such a performance argues that the legislature could handle monetary policy only in broad terms; that is, that Congress might have set up some goals or rules and a general institutional framework for their attainment, but that details of policy had to be left to a relatively small, close-knit unit that could achieve both force and direction.

Woodbury's only reference to his new discretionary powers over the specie reserves of the selected depository banks was that measures (unspecified) had been adopted "and recommendations urged, that the specie in the vaults of the selected state banks should be still more increased in comparison with their [note] issues and deposits."[24] In his report for 1836 he said vaguely that the state banks had been selected "according to the discretion of this Department" because they were "regulated in a manner considered most secure to the Treasury and convenient to the community."[25] Notwithstanding his official confidence, the deposit banks were practically unregulated, did not even face state restrictions, and would soon show that the public deposits were not "safe," that is, redeemable in specie on demand.

Although Woodbury did not use his discretionary power to control the reserves of the deposit banks, he was aware that bank paper was increasing substantially and that bank credit was expanding more rapidly than the large importations of specie. The ratio of specie to paper money had "improved" from one-third to one-half between 1833 and 1835, he said, but had "much deteriorated in the last year and a half [to the end of 1835] . . . The currency may be considered as too redundant [sic], and in an unnatural and inflated condition." Such redundancy, he held, was a result of "numerous incorporations of new banks, without suitable legal restrictions, in many states, on either the amount of discounts or of the paper issued, in proportion to the specie on hand." He recommended that the states repress small issues of notes and restrict paper issues of banks to three times their holdings of specie; but he gave no indication that he could exercise exactly this control over the deposit banks if he so chose.[26]

At the same time that he was urging state laws for prescribing reserves of specie against outstanding notes, Woodbury held that the economy needed more specie because specie was a "substitute" for paper. At the same time, he saw paper money advantageously "economizing" specie.[27] Obviously he was reasoning tautologically. If the economy "needed" more specie to drive out paper, but then "needed" more paper to economize the use of specie, the result would have been continuous inflation.

Woodbury expressed the narrow view that the power of Congress to coin money and regulate its value "is a power evidently referring to specie and not to paper, as the latter is not coined, nor its value regulated by law." In contrast, John C. Calhoun had stated: "Whatever the Government receives and treats as money, is money; and if it be money, then they have under the Constitution the right to regulate it."[28]

5. The Specie Circular and Distribution of the Surplus

[The suspension] was the effect of necessity with the deposit banks, exhausted by vain efforts to meet the quarterly deliveries of the forty millions to be deposited with the States. (Thomas Hart Benton, *Thirty Years View*)

The Act to Regulate the Deposits of Public Money was passed by Congress after prolonged debate on June 23, 1836. The first dozen sections of the act defined the terms on which the deposit ("pet") banks might hold the fiscal balance due the Treasury of the United States,[1] and the last three sections ordered the distribution of the surplus fiscal balances in these banks. The cash balance of the government was already on deposit in the eighty-odd depository banks as a credit to the Treasury; the new statute simply prescribed that these balances be transferred to the credit of the state governments.[2]

Daniel Webster voiced the majority sentiment of contemporary legislators: "[The public money] is hoarded. It is withdrawn . . . and with great inconvenience and injury to the general business of the country."[3] But his observation contained only specious truth. Far from being locked up and withdrawn, the public money had been deposited in the chosen deposit banks and subjected to the multiplying effect of fractional reserve bank-credit expansion. "Depositing" the money with the states could have had the liberating effect implied by Webster only if the federal government had held a balance of hard cash independent of the banking system and the economy in general.[4]

The bill finally passed both houses of Congress by large majorities and was sent to Jackson. Senator Thomas Hart Benton, a presidential intimate and confidant on monetary and banking policies, reported that the

president signed the bill "with a repugnance of feeling," primarily because he realized that the popularity of such a measure might facilitate the election of Van Buren in the fall of that year.[5]

Even though he felt constrained to sign a bill he did not want in order to help elect a successor he did want, Jackson found a neutralizing executive order for which he could take personal responsibility, thereby causing no detriment to Van Buren. This order became the Specie Circular. It was issued to the collectors and disbursors of the public money on July 11, 1836, less than three weeks after passage of the Act to Regulate the Deposits and, more significantly, two weeks after Congress had adjourned. It was technically an order from the secretary of the Treasury to the collectors of public revenue and the deposit banks, which stated that after December 15, 1836, only specie would be acceptable for payment of public lands in parcels over 320 acres.

Secretary of the Treasury Levi Woodbury signed the order, although he had had no initiative in the action. Initiative had come from Senator Benton, who had sponsored a very similar bill in the session just ended. He had been the only senator to favor such a bill, so congressional antagonism to such a measure was abundantly clear.[6]

The Specie Circular was surely intended to operate as a deflationary device to prevent distribution of the surplus, first, by reducing the volume of spending on public lands and, second, by tending to reduce the amount of treasury balances available for distribution.[7] Simple analysis shows, however, that this dramatic political flourish had only negligible economic results.

Sales of public lands during 1836 yielded $25 million, or about one half of total government receipts (see table 5.1). Even if the Specie Circular had had the absolute effect of reducing sales of public lands to zero, the result on the general economy would have been infinitesimal. Aggregate spending in the economy at the time was about $1,000 million a year.[8] If no public land had been sold between July 11 and the end of the year, total spending would have been reduced a maximum of 1 percent. Since the amount spent on public lands did not fall to zero, the direct decline in spending exerted by the Specie Circular was at most a fraction of 1 percent. People who had only state bank notes and were thus unable to buy land might still have bought other goods and services currently produced. In fact, taken alone, a policy that tended to make the public unavailable would have had slightly inflationary effects and would have opposed the principal thrust of Jacksonian policy at that time. Finally, in almost all sections of the country, state bank notes were redeemable in specie on demand for ten months following the issuance of the Specie Circular. General economic effects can hardly be imputed to an alleged cause that involved such a lag.

Whether the Specie Circular decelerated total spending and whether it affected the size and location of the federal government's balances are distinct questions. In fact, the deposit balance to the credit of the Treasury in the deposit banks *increased* from $37.28 million to $45.06 million between June 1, 1836, and November 1, 1836, while the specie in these banks increased from $10.45 million to $15.52 million.[10] Secretary Woodbury's report for 1836 stated that weekly selections of new depository banks had been necessary because revenues had "increased over our expenditures so constantly and in such large amounts."[11] The damping effect of the circular on government receipts, then, was also negligible.

Another observation argues against a significant effect of the Specie Circular: the lack of any recurrence of large-scale purchases of public lands after the repeal of the circular in the middle of 1838. Sales of public lands resumed their normal level of $2 million to $3 million per year even though the economy experienced a substantial recovery during fiscal 1838-39.

Analysis of the real prices paid for land readily explains the land boom of the middle 1830s. The nominal price of land was fixed by statute at $1.25 per acre. When the general price level increased, the real price of land declined proportionally and land became a profitable investment for households and firms. But as the extensive margin of good land was

TABLE 5.1. Land sales in the United States by quarters, 1836-1838 (calendar years, millions of dollars).

| Year | Quarter | | | | |
	First	Second	Third	Fourth	Total[1]
1836	6.05	8.42[2]	5.86[2,3]	4.83[3]	25.16
1837	3.40	1.90[4]	0.35	1.13	6.78
1838[5]	0.50	0.50[6]	0.70	2.20	3.90

Source: *Treasury Reports, 1836-1838.*
1. Total land revenues for 1835 were $14.26 million.
2. For the second and third quarters of 1836, data were provided by Professor Harry Scheiber.
3. Specie Circular was issued July 11, 1836, and became effective December 16, 1836.
4. Banking system suspended specie payments.
5. Data for 1838 taken from W. B. Smith and Arthur Cole, *Fluctuations in American Business, 1790-1860,* (Cambridge, Mass.: Harvard University Press, 1935), p. 712.
6. Specie payments resumed and Specie Circular repealed.

pushed back—as better land was picked over and acquired—the remaining land was not so economically desirable even at the lower real price, and sales resumed their normal volume. This pattern of behavior can be inferred without recourse to the Specie Circular, and it is confirmed by the data in table 5.2.

Even though much new land (including much supermarginal land) was offered for sale through 1837, large volumes were purchased only when the real price fell in 1835 and 1836. By 1836 the real price was 25 percent less than in 1834. This result is respectably economic and demonstrates the high elasticity of demand for land.

Although the Specie Circular was of no consequence, the same cannot be said for the distribution of the surplus under the provisions of the Deposit Bank Act. Most descriptions and analyses of the distribution and the consequent panic of 1837 draw heavily from the first documentation on the subject, *The History of the Surplus Revenue of 1837*, by Edward G. Bourne. According to the usual treatment, the orders of the federal government for distributing the surplus among the states caused a flow of funds in opposition to the normal course of trade. Specie was allegedly forced west to further the sales of public lands in accordance with the Specie Circular, but was needed in the East in order to provide for the surplus distribution.[12] All the accounts base their analyses of the distribution on the assumption that an actual disbursement of funds was primarily responsible for the general economic collapse of the times. No one has examined the actual flow of funds to see whether the quantity of specie

TABLE 5.2. Sales and prices of public lands, 1833-1837.

Year	New land offered (millions of acres)	Land sold (millions of acres)	Receipts from land (millions of dollars)	Nominal price per acre ($)	Real price per acre ($)[1]
1833	6.615	3.856	4.972	1.29	1.36
1834	13.057	4.658	6.100	1.31	1.46
1835	13.767	12.564	16.000	1.27	1.27
1836	0.509	20.071	25.168	1.25	1.10
1837[2]	—	4.805	6.127	1.28	1.11

Source: U.S. Congress, 25th Cong., 2nd sess., *Senate Doc. No. 85*, p. 3.
1. Computed using Warren and Pearson's series for WPI, 1789-1890 (1910-1914 = 100), *Historical Statistics*, p. 115.
2. To September 30.

moved was significant, nor has anyone included the possibility of bank-credit contraction in general as a primary cause of the panic. The argument developed here is that the form and not the substance of the distribution was important, that plenty of specie was available in any section of the country to satisfy the distribution of funds in that section, but that the relatively small amount of specie actually withdrawn from the deposit banks initiated a critical bank-credit contraction.

That the distribution involved more than a transfer of specie was recognized by many influential men inside and outside government. Secretary Woodbury reported in December of 1836 that "the utmost care had been exercised . . . to prevent any unnecessary derangement or pressure in the money market, by affording reasonable time for all those transfers to be effected."[13] In another part of the same report he registered a less confident attitude: "The embarrassments incident to the transfers of such large sums of money, . . . and the consequent temporary withdrawal of considerable portions of it from immediate use, are embarrassments inseparable from the provisions and faithful execution of the law in its present form."[14] Here Woodbury demonstrated his awareness that the banking system might lose specie to the various state treasuries. He thus showed insight into the impending troubles, so his "embarrassment" (his key word) was probably well advised.

Many others also registered apprehension. Nicholas Biddle declared that banks had tolerated each other's notes in payments due the government, "and now that government has let loose upon them a demand for specie to the whole amount of these notes."[15]

Henry A. Wise, of Virginia, one of the most articulate critics of the government's financial policies, said in the House of Representatives before passage of the Deposit Bank Act that "to touch the surplus would be to lose it in the ruins of the deposit banks." He felt that the surplus would not be distributed, but he reckoned without his less determined colleagues.[16] And Senator Benton observed in retrospect that "the first installment [was] delivered the first of January, in specie or its equivalent; the second in April, also in valid money." But for the third installment, "the federal government could only do as others did, and pay out depreciated paper." The government, he alleged, was "taken by surprise in the deprivation of its revenues."[17]

Woodbury, who had already shown some misgivings, added after the event: "It is not to be expected that several of [the banks] would be able to pay over at once, and in specie, the whole of the large amount then in their possession."[18] If the probability of the payments had been in doubt, Woodbury's failure to impose defensive fractional reserve requirements on the deposit banks when deposits were building up in the latter half of 1836 is a major fault in his administration of the Treasury Department.

Previous analyses based on the statistics of the distribution have not sharply distinguished between government deposits in the banks and the specie reserves available to pay such deposits. As tables 5.3 and 5.4 show, the deposit banks had specie reserves of only $15.52 million against government deposits alone of $45.06 million. The specie reserves of the whole banking system, being only $40.02 million, could not have satisfied the government's potential specie demand; and obviously the government would not and did not demand specie for the bulk of the funds it distributed. One can deduce that about $5 million of specie was put into transit, and other evidence supports this estimate.

Table 5.5 groups the states into North and East, West, and South, and shows the amounts on deposit in these regions, the amounts due them as a result of the distributional statute, and treasury balances available for satisfying the distribution requirement. If the regions are accepted as defined, and the assumption is made that each region took care of itself insofar as it was able, only the South would have required funds from other regions. The Northeast had $8.57 million of government deposits in "surplus" states with which to pay off $1.58 million to "deficit" states; the West had $10.32 with which to pay off $0.72 million. Even the South required only $1.90 million more than was at the disposition of the Treasury in that region for the distribution, and the total amount that had to be transferred from all surplus states to all deficit states in any case was only $5.58 million.[19]

Such a statistical breakdown explodes the East-West funds-in-transit hypothesis. The deposits in both regions were many times the amount necessary for satisfying the demands of those regions. The critical factor was the amount of specie reserves that had been stretched thin in the support of bank credit.

TABLE 5.3. Principal assets and liabilities of all banks (millions of dollars).

Item	Jan. 1, 1836	Jan. 1, 1837	July 1, 1837	Change from Jan. 1, 1836 to July 1, 1837
Specie	40.02	38.71	30.03	− 9.99
Circulation	140.30	151.31	117.76	−22.54
Deposits	115.10	129.66	93.76	−21.34
Total	295.42	319.68	241.55	

Sources: *Treasury Report to Special Session,* 1837, p. 61, and *Treasury Report,* 1837, p. 39.

TABLE 5.4. Principal assets and liabilities of deposit banks (millions of dollars).

Item	Nov. 1, 1836	May 1, 1837	Aug. 15, 1837	Change from Nov. 1, 1836 to Aug. 15, 1837
Specie	15.52	13.33	10.53	− 4.94
Circulation	41.48	37.62	32.63	− 8.85
U. S. Treasury	45.06	26.86	12.94	−32.12
Private deposits	26.57	30.78	29.49	+ 2.92
Total	128.63	108.59	85.68	

Sources: *Treasury Report to Special Session,* 1837, p. 61; and *Treasury Report,* 1837, p. 39.

This analysis rests on the assumption that no specie would be transferred to a state or even within a state unless the amount due from the distribution was greater than the amount of treasury deposits in the banks of that state. Such an assumption is reasonable and proper. State treasuries, to which the federal Treasury sent checks drawn against the deposit banks, would deposit the checks themselves in the banks they used for the same purpose. In many cases both state and federal governments would use the same bank; or if a state government did not employ a depository bank within its boundaries against which the federal government had drawn a check, chances were good that the state would begin to employ that bank in order not to embarrass the bank by a withdrawal of funds.

Such charity could not be imputed to a state government that received a check drawn against an out-of-state bank, especially if that state was very distant. In addition, some states in which few or no banks existed might well keep the funds as specie in their own treasuries until disposition was made sometime in the future. Only when specie was pulled out of the depository banks would the banking system find its position precarious; and the fractional reserve nature of the system magnified the delicacy of the situation.

The absolute loss of $4.94 million of specie from the deposit banks (table 5.4) during the distribution is significant because it is between the $1.90 million the South required on net balance and the $5.58 million estimated as the maximum interstate transfer necessary for effecting the distribution. The loss of this much specie was matched by a sevenfold contraction of bank credit, an event that goes much further in explaining the panic of 1837 than the mere assumption of funds in transit. The rest of the banking system also lost specie and correspondingly contracted.

TABLE 5.5. Statistics of Treasury balances in state banks and distributional shares due each state and each region (thousands of dollars).

State	(1) Due from distribution in three installments	(2) Treasury deposits with banks as of Dec., 19, 1836	(2) − (1) Deficit (−) or surplus (+)
Maine	956	508	− 448
New Hampshire	669	632	− 37
Vermont	669	162	− 507
Massachusetts	1,338	2,386	+1,048
Rhode Island	382	350	− 32
Connecticut	765	741	− 24
New York	4,015	11,536	+7,521
New Jersey	765	534	− 231
Pennsylvania	2,868	2,685	− 183
Delaware	287	170	− 117
Totals East and North	12,714	19,704	6,990
Maryland	956	·1,225	+ 269
Virginia	2,199	1,239	− 960
North Carolina	1,434	661	− 773
South Carolina	1,051	937	− 114
Georgia	1,051	559	− 492
Alabama	669	1,408	+ 739
Tennessee	1,434	492	− 942
Kentucky	1,434	1,803	+ 369
Totals South	10,228	8,324	−1,904
Mississippi	382	1,791	+1,409
Louisiana	478	4,382	+3,904
Ohio	2,077	3,131	+1,054
Indiana	860	2,136	+1,276
Illinois	478	46	− 432
Missouri	382	1,881	+1,499
Arkansas	287	0	− 287
Michigan	287	1,462	+1,175
Totals West	5,231	14,819	9,598
Total	28,173	42,857	net 14,684

Source: E. G. Bourne, *The History of the Surplus Revenue of 1837* (New York, 1885), p. 142, with corrections to the arithmetic in the original.

But nondepository banks lost less in absolute terms, even though they held a greater total of specie, and their credit contracted less relative to the specie reserves lost.

Specific details on the transfer of moneys for the three installments of the distribution are given in *Letters on State Deposits* in the National Archives.[20] These letters were sent from Secretary Woodbury to the state bank depositories just after November 1, 1836, apprising them of the amounts that would be drawn against the government's accounts. Starting in January 1837, Woodbury sent other letters with warrants for these amounts to the state treasuries. No records exist showing in what form the states cleared the warrants they had against the depository banks; but each state was sent checks from the Treasury drawn against banks in that state insofar as such coordination was possible. The residual, that part drawn in favor of states *not* from banks in those states and presumably paid in specie, was divided as indicated in table 5.6.

These values show that of more than $18 million distributed to the states in the first two installments, only $2.29 million involved an inter-

TABLE 5.6. Interstate transfers ordered by Treasury for first two installments of the surplus.

Transfer	Amount, (millions of dollars)
From Massachusetts (all Boston banks and payable to Maine and New Hampshire)	0.395
From New York (almost all New York City banks and payable to Vermont, New Jersey, North Carolina, Connecticut, and Virginia)	1.431
From Mississippi (from Natchez banks to Arkansas)	0.115
From Indiana (State Bank of Indiana and branches to Illinois and Missouri)	0.351
Total	$2.292

Source: National Archives and Records Service, Record Group No. 56, *Letters on State Deposits*, June 27, 1836 to Sept. 11, 1837 (Washington, D.C.)

state transfer. The New York City depository banks were the ones drawn against most heavily for the whole distribution. These banks saw their Treasury deposits reduced by $9.90 million between November 1836, and August 1837, but they lost only $2.39 million in specie.[21] Their specie loss was over half the total amount lost from all depository banks; but the fact that this loss was only one-fourth the decrease in their Treasury deposits implies that three-fourths of New York City banks' payments to the states were made either in their own notes or in deposit accounts credited to the different states.

Woodbury's reports, both before and after the distribution, suggest the same pattern of specie losses and bank-credit transfers. In December 1836 he foresaw the "trouble and embarrassment" of sudden transfers of money in January but anticipated that these effects could be minimized "by combining . . . the transfers ordered by Congress to be soon made from banks having an excess [of Treasury deposits] with transfer of that excess to other banks in the States where it was to be paid—and in which last-described banks and States a deficiency existed."[22]

An interesting case that developed during the distribution again demonstrates the validity of the intrastate deposit-distribution hypothesis. Woodbury issued warrants for first installment payments of $225,000 against the Agricultural Bank of Mississippi at Natchez as part of the allotments going to Tennessee and Arkansas. Payment was demanded in specie by the state of Tennessee, but the Agricultural Bank refused to honor the drafts: It would not or could not pay specie. Woodbury then shifted the payments due Tennessee and Arkansas to banks in Louisville, Cincinnati, New York, and New Orleans and issued warrants for $255,000 against the Agricultural Bank of Natchez for the second and third installments to the state of Mississippi, *because* this bank had not honored the specie request from Tennessee. Obviously, the Mississippi draft did not require specie in order to clear.[23]

The financial crisis of 1837 provoked President Van Buren to call a special session of Congress in September of that year. In his report to that session Woodbury again confirmed this hypothesis when he stated that "a considerable portion of the money since [the beginning of the suspension], as well as formerly, paid by the banks on transfers and drafts [for the distribution] has not been demanded nor paid in specie."[24]

The most logical conclusion on the substance of the distribution is that the depository banks and the state treasuries cooperated in great part, but that in cases of interstate demands (particularly against New York banks), the state treasuries required specie, provoking a bank-credit contraction that initiated the crisis of 1837. Once the state treasuries had divested themselves of these funds (one year later), specie payments were resumed.[25]

Secretary Woodbury had the deposits in the depository banks as judiciously placed as possible for an efficacious transfer of titles to the state governments. However, his responsibilities under the Deposit Bank Act required more of him. Since he had been given the authority to regulate the reserves in the deposit banks almost six months before the distribution began, he could have specified a specie requirement that would have forced the depository banks to hold extra reserves. If he had assumed an excess of only $5 million, a reasonable assumption in view of the insights he and others had shown into the increased demand for specie that distribution might provoke, a 20 percent specie requirement would have sufficed to neutralize the specie loss induced by the distribution. The depository banks would have had to restrain note and deposit liabilities to about $77 million instead of letting them expand to $113 million as they did (see table 5.3). Since treasury deposits in the banks increased by $8 million and specie reserves by over $5 million between June 1 and November 1, 1836, increased reserve requirements would have been sufficient to restrict bank-credit expansion and the magnitude of the subsequent contraction. As the titles to the deposits were transferred to the states, the requirements could have been eased accordingly.

Any such imposition on the banking system at this time would have resulted in protests from the banks and from some legislators.[26] It would have been dangerous, too, as some observers would have claimed that such a maneuver would trigger a depression. Playing it safe, as Woodbury did, by following the letter of the distribution law absolved him of any responsibility for the collapse that followed. He recognized that the bank failures were serious but reported with "pleasure" that most of the deposit banks had reduced circulation and discounts.[27] In an earlier year he had piously denied that treasury deposits had been moved from one section of the country to another for any but fiscal reasons. At the time he had said that whatever transfers had been made had tended "to obviate rather than create any pressure in the money market."[28]

The conclusions here are criticisms—substantive and methodological—of what actually happened and of the reasoning usually applied to what actually happened.

First, the Specie Circular was dramatic but innocuous.

Second, the effect of the distribution was appreciable almost entirely because a small portion of it was a quasi-increase in the demand for hand-to-hand specie by the state governments, a demand that had to be fulfilled by an internal specie drain from key metropolitan commercial banks. Since the commercial banking system operated on a fractional reserve basis, a decline of the banks' specie holdings forced a manifold contraction of their demand liabilities, the medium used by the general public for conducting almost all its purchases and sales.

Third, a nominal but courageous treasury policy for increased reserve ratios in the deposit banks during the predistribution period would have largely mitigated any specie losses the banks suffered.

The preceding analysis and conclusions deny that the Specie Circular had any fundamental economic effects. Political it may have been; economic it was not.[29]

The distribution of the surplus, on the other hand, had pervasive effects on the banking system and the economy. It distributed titles to bank deposits from United States Treasury offices to state treasuries. It thus transferred discretion over this money to twenty-six state governments. This windfall—a nineteenth-century version of revenue-sharing—required time for its ultimate disbursement. Once the state legislatures had the money, they had to go through the process of debating and negotiating its disposition. In addition, some state governments demanded redemption of their claims in specie from the federal government's depository banks. The thesis just argued is that this small but significant and unavoidable demand for specie provoked a fractional reserve bank-credit contraction of substantial proportions in 1837.

This view is relatively short run. It ignores external specie movements for the period under consideration. The demand for redemption of bank obligations in specie may be viewed as an increase in the ratio of specie to bank-created money,[30] while the contraction of bank credit was simply an increase in the specie reserve-deposit ratio. These changes could have occurred independently of external specie flows that altered the stock of high-powered money. These two ratio changes, with changes in the specie base held constant, occurred during the year in which the Distribution Act was passed and the bank-credit contraction and specie suspension also took place.

A more comprehensive study by Peter Temin specifically treats the issue of the specie flows. In his book *The Jacksonian Economy* Temin argues persuasively that the "bank war" did not initiate the bank-credit expansion and inflation of 1834-1837. Temin attributes the boom at this time directly to voluminous specie inflows, which were primarily a result of capital exports from England to the United States. This flow allowed the United States to keep its specie [silver] in the face of a trade deficit rather than lose it through trade to the Orient. The inflation of the period, Temin concludes, was specie-inspired.[31]

The increases in the specie-money and reserve-deposit ratios in 1837 subsequently caused the money stock to decline. Specie inflows continued but at a rate only half as great as the average for the preceding three years.[32] Thus the rate of increase in what is now called the monetary base declined greatly as the critical money-determining ratios increased. These changes had predictable effects. The banks' attempts to stay solvent resulted in suspension of specie payments. Loans were restricted, and the banks' demand obligations were reduced. By July 1, 1837, bank-held specie was down to $30 million from $38 million in January. (See table 5.3.)

Temin argues that the distribution, "while it posed a burden for the banking system, and while it created much trouble after the suspension of payments, did not cause the suspension."[33] Temin attributes the primary cause of the suspension to the actions of the Bank of England in the summer of 1836 when it raised its discount rate and imposed other credit restrictions. These policies had repercussions in the United States on interest rates, on the price of foreign exchange, and eventually on the price of cotton.[34]

Since all these events, including the distribution, are correlated, assigning primacy of cause to any one is difficult and perhaps only of limited importance. The fact remains, however, that in the first half of 1837 the banking system lost considerable specie at the same time that specie inflows to the United States were still substantial. The specie held by people and by state governments increased at the expense of bankheld specie. Even if the state governments had simply transferred their claims on the distribution from the federal government's depositories to the institutions they used for the same purposes, the ratio of specie to bank obligations would have increased. The specie-losing banks would have had to contract. Then only after a lag would the specie-receiving banks have been able to expand commensurately. Add to this lag the fact that some state governments kept the specie in their own state treasuries until it was distributed within these states, and much of the decline in bankheld specie is explained. Thus the initiating factor may well have been the Bank of England's policy in the latter half of 1836; but without the distribution of the surplus as an aggravating factor, the bank panic and suspension would probably have been nothing more than a gentle decline to the position the economy came to assume by mid 1838.

6. The Independent Treasury System before the Civil War

You propose to enable . . . the Secretary of the Treasury . . . to purchase said stocks at their "market value" . . . Why to purchase it at the market value, you make your Treasury Department a broker! And I shall move that "market value" be stricken out, and "par value" be substituted . . . There is no reason why this engine of corruption should be placed in the hands of any party, or any officer in any department of the Government. (W. F. Giles, House of Representatives, 21 January 1847)

Much debate has centered on whether recovery after the panic of 1837 was genuine or merely a stage in a longer decline to the trough of 1843. Events of 1838 and contemporary opinion on the state of that economy confirm that no downward *trend* was evident at the time. Most states permitted banks a year of grace, either by custom or by law, in which to reestablish specie payments after a suspension; and by May 1838 specie payments were again general and genuine. Specie imports of $14 million to the United States between September 1837 and September 1838 considerably helped the processes of resumption and recovery.[1] The unpopular Specie Circular was also repealed by overwhelming majorities in both houses of Congress on May 29, 1838. This action had little effect—it was more of an afterthought, as specie payments had already been resumed several weeks earlier.

In his Treasury report of December 1838 Secretary of the Treasury Levi Woodbury exuded optimism over the state of business. The banking system had more specie reserves than it had ever had before, but it had refrained from expanding notes and deposits to their inflated volume of a few years earlier.[2]

During 1839 the prospects for continuing prosperity, which had seemed so bright at the beginning of the year, dimmed. The constant specie imports of the preceding six years were replaced by a specie export of $3 million to help finance a trade deficit of $39 million for the year.

Prices, which had held steady from the middle of 1837, started to decline about the middle of 1839 and continued falling until 1843 when they reached a trough 30 percent below their 1837-1839 level.[3] Recovery was a mirror image of recession, although business activity did not really become buoyant until after the gold discoveries of 1848-1850.

The institution most prominent in the development of monetary policies during the later thirties and early forties, and for a long time afterward, was the independent treasury system. Its emergence was pragmatic and circumstantial; but it initiated many of the monetary policies in use today, including open-market operations in government securities. Advocates and detractors of this system debated most of the controversial issues still current in contemporary policymaking.

Sentiment favoring such a system was voiced in Congress as early as 1834 when William F. Gordon of Virginia, an anti-Jackson Democrat, offered the plan. He opposed the increase in power of the executive branch under Jackson and wished "to make those who received the revenue the agents for its custody . . . and also for its disbursement."[4] Gordon's proposal lost by a vote of 33 to 161 in spite of the favor it received from hard-money Democrats such as Senator Thomas Hart Benton and William M. Gouge, an influential Treasury official.[5] In 1835 R. T. Gamble of Georgia again tried to put forth the same proposal, but his resolution was also rejected. Congressional sentiment leaned toward a trial for the state bank depository system.

The Deposit Bank Act was passed in lieu of an independent treasury act and by its provisions permitted selected state banks to assume the custodial role of the government's funds. Congress tried to incorporate banking regulation in this act in order to prevent executive control over the purse and commercial bank inflation of the credit structure. The net effect of this legislation was to leave control of the Treasury's moneys to the discretion of the secretary of the Treasury.

When the state depository bank structure collapsed in 1837, the doctrinaire group of hard-money men favoring an independent treasury was joined by a second force of disillusioned "pet bank" supporters. By 1840 this alliance was able to pass the Independent Treasury Act and to pass it again in 1846 after the Whigs had made one more attempt to reinstitute a national bank in 1841.[6]

The independent treasury did not simply begin operations upon enactment of a statute; it developed gradually as a result of the inefficacies within the state bank depository system in conducting the monetary affairs for the government during the later 1830s. When the state bank depositories were paying specie, that is, were not operating on a suspended basis, their notes, specie, and treasury notes were by law all payable and receivable in government transactions. When the state banks were not paying specie, only treasury notes and specie were acceptable by law. (Banks that did not pay specie on demand could not qualify as government depositories.) Therefore, while the state bank depository system was operating properly, no immediate depository problems or monetary crises called for a change in that system; and when the state bank system defaulted, the government was practically operating on an independent treasury basis anyway. Only after approximately ten years of this makeshift did a majority of Congress and a Democratic administration establish the independent treasury de jure.

A bill to create an independent treasury was brought up in a special session of Congress in 1837 but was postponed. It came up again in 1838 and was passed in the Senate but rejected in the House. It was then introduced and passed in 1840 by decisive margins. Debate over the bill in the House was extensive and became heated. When it finally passed, Caleb Cushing of Massachusetts, an outspoken Whig, moved that the title be changed to "An act to enable the public money to be drawn from the Treasury without appropriations made by law." His reference was to the discretionary power of the secretary, granted by the tenth section of the act, to transfer money from one depository to another. As soon as Cushing had made this motion, a disordered debate "was renewed with tenfold fury, and some members made use of some very hard words, accompanied by violent gesticulation."[7] Lawmakers seem to have taken their responsibilities very seriously in those days.

The general Whig victory in November 1840 changed the whole political picture. The Whigs now had their chance to incorporate another national, quasi-central bank. It was believed that such an institution might somehow be able to reverse the downward course of business activity. Accordingly a special session of Congress was called for the summer of 1841. Before the newly elected Harrison could assume any presidential leadership or duties, he died and Vice-President John Tyler took office. Tyler had been a senator from Virginia when Jackson was president, and his secretary of the Treasury, Thomas Ewing of Ohio, had held similar office.

With large majorities in Congress, the Whigs easily repealed the Independent Treasury Act. They then turned their attention to the creation of a fiscal bank, their new name for a third bank of the United States. Henry Clay, the leader in the Senate, asked for a report from the secretary of the Treasury on the feasibility of incorporating a national bank, a report that would presumably include all the qualities that would make a bank bill acceptable to the president.[8] Ewing and the rest of the cabinet had been appointed by Harrison, not Tyler, but no one felt that any incompatibility existed between Tyler and his cabinet; so Ewing's report was understood by Congress as one that essentially met the predilections of the president. This report stated, among other things, that the fiscal bank should be "so selected or framed as to exert a salutary influence over the business and currency of the country . . . The active business of the country . . . [is] intimately connected with and dependent upon the financial arrangements of the General Government. If they be wise and beneficient, they indirectly, but efficiently, promote those great interests of the people; if constant and uniform in their action, they give to those interests confidence and stability."[9] This statement brings out three important facets of Whig monetary principles: first, a clear acceptance of a policy-making national bank; second, the liaison of this bank with federal government fiscal affairs; and third, the use of monetary policy for the promotion of general economic stability.[10]

The bill for the fiscal bank reported out by Congress called for a reserve requirement of at least 33 percent specie to bills (paper currency) in circulation, while it limited deposits to 175 percent of capital, or a total of primary deposits plus $20 million.[11] The bill passed by a narrow margin in the Senate, but by a much larger majority in the House, and went to the president on August 7, 1841.

Even though Ewing had worked very hard to get out a bill that, according to Benton, would "avoid the President's objections, and save his consistency—a point upon which he was exceedingly sensitive," Tyler vetoed the bill—much to the surprise of both those for and those against it.[12] Not suspecting that any underhandedness was involved, supporters of the bill in the House then revived a dormant currency bill, dressed it up as a fiscal corporation bill, and rushed it through Congress. Every conciliatory gesture to the president was made by the Whig congressmen in framing this second bill, but again the measure was vetoed, and nowhere near enough votes were present to override the veto.[13]

The most valid analysis of Tyler's unseemly actions is given by Benton. According to Benton's account, a political splinter of the Whig party approached Tyler early in the special session with the idea of forming a third party that would be anti-Clay, anti-national bank, and pro-state's rights. It hoped to draw enough support from the Whigs and the Democrats to form a new political majority. By enlisting Tyler as its leader, the new movement would have some initial momentum and prestige. Tyler accepted the scheme.[14]

The orthodox Whigs went to great lengths to conciliate the splinter group, as they did not know that the new party would not allow *any* bank bill to get through. Tyler's ostensible compromise on the fiscal corporation bill after the defeat of the fiscal bank bill was deceitful. He had to give the appearance of support, but he hoped that enough negative votes would be negotiated in Congress to defeat the bill before it reached him. When the bill passed both houses of Congress, Tyler had to veto it because this veto was "the edifice of the new party, and the democratic baptismal regeneration of Mr. Tyler himself."[15]

All Tyler's cabinet except Webster resigned.[16] In his letter of resignation Ewing pointed out that he had been asked by Tyler to be agent and negotiator for the bill and that the bill had been "framed and fashioned according to your own suggestions." The veto message, he continued, "attacks in an especial manner the very provisions which were inserted at your request."[17]

Ewing's indictment emphasized Tyler's hypocrisy. Far from structuring a viable third party, Tyler's actions simply provoked repudiation and condemnation by the Whig Party. This schism proved crippling to any further Whig legislation. And the first regular session of Congress in Tyler's presidential term was yet to meet! Benton summed up the situation: "To the Whigs, it was a galling and mortifying desertion, and ruinous besides. A national bank was their life—the vital principle—without which they could not live as a party—the power which was to give them power . . . To lose it, was to lose the fruits of the election, with the prospect of losing the party itself."[18]

During the next four years the Tyler administration had to operate as a lame duck; only a handful of Virginians stayed with it. The remainder of the Whigs simply repudiated it, and no cooperative program was possible. The administration still had to carry out routine operations. A new cabinet was subsequently appointed, with Walter Forward of Pennsylvania as secretary of the Treasury. Forward had been a member of Congress from 1822 to 1825 and had played an important role in the original formation of the Whig party. As a reward for his services in the campaign of 1840, he had been appointed first comptroller of the currency, and he accepted the secretaryship when Ewing resigned.

Tyler, perhaps in some spirit of reconciliation, suggested yet another fiscal-banking organization in his message to Congress in late 1841. The Senate Committee on Finance then dutifully asked the secretary of the Treasury to submit the draft of a bill for a "board of exchequer" in compliance with the president's message. Forward in his reply went even further than had his predecessors in arguing for a policymaking institution. He said that the question to be considered was whether the "Government shall attempt to supply a sound paper medium for payments to the Treasury, and for the general uses of the people . . . [and whether] it shall attempt to benefit the general business of the community."[19] He stated that the government had the *duty* of furnishing a paper money with a countercyclical bias. A board of the exchequer would further such a duty, because it "would furnish [Treasury] notes for disbursement and receive them for taxes. With these means, and, by faithful and skillful management, though it might be embarrassed by the prostration of other institutions around it, it would still retain its own credit; and that credit would be a fructifying and vivifying germe, amid general blight and barrenness [*sic*]."[20]

Forward's report showed that the board would have to exert some control over the banking system in order to control the stock of money advantageously. "Whenever a bank makes a loan, or a discount, by the issue of its bills, it adds so much to the circulating medium of the country. To such a system there must be some check." He confessed that he was "to some degree uncertain" on just how note issues by the board should be proscribed; but such issues would convert "the most austere . . . duty of the Government, the collection of taxes, into the very means of sustaining the industry . . . by whom taxes are paid."[21]

Although the plan for a board of exchequer showed sophistication in the development of purposive monetary policy, it never came up for consideration in Congress. Benton reported that in the House of Representatives "[i]t died a natural death on the calendar on which it was placed. In the Senate the fate of the measure was still more compendiously decided." The Committee on Finance, "deeming [the bill] unworthy of consideration, through its chairman, Mr. Evans of Maine, prayed to be discharged from the consideration of it, and were so discharged accordingly."[22]

Tyler mentioned the plan again in his message to Congress the following year, but nothing more was done about it. The Whigs in Congress were too disillusioned by Tyler's inconsistencies and political machinations to bother with anything except routine legislation. The Democrats obtained control of Congress in the elections of 1842, thus completely ruling out the adoption of any Whig financial institution.

The Whig attempts to promote a central banking institution during their short-lived political dominance of 1840-1842 have been largely neglected in monetary history. Equally overlooked have been the policies of Whigs and Democrats with regard to issues of treasury notes. These notes were usually reserved for "emergencies," for example, the War of 1812. For the twenty years following the formation of the Second Bank no fiscal emergencies had developed, so no issues of treasury notes had been authorized. Government revenues again proved inadequate after the distribution of the surplus in 1837, and treasury notes reappeared for several years running. The government's primary source of income, tariff revenues, had become progressively smaller in the late 1830s due to revised tariff schedules and a decline of trade, and sales of public lands had also fallen. The deficits that arose were optimistically seen as temporary, so the temporary expedient of issuing treasury notes was frequently authorized to finance them.

These notes had slightly different characteristics from one issue to the next. Usually they were not reissuable and only drew interest for one year. But they were legal tender for all payments due to and from the government, and many of the issues were generally regarded and used as bank reserves. Henry Clay believed that the measure authorizing the notes in 1837 would turn the government into a bank "with Mr. Woodbury [the current secretary] as the great cashier."[23]

In a debate over a similar bill in 1840 Daniel Webster alleged that Woodbury had been depositing the notes in the state banks still used as depositories and checking against the accounts thus created.[24] A deposit implied that the banks and Treasury were willing to treat the notes as liquid, primary reserves on which the banks could expand credit. A sale would have implied much less liquidity; the treasury notes would have been regarded as income-earning assets in competition with other income-earning assets held by the banks, and they would have been conducive to an expansion of credit only if the banking system had purchased them with "excess" reserves.[25] Since the notes could be deposited in banks by the general public, prohibition of similar action by the Treasury was incongruous no matter how the banks subsequently treated the notes. Nonetheless, Webster's protest stimulated a special inquiry from the Senate to Woodbury asking "whether Treasury notes, bearing interest, have been deposited in banks for the purpose of raising a credit to be drawn against by the Treasury Department."[26]

Woodbury replied that treasury notes had been utilized as a fiscal expedient since 1837. When the notes could be sold to the banks for specie, their interest rate was 5 or 6 percent. Otherwise the notes were issued as currency at infinitesimal rates of interest.[27] He pointed out that the Treasury Department had discretion over the rates at which the notes were issued and that the rates had been changed from time to time "so as to accommodate the state of the money market and the condition of the currency, as well as to sustain the public credit."[28] He then gave statistics for the issues made during the three years 1837-1839. Of $19.57 million issued, $7.78 million had been either sold or issued to banks as interest-earning assets, and $11.79 million had been issued as currency.[29] Interestingly enough, $7.44 million (almost 40 percent) of the total amount issued during the three-year period was expended in the second quarter of 1838 just before the resumption of specie payments in May of that year. (See table 6.1.)

Woodbury made available some correspondence he had had with a treasury agent in New York in April and May of 1838. The agent, John Barney, wrote that he could not get specie for the notes in New York, but that he was sure he could get $5 million from the Bank of France. Obtaining the specie from abroad, he thought, would "prevent the whole ten millions [of securities] being brought into market here, to absorb all the floating capital [specie], and increase distress." Then on May 20, 1838, Barney wrote that since the new treasury note act would probably pass Congress that day, "there is a constant demand for six percent Treasury notes in exchange for specie, at par,"[30] and all the notes were subsequently floated to banks on "special deposite" at 6 percent.

In what regard the banks held the treasury notes and how many of the notes not bearing interest they held as reserves are difficult questions. In an exchange with John Brockenbrough, president of the Bank of Virginia, that took place in early 1839, Woodbury reported that he had offered Brockenbrough some of the current listing of treasury notes at 6 percent, with redemption anticipated in about six months. Brockenbrough had said that his bank could not accept the offer unless the notes could be used if necessary "to meet the reflux of our circulation," that is, unless the

TABLE 6.1. Stock of money, prices, and specie flows 1833-1860 (all values except prices in millions of dollars).

Year	Beginning-of-year state bank notes and deposits		Specie in banks	Prices (1913=100)	Export (−) or import (+) of specie
					(Oct. 1-Sept. 30)
1833		170	25	56	+ 4.5
1834		190	26	57	+15.6
1835		204	44	60	+ 6.7
1836		278	40	68	+ 9.1
1837	288	160[1]	38	72	+ 4.5
1838	201	158	35	71	+13.2
1839	225	176	45	71	− 3.1
1840	183	159	33	60	+ 0.4
1841	172	139	35	60	− 5.0
1842	146	144	28	55	− 0.7
					(Oct. 1-June 30)
1843	115	128	34	51	+20.8
					(July 1-June 30)
1843-44	160	137	50	52	+ 0.4
1845	178	165	44	54	− 4.5
1846	178		44	54	− 0.1
1847	203		42	58	+22.2
1848	198		35	58	− 9.5
1849	232		46	54	+ 1.3
1850	206		44	51	− 2.9
1851	241		45	54	−24.0
1852	284		49	60	−37.1

TABLE 6.1. (cont.)

Year	Beginning-of-year state bank notes and deposits	Specie in banks	Prices (1913=100)	Export (−) or import (+) of specie	
1853	298		60	−23.3	
1854	292	47	64	−34.4	
1855	393	59	64	−52.6	
1856	377	54	67	−41.5	
1857	409	59	68	−56.6	
1858	445	58	70	−33.3	
1859	341	74	69	−56.5	
1860	453	105	63	−58.0	
1861	461	84	61		+16.5

Sources: Most of the data in this table for bank notes, deposits, and specie were taken from *Historical Statistics of the United States* (1789-1945) (Washington D.C.: Department of Commerce, 1949). These values are probably fairly accurate for years after 1845. For years before 1845, the figures compiled by George Macesich "Monetary Disturbances from 1834-45," (Ph.D. diss., University of Chicago, 1958), are superior.

The price index and the import and export of specie were also taken from *Historical Statistics*. The price index was compiled originally by the Federal Reserve Bank of New York and drew from work done by Alvin H. Hansen.

Note: Due to a change in statistical measurement in 1843, the values for specie import and export begin a quarter of a year before the year indicated, while the other values are as of January 1. After 1843 the specie values lead the other values by six months.

1. Macesich's data, from "Monetary Disturbances from 1834-45."

notes could be used as bank reserves. Woodbury said that they could not be so used and would have to be held to maturity, thus indicating that *he* would not sanction deposit of the notes.[31] Woodbury's opinion had no force of law, or even custom, behind it. The banks did not face legal reserve requirements. So the only question was whether the general public would accept the notes in the reflux function. Since the notes were legal tender for government dues and were generally treated as money, their reserve function was practically established. Of course, the notes issued at nominal interest rates (0.01 percent) were accepted as bank reserves and as currency without question.

Congress's recognition of the liquidity of the treasury notes, especially the leverage these notes might exert through the banking system, is comment enough on the position the Treasury then held. Only Woodbury's ambivalences over the Treasury's role in monetary affairs—his general mugwumpism—prevented the Treasury from assuming central banking functions of a more obvious bent.

In 1841 several opinions by Whig leaders in the House of Representatives over subsequent treasury note bills focused the Treasury's monetary position even more sharply. Daniel D. Barnard of New York objected that under the treasury note act proposed for that year "paper may be issued designed to become, and which would become, a common medium of payment and circulation between the Government and its creditors and debtors, and, as far as it would go, a common money medium in circulation in the community."[32]

John C. Calhoun, a leader in congressional monetary thought, had earlier voiced the very practical opinion: "Whatever the Government receives and treats as money, is money; and, if it be money, then they have under the Constitution the power to regulate it."[33] He expressed himself in favor of treasury note authorizations as he felt "that the elements of a true and stable currency . . . would be found to consist partly of gold and silver, and of paper, resting not on the credit and authority of banks, but of the Government itself."[34]

Even the Whigs found themselves forced to rely on treasury notes after their attempts to establish a fiscal bank in 1841. Walter Forward, secretary of the Treasury, wrote a special message to the House Committee on Ways and Means in January 1842 calling for a treasury note issue. Then John Spencer of New York, Forward's successor, issued a relatively small amount of treasury notes in 1844 with a convertibility feature. That is, the notes were convertible into specie at par at either treasury depository in New York City. That the notes were redeemable on demand, and not after some intervening time period, confirmed that they were not issued in anticipation of tax payments but were issued as if they were paper money. The House Committee on Ways and Means condemned Spencer's action on the obvious grounds that the Treasury had no need to issue notes if specie was available, and that such an issue could only be regarded as an unconstitutional emission of paper money.[35]

The use of treasury note issues to cover government deficits gave the independent treasury one characteristic of a central bank of issue. Whether its sponsors intended it to conduct monetary policy in this fashion is an academic question. Given (1) an international specie standard, (2) a fairly fixed volume of government expenditures, (3) tariff revenues that were highly elastic with respect to domestic money income, and (4) government revenues that were an appreciable fraction of national money income, two stabilizing monetary forces would act on the economy. If, for example, the internal price level declined, then a favorable balance of trade would arise that would lead to a specie inflow. Long-term credits granted by the creditor country would—and frequently did —modify this process (for example, in 1839-1841). In addition, the decline in the internal price level with the proportionally greater decline in tariff revenues would result in a fiscal deficit to the government. The debt created by the government to meet such a deficit would generally consist of liquid assets. Treasury notes were certainly as liquid as specie, and even long-term bonds if sold to banks with "excess" reserves would also generate new bank notes and deposits. With the combined effects of the specie inflow and the fiscal deficit, buoyancy in the economy would most likely be experienced when a low absolute volume of imports was joined with a large surplus in the balance of payments and a large federal deficit. The reverse of these conditions could be expected to be correspondingly constraining.

The time series in table 6.2 tend to support this general hypothesis. Gold imports were over $13 million in 1838, for example, while treasury note issues were almost $5 million net for the whole year. Since the total stock of bank-held specie was $35 million, these liquidity inputs were large enough to have resulted in the short-lived but well-defined prosperity of 1838-39.

The unique monetary-fiscal footing enjoyed by the independent treasury practically ordained that it would become an agent of monetary policy, especially when fiscal deficits were financed by treasury notes. Congress implied its awareness of this position in its debate over the treasury note measure in 1847, when a fiscal deficit was impending due to the expenditures on the Mexican War. W. S. Miller, a representative from New York, voiced much Whig sentiment when he said that the new treasury notes would offset to some extent a principal evil of the independent treasury system—the evil of tying up specie. But sooner or later, he thought, the Treasury would provoke mischief, "and at that moment the Secretary of the Treasury will hold in his hands the destinies of the trading community." Proponents of the independent treasury, he said, "disturb the commercial world by a pretended adoption of a government currency exclusively metallic, and the actual issue of mere government paper."[36] In general, other opinions were in agreement with Miller's. The opposition was mainly from the Whigs and a few hard-money Democrats. Thomas Hart Benton, for example, continually alleged that the power to emit treasury notes made the Treasury a bank of issue.[37]

Benign or hostile, these opinions indicated that Congress was aware of the policymaking powers inherent in the Treasury Department. When the last pre-Civil War spate of notes was issued between 1857 and 1860, opinions about them seemed much less cautious than those expressed ten and twenty years before. Senator R. M. T. Hunter, chairman of the Committee on Finance, believed that the forthcoming issue of notes in

TABLE 6.2. Governmental expenditures, receipts, cash balances, and changes, 1832-1861 (millions of dollars).

Year	Total expenditures excluding payments on debt	Total receipts from customs, lands, and miscellaneous	Jan. 1 Treasury notes Out	Change	Jan. 1 Long-term debt Out	Change	Treasury cash balance Jan. 1	Change over year
1832	34.36	31.87	—		—		4.50	− 2.49
1833	24.26	33.95	—		—		2.01	+ 9.69
1834	24.60	21.79	—		—		11.70	− 2.81
1835	17.57	35.43	—		—		8.89	+17.86
1836	30.87	50.83	—		—		26.75	+19.59
1837	33.81	18.03	—	+ 2.99	1.50		46.34	−37.27
1838	31.42	19.37	2.99	+ 4.76	1.50		5.09	− 0.09
1839	25.00	30.40	7.75	− 6.67	1.50		5.00	− 3.26
1840	22.35	16.99	0.98	+ 1.60	1.50		1.74	− 0.58
1841	26.39	15.95	2.58	+ 4.80	1.50	+ 3.17	1.16	1.16
1842	23.92	19.61	7.38	+ 2.71	4.67	+ 4.13	—	—
1843 (first half) (July 1-July 1)	11.56	8.07	10.09	+ 0.34	8.80	+13.54	0.04	+10.39
1843-44	21.84	27.50	10.43	− 8.17	22.34	− 0.06	10.43	− 2.57
1844-45	22.84	29.77	2.26	− 1.47	22.28	− 5.66	7.86	− 0.20
1845-46	27.66	29.50	0.79	− 0.24	16.62	+ 0.13	7.66	+ 1.47
1846-47	57.79	26.35	0.55	+14.99	16.75	+ 9.02	9.13	− 7.43
1847-48	45.21	35.43	15.54	− 0.82	25.77	+ 9.05	1.70	− 1.55
1848-49	44.75	31.07	14.72	−11.09	34.82	+26.80	0.15	+ 2.03
1849-50	40.06	43.38	3.63	− 2.95	61.62	+ 4.05	2.18	+ 4.42

1850-51	47.48	52.31	0.68	—	65.67	− 3.11	6.60	+ 4.31
1851-52	43.73	49.73	—	—	62.56	+ 2.57	10.91	+ 3.72
1852-53	47.22	61.34	—	—	65.13	+ 2.21	14.63	+ 7.31
1853-54	54.35	73.55	—	—	67.34	−20.10	21.94	− 1.80
1854-55	59.55	65.00	—	—	47.24	− 6.67	20.14	− 1.21
1855-56	62.51	73.92	—	—	40.57	− 6.61	18.93	+ 0.97
1856-57	66.92	68.63	—	—	33.96	− 4.90	19.90	− 2.19
1857-58	74.05	46.55	—	+19.75	29.06	− 3.90	17.71	−11.31
1858-59	68.98	53.40	19.75	− 5.03	25.16	+18.54	6.40	− 2.06
1859-60	63.03	55.97	14.72	+ 4.97	43.70	+ 1.38	4.34	− 0.71
1860-61	66.44	41.34	19.69	+ 0.35	45.08	+23.36	3.63	− 1.37
			20.04		68.44		2.26	

Source: The data in this table were derived from the *Treasury Reports* for the years shown.

Note: Total expenditures includes interest payments on the national debt, but not debt repurchases. Total receipts does not include "receipts" from issues of treasury notes or long-term debt. The values for notes and debt are contained in columns further to the right, as are year-to-year changes in these values. The same procedure is followed for the Treasury's cash balance.

This table cannot be taken too literally, not only because of the variable accounting practices followed by different secretaries, but also because of events such as the Texan Indemnity issue, which unilaterally increased the outstanding debt of the federal government in 1850-1852 by $10 million. At the same time this issue of debt had no offsetting "deficit" to fulfill, and other debt was being retired at the same time by ordinary repurchase. Thus at times the values in this table will not appear to be consistent nor complete. They are generally correct and give a useful fiscal-monetary picture of the federal government's role in the period covered.

late 1857 "would relieve the community more . . . than any other mode in which we can borrow money." He also observed that by serving as bank reserves the notes would help the banks resume specie payments: "We offer incidentally to the merchant and to the banks a great advantage in Treasury paper of this sort, which is equivalent to specie."[38]

Senator John Crittenden of Kentucky was even more explicit than Senator Hunter. "One of the circumstances which invite, at this time, to the issue of a paper currency by the Government," he said, "is the ease and alleviation it may give to the commercial and pecuniary distresses and wants of the country." Senator John Bell replied that he did not think the issue of treasury notes would furnish much relief, but he would favor such an issue if it would help. He did not deny the monetary character of the notes.[39]

Secretary of the Treasury Howell Cobb, although he favored an issue of treasury notes during this crisis, did so primarily for fiscal reasons. He doubted the constitutional ability of the government to provide relief as such.[40]

James A. Dixon, a Whig senator from Connecticut, took exception to Cobb's negative attitude. He saw the issue of treasury notes as not only consistent with but complementary to subtreasury policy, although it was a policy he and other Whigs felt they could improve. "We were told," he said, "that the sub-Treasury was to prevent all contraction or expansion; . . . that it was to save the banks, or at least, to save the Government. The Secretary of the Treasury . . . only offers to us a bankrupt law for the banks [and] . . . this issue of paper money."[41] In company with other Whigs Dixon felt that a national bank was the best medium for conducting monetary policy. Bell seconded Dixon in a speech that concluded: "If the Government has no power to regulate the currency, it fails in one of its great purposes."[42]

The Whigs were in a more secure position when arguing for control over the currency than were the Democrats. They wanted regulation of the currency by a quasi-central bank and openly avowed this principle. The Democrats, on the other hand, constantly had to arbitrate a schism. Many of them opposed central banking control over the monetary system; and to some, such as Thomas Hart Benton and other sound-money men, hostility to central banking was consistent with antipathy to all banks and unremitting advocacy of a completely metallic currency. The less-than-hard-money Democrats had to develop a compromise philosophy; and since their policies were generally the dominant ones in this period, they must have succeeded. Part of such a development is seen in their policy toward issues of treasury notes; the other major policy development was their acceptance of treasury open-market operations.

The Whigs, being descendants of the banking school of monetary thought, argued that they wanted metallic standards, but that a national bank would act as a shock absorber and prevent the extreme variations in prices and employment that sometimes occurred under metallic standards. They would allow, even assist, adjustments to the economy, but with the cushions of national bank policy in convenient spots.

The sound-money men were responsible for the formal thesis that provided for the enduring existence of the independent treasury system starting in 1846, but they also had a lot of support from disillusioned state bank supporters. Both these groups wanted a separation of all banks from the state, but the institution they created as independent emerged with more central banking potential than any of the Whig schemes they had so virtuously crushed. Its central banking functions developed only as a pragmatic result of its fiscal position and because of the innovative skill of some of its executives. These latter men constituted a third force that was an essential element for an effective policymaking institution.

The independent treasury had hardly started operations when policy developments suggested that the divorce of the state from the banks had not necessarily released the banks from the state. The words and the actions of key treasury officials under the new system reflected an emergence of policies not seen as a part of the original scheme.

Robert J. Walker was the first secretary of the independent treasury. The promotion of an independent treasury was a major goal of President James Polk, Walker's chief, but Walker was its most vociferous, energetic, and capable supporter.[43] Under the independent treasury, he held, specie would "neither expand nor contract beyond the legitimate business of the country"; while if left to the capriciousness of the banking system, specie would be "made the basis, as often heretofore, of bank paper expansions, and if so, ruinous revulsions would not fail to ensue."[44] He stated further that the independent treasury would give "stability to all [manufacturers'] operations, and insure them, to a great extent, against those fluctuations, expansions, and contractions of the currency so prejudicial to their interests . . . Stability, in both the tariff and the currency, is what the manufacturer should most desire. Stability [again] is what the manufacturer should most desire, and especially that that question should be taken out of politics by a just and permanent settlement."[45]

Walker could not have been cognizant of all the policy measures that he and successive secretaries might promote, and his implication that the independent treasury would buttress a hard-money policy was hardly more than window dressing.[46] He nevertheless regarded the independent treasury as a policymaking institution; his subsequent activities, in fact, implied a degree of control over the monetary system that this institution could not sustain so early in its career.

During the Mexican War the independent treasury under Walker operated unexceptionably. While its monetary policies were limited, it transferred specie for military purposes without even rippling the money market, and it floated three major loans to finance the war.

Congress included in the second of these war loans the incongruous limitations that the securities had to be sold *at par or above* but could only be repurchased, when a fiscal surplus was available, *at par or below*. Both Polk and Walker felt that such proscription dampened optimum debt policy, and at the end of the war they asked Congress for authorization to repurchase outstanding government debt "at the market rate above or below par."[47]

Walker's repeated entreaties did not settle comfortably on Julius Rockwell, a very Whiggish Whig from Massachusetts. Rockwell felt that government repurchases at that time would inflate the prices of the securities, embarrass the incoming (Taylor) administration, and give too much discretionary power to the secretary of the Treasury.[48]

Rockwell criticized Walker for what may have been one of the first policy-loaded, open-market operations in government securities that a central monetary agency of the United States ever conducted. Walker had repurchased $800,000 of the loan of 1847 at a time when the market price of the securities was well above par. He had contrived this apparently illegal feat by buying them at par and agreeing to resell them to those who made them available, again at the par value, thus effectively granting a loan using the securities as collateral. According to Rockwell, specie had accumulated in the subtreasury in New York, and "the Secretary was urged to this unauthorized proceeding by many gentlemen of great respectability in business, as well as by those dealing largely in stocks, with the view of relieving the pressure upon the money market in New York, and indirectly other parts of the country."[49]

Walker's procedure clearly anticipated central bank repurchase agreements, a common twentieth-century device. The volume of his operations was small, although it may have significantly affected the New York money market at that time. He clearly intended to influence the economy by a contrived monetary operation. Rockwell's criticisms confirmed such intentions and indicated a recognition that stability in the money market was an objective of treasury policy.

Walker verified the intentions of his money-market activities by declaring that the independent treasury would check "not the issues, but the over-issues [of banks], and [would] mitigate if not prevent those revulsions which are sure to ensue when the business of the banks, and as a consequence that of the country, is unduly extended."[50] Such an overt expression of banking policy, together with the open-market operations he modeled, readily suggests that Walker would have developed the independent treasury into a thoroughgoing monetary authority and substantiates the thesis that the independence of this institution was destined to be one-way.

Even though the Whigs generally won the elections of 1848, thus ending Walker's tenure as secretary, they made no serious attempt to overthrow the independent treasury or to incorporate another national bank. The Whig secretaries had no particular affinity or zeal for the system fathered by the Democrats, so they showed no imaginative insights or developments in monetary policy at this time.[51] The Whig secretary of the Treasury continued to ask Congress for authorization to repurchase the outstanding debt at the market price; and because a sizable specie balance had accumulated in the subtreasury offices by early 1853, Congress finally repealed the provision of the Loan Act of 1847, which had prohibited such repurchases. Although this action was momentous in monetary policy history, it was then regarded as so perfunctory that it was not even recorded in the *Congressional Globe*, but was buried in the Appropriations Act.[52]

Since the bulk of government income came from tariff revenues, a source decidedly sensitive to changes in the flow of national money income, total government receipts increased appreciably after 1850 with the general prosperity of the times generated by gold discoveries in California and Australia. Expenditures tended to increase much less rapidly. So the Treasury's gold balance by late 1852 had become an appreciable fraction of the total stock of specie and other reserves held by the banks. The total treasury balance was $14 million, bank reserves were $45 million, and notes and deposits were slightly less than $300 million. Thus a $10 million transfer of specie, say, from the Treasury to the banks would have permitted the outstanding stock of bank notes and deposits to increase by more than 20 percent without changing the existing reserve ratio of the banking system.

The new secretary of the Treasury under President Pierce was James Guthrie, an industrialist and banker from Louisville, Kentucky. Though Guthrie had not held public office before his appointment, he was prominent in state politics and in railroad and banking enterprises. He later became a United States senator.[53]

Guthrie noted in his annual report for 1853 that his predecessor, Thomas Corwin, had made a few private arrangements for debt repurchases at the beginning of the year, but he himself felt that a continuation of such cryptic methods might lead "to a misapplication of the public funds, and to favoritism. Public notice was at once given that the $5 million of the loan of 1843 would be redeemed at the Treasury on July 1, 1853." Other portions were also repurchased in New York and Philadelphia until July 1. Then, Guthrie reported,

> the amount still continuing to accumulate in the Treasury, apprehensions were entertained that a contraction of discounts by the city banks of New York would result, . . . and combining with the fact of the large amount in the Treasury, might have an injurious influence

on financial and commercial operations. With a view, therefore, to give public assurance that money would not be permitted to accumulate in the Treasury, . . . a public offer was made on the 30th of July to redeem . . . the sum of $5 million of the loans of 1847 and 1848, at a premium of 21%, and interest from the 1st of July, 1853, on the principal. And on the 22nd of August another public offer was made for $2 million.[54]

As a result of this policy, the Treasury repurchased $20.9 million of the debt during 1853-54 at an average premium of 15 percent and effectively replaced income-earning assets of the economy with high-powered specie. That a premium of such magnitude was paid indicates that these transactions were no mean fiscal dabble.

Guthrie's intentions were accentuated by his silver-purchase policy. The surplus, he said, had become a cause for alarm in commercial and financial circles, and to relieve this situation advances were made to the mint "for the purchase of silver for the new coinage, and to enable the mint to pay promptly and in advance of coinage for gold bullion."[55]

The New York money market had shown some signs of stringency in the fall of 1853. In 1854 a more serious situation developed. As a result of a decline in the value of railroad securities, banks in Ohio, Indiana, and Illinois were forced to suspend specie payments in the spring, while call rates went to 8 percent and good short paper to 12 percent in the money market.[56] Indexes of prices and the stock of money, as well as Guthrie's report for 1854, confirm the supposition that the economy was on the verge of a crisis. Total bank notes, deposits, and specie declined approximately 5 percent during the year, and Guthrie remarked on the "pressure in the money market" and "disorder in money matters . . . [from] the failure of many of these . . . banks, and the curtailment of the circulation and discounts of others—which in the last six months must have reached forty or fifty millions of dollars."[57] His debt repurchases continued at a rate of $6-$7 million per year, and in December of 1855 he was able to report that the stock of money, so reduced in the latter half of 1854, had "more than recovered."[58]

Guthrie continued to advocate hard money. He felt that the use of banks as depositories of public funds would cause specie to leave the country. Bank paper (less-good money) would drive out specie (better money). He reasoned from this postulate that the federal and state governments could "increase the specie in the country to any amount that is desirable . . . by creating an effective demand for specie"; that is, by permitting only specie in the collections and disbursements of local governments.[59] He hardly imagined that the country would be able "to dispense with banks of issue, and their attendant evils, and have the gold and silver contemplated by the constitution,"[60] as he alleged. He was nonetheless one of the first influential government officials to recommend an excise tax on bank notes.[61]

That Guthrie's policies evolved as a pragmatic result of the problems he faced in office is evidenced by a letter from A. T. Burnley to Guthrie in July 1854. Burnley, an obscure lobbyist of some sort, had asked Judge George Bibb, a Whig predecessor of Guthrie's in the secretaryship and a fellow Kentuckian, for some definition of the implied and discretionary powers inherent in the office of secretary. Bibb cited a Supreme Court judgment (McDaniels case VII Peters 14) which stated that a cabinet officer was often compelled to exercise discretion in the execution of the duties and responsibilities of his office. "Numberless things," the opinion concluded, "must be done that can be neither anticipated nor defined."[62]

After several years of open-market operations during which $38 million of a total of $63 million of government securities were repurchased, Guthrie was moved to give a seasoned dictum of monetary policy. Uncertainties in economic life due to wars, political strife, and other phenomena, he said,

> destroy confidence and with it credit, inducing the hoarding of the precious metals, the withdrawal of deposits, the return of bank notes for redemption, the consequent stagnation of commerce, in all its channels and operations, the reduction of prices and wages, with inability to purchase and pay, bank suspensions and general insolvency . . . The independent treasury, when over-trading takes place, gradually fills its vaults, withdraws the deposits, and pressing the banks, the merchants and the dealers, exercises that temperate and timely control, which serves to secure the fortunes of individuals, and preserve the general prosperity.
>
> The independent treasury, however, may exercise a fatal control over the currency, the banks and the trade of the country . . . whenever the revenue shall greatly exceed the expenditure . . . [Without the repurchases of debt since March 4, 1853], the accumulated sum would have acted fatally on the banks and on trade.[63]

Although this exposition by Guthrie seems to overemphasize the downswing of business activity, it describes well the balancing effect that the independent treasury could have on the private economy. He thought of the restrictive policies of the Treasury as largely automatic. Specie would accumulate in its vaults as a result of overtrading, but more specie in the Treasury would leave less in the banks and thus restrain the expansion of the banks. Too much restraint by the Treasury, however, would result in a "fatal control." In the recent past such a contingency had been avoided by debt repurchases. Guthrie simply stated the case for a Treasury policy that had developed circumstantially from the expansion of business activity due to the gold boom.

In March 1857 Guthrie was replaced as secretary by Howell Cobb of Georgia, a long-time congressman and a former Speaker of the House. As the panic developed in the autumn of that year, Cobb continued the open-market purchase policy innovated by Walker and continued by Guthrie. He saw "the large sums from the Treasury . . . affording relief to the commercial and other interests of the country."[64]

But the Treasury's specie balance had been used too prodigally, not only in purchasing securities in the open market, but also in financing the fiscal deficit of 1857. When the balance reached the minimal value thought necessary for routine transactions (about $6 million), Cobb seemed to lose the confidence that complements a positive theory. He defensively backpedaled completely denying any governmental responsibility for restoring monetary or business equilibrium. He sermonized with a handwashing statement in marked contrast to what Walker and Guthrie had declared: "There are many persons who seem to think that it is the duty of the government to provide relief in all cases of trouble and distress . . . And their necessities, not their judgments, force them to the conclusion that the government not only can, but ought to relieve them." He then prescribed the orthodox and austere alternative of "liquidation and settlement as the surest mode for the restoration of the equilibrium." Whereas Walker and Guthrie had been incisive and positive, Cobb was unconvincing and desultory. He recommended the issue of treasury notes, not for any countercyclical purposes, but because he felt that the government's deficit would be temporary and should therefore be met by temporary means.[65]

Issues of notes as well as longer-term debt were authorized by Congress in 1857 and in the following three years to provide for fiscal deficits. The economy recovered quickly from the panic, and the only improvidence felt was in the flow of receipts to the Treasury itself. In such a situation treasury policy was primarily fiscal.

The central banking performances of the pre-Civil War independent treasury and of the other institutions that attempted monetary policies during the nineteenth century were less important than the ideas they fostered. The function of central banking and the central bank's position vis-à-vis the private economy were not sharply defined. Neither the early Bank of England nor the Banks of the United States were created as central banks nor dared recognize themselves as such. The Bank of England in fact became famous for declaring what it could *not* do in the area of monetary policy and at times led as precarious an existence as the Second Bank of the United States in the early 1830s. The Bank of England was perhaps tolerated because of its self-effacing and seemingly ineffectual character. By contrast, the Second Bank of the United States was cut down because of its more purposive attitude with respect to monetary policy.

Other factors retarded the development of policymaking institutions. The states, for example, were properly jealous and fearful of encroachment by the federal government. Since a central bank would necessarily be a federal bank and would maintain and operate state branches from a distant nucleus, proponents of states' rights found opposition to national (central) banking almost axiomatic.[66]

The institution of metallic standards also deterred central banking development. Although the Whigs thought they could marry the principles of metallic-standard self-regulation to central-bank manipulation of the credit structure, long-run adherence to a policy of metallic standards was inconsistent with the usual central bank policies. Even a central bank with bountiful gold reserves could not permanently retard an external gold drain without allowing prices to fall. Ultimately, the price-specie flow mechanism would have to dominate—barring the unlikely event of devaluation.[67]

The policies pursued by the independent treasury were exactly what it was ostensibly created to avoid. They developed through force of circumstances and were sporadic and opportunistic, but they were a natural emergence. When would an independent treasury *not* be forced into a policymaking role? When evaluated in its full sweep of history, the independent treasury may well appear in retrospect as the optimal monetary-fiscal institution. It was indeed a unique institution, for it contained all the prerequisites for employing monetary-fiscal coordination of a high order. With the dualistic structure of national banking that the Whigs subsequently developed, or such as the United States ultimately obtained in the Federal Reserve system, powers and responsibilities were destined to overlap and duplicate because of the impossibility of rationalizing precisely and permanently the bounds of authority for each of the agencies.

7. Civil War Inflation and Postwar Monetary Policies

> No human intelligence can fix the amount of currency that is really needed . . . So long as the volume of currency depends upon legislative enactment, uncertainty and instability will pervade all financial operations. (Hiland R. Hulburd, 1869)

> If we cannot [get free coinage of silver] I am in favor of issuing paper money enough to stuff down the bondholders until they are sick. (Richard P. Bland, 1878)

The banking and monetary system on the eve of the Civil War had enjoyed fifteen years of relative stability, a condition often aspired to by secretaries of the Treasury during that era. Strangely enough, historians and analysts have not given the era a good press. The currency system, for example, was seen as "far from satisfactory" by Hepburn. There was, he said, "no central place of redemption, hence most notes were at a discount, varying with the distance from the bank of issue. It was estimated that there were 7000 kinds and denominations of notes, and fully 4000 spurious or altered varieties were reported."[1]

This common concept of the chaotic state of the banking system was magnified in the eyes of most observers by the noxious presence of wildcat banks. Yet very little authentication has been offered to support such a dismal picture. In fact, a recent study by Hugh Rockoff reliably indicates that by 1860 note holders' losses from all "free" banks, including wildcats, were less than what they would have lost in that year from a 2 percent inflation. Rockoff also points out that the thousands of "spurious and altered varieties" of notes reported by Hepburn were a *cumulative* total over decades. The bank note reporters and counterfeit detectors continued to list such notes for fear that batches of worthless notes from broken banks would be circulated long after the books of such banks had been closed.[2]

At the base of the disorganized monetary system was seen a bumbling, destabilizing independent treasury that not only had no control over the banking system and the note issues of the banks, but also tied up specie and disturbed the money market by its unsynchronized fiscal receipts and expenditures.[3]

The records for the period 1845-1860 imply an economic tranquility that contradicts this critical view of the Treasury and the monetary system. Growth in bank credit and the stock of money was as orderly as it had been or would be in any other period of United States financial history. The independent treasury behaved creditably. It deliberately prevented pressures from developing in the money markets, and hence in the economy, by its monetary-fiscal stabilizing actions. Its separation from the banking system allowed it to exert objective influence it might not otherwise have had, and the banking system seemed no worse for its independence. Only the panic of 1857 rippled the surface, and even this event was short-lived and relatively harmless.

The Civil War put an end to these idyllic conditions. Its real demands on the economies of both North and South were long-run and pervasive, as were its institutional effects on the banking and monetary systems.

The development of hostilities in 1861 provoked major economic and financial questions for both North and South. The principal monetary question was where to get the money to prosecute the war successfully. The three timeworn methods of answering this question included (1) taxing a larger part of the national product, (2) borrowing by issues of interest-bearing fixed-dollar claims (government securities) redeemable sometime in the future, and (3) simply printing paper money.[4] Each of these means had its recommendations and its failings.

Taxes were principally tariffs. Since the international trade that gave rise to tariff revenues was seriously impaired during such a conflict, revenues from this source were more likely to decrease than increase. Government expenditures ultimately increased tenfold, and the tariff system just could not handle such a load even in the beginning. Internal taxes were a second possibility. An income tax and other domestic taxes were imposed. These programs, however, were ponderous to get into operation and slow to yield revenues.[5]

Bond sales were a natural and legitimate alternative. Congressional authorizations could be obtained quickly; and for the long-run operation of the war, sales of government securities raised the bulk of the increased revenues.

The third method of raising money was the printing of fiat money. Most of the paper money printed in the North was the famous United States notes, more popularly known as greenbacks, or legal tenders. The precedent for the issue of such currency was seen in the frequent recourse to issues of treasury notes during the previous fifty years. A large fraction of these notes had looked like money and had been treated as money —to a limited extent as hand-to-hand currency and to a large extent as bank reserves. However, the quantity of notes issued had been confined to amounts between $3 million and $20 million. Most of the time the notes had been issued for only one year and were not reissuable, although they frequently stayed out for an extra year or two. They were legal tender only for debts due to and from the government.

The new issues were unpredented in that they were full legal tender, in seeming violation of constitutional proscription, and were issed in quantities that were massive compared to the amounts of earlier decades. While they were considered temporary and were supposed to be redeemed sometime (two years) after the end of hostilities, no one imagined that they would circulate for only a year. They were also reissuable when they came back into the Treasury as payments for taxes and tariffs to the government. The common feature of the United States notes of the 1860s and the earlier treasury notes was that both looked like and were treated as currency and bank reserves.

The stock of money in general circulation in 1860 was on the order of $500 million, composed of roughly equal amounts of currency and bank deposits. Virtually all the money stock at this time was bank-issued. When the issues of United States notes began to appear, prices began to rise. Imbedded in the general price level was the price of gold, whose market price would not rise as long as its mint price could be maintained. But the issues of new currency gave the commercial banking system additional reserves, and the commercial banks reacted by extending credit and issuing more bank currency. As the price level responded, people anticipated that the mint price of gold could not sustain the pressure. Government gold, which had been obtained by sales of interest-bearing securities to the banks, was demanded in redemption of notes. Bank gold likewise was called for. Then the gold was either hoarded or shipped abroad to settle foreign accounts. These drains forced the banks and the government to suspend specie payments on December 30, 1861.

Suspension of gold payments did not mean the end of the monetary system. Prices, including the price of gold, rose as people tried to get rid of unwanted money balances. Obviously they could not get rid of them; all they could do was bid down the value of each money unit until the total stock of money was held with no further change in prices. By the time the war ended in 1865 the price level was about double its 1860 value, while the market price of gold peaked at 258 percent of its prewar value in July 1864.

The issue of greenbacks was not the only intrusion of the federal government into the currency structure. The organization of the national banking system introduced yet another governmental control over the monetary system.

The secession of Southern states was also a secession of Southern congressmen from the federal Congress. Since these men were all Democrats, their absence left the Whig-Republicans as a congressional majority, a position they had not enjoyed since 1840. They could now bring out of mothballs some of their more treasured projects, one of which was a national bank, and feel fairly certain of favorable legislative action.

The National Bank Act (or National Currency Act, as it was formally labeled) passed in 1863 as a war measure, but the national banking system did not really become an established institution until after 1865. While the act had its roots in Whig banking philosophy, the system that finally emerged was a multibank organization and not a monolithic bank of the United States with branches. The system nevertheless embodied the concept of a central reserve-holding core of banks in the central reserve cities, or redemption centers, as well as a satellite system of "country" banks in all the smaller communities.

All banks in the national system had to be chartered by the federal government—specifically by the office of the Comptroller of the Currency, the agency in the Treasury Department expressly authorized to oversee the national banking system. Membership in the system was permissive, but to some degree exclusive. Banks were not forced to join, but some banks could not meet the requirements. However, the systemwide regulation to which all would be subject promised a degree of assurance to reasonably sound banks that other national banks would also be sound.[6]

Reserve requirements were specified for all banks in the system: 25 percent for banks in reserve cities, and 15 percent for all others (country banks). Note issues of national banks were to be uniform in design, and the notes had to be accepted by all other national banks at par. National banks had to hold government bonds as collateral for the notes,[7] and each national bank had also to hold government securities up to at least one-third of its capital.

Many state banks found they had little to gain by joining the new system; and, of course, until the war ended, Southern banks could not join. To make participation more attractive, Congress in 1865 amended the original act so that nonnational banks had to pay a 10 percent prohibitory tax on bank note issues. This move had two results. First, many more banks became national banks; and, second, banks that still did not want to be coerced avoided the tax by using demand deposits exclusively to finance loans and investments. Thus the use of demand deposits was greatly accelerated, and state bank note issues became a thing of the past.

The national banking system did not become fully operational until after the war's end. But by 1867 the economy had two major paper currencies roughly equal in volume: government-issued legal tender currency composed of United States notes, demand notes, and three percent certificates, and the national bank notes, which were limited by the National Bank Act to $300 million.

The presence of inconvertible paper currencies meant that the monetary system was subject to political control and would continue to be until the resumption of specie payments. Politicians were not accustomed to making decisions for the monetary system and perhaps were ill-fitted for the task. Ultimately the stock of money was reduced and resumption did occur at the prewar parity of gold and the dollar. So something worked. The question is, was that something devious bureaucratic hypocrisy, fortunate happenstance due to external factors, lucky blundering that resulted in the desired results, or some combination of all three?

In the fourteen-year interval between 1865 and resumption, political, social, and economic forces clashed and compromised over the base on which the monetary system should rest. The traditionalists wanted gold, the opportunists wanted silver, and the innovators favored a paper money. The struggle that took place among the proponents of the various systems is instructive even if the question of hypocrisy or happenstance is left unsettled.

Resumption of gold payments was the long-run policy to which all parties agreed at the end of hostilities in 1865. But progress toward resumption proved to be anything but simple and straightforward. The struggle to achieve it witnessed the following developments: (1) Congressional opinion was not sharply polarized into gold-standard resumptionists and paper-money inflationists. (2) The price level discipline necessary to effect resumption was hedged by numerous compromises that allowed monetary expansion in some sectors of the financial system to counteract constrictions in other parts. (3) The Treasury Department, with little more than a congressional prescription to do good (resume), undertook certain central banking functions to obtain the desired end. (4) The strategic position silver was obtaining, even though little silver currency came into circulation before 1879, exerted political leverage on the course of resumption policy.

The seventeen-year suspension period of specie payments (1862-1879) has provided data for much monetary analysis. For example, James Kindahl has described the price level path that the preresumption economy had to take for specie payments to be reestablished. Kindahl's statistical analysis is both competent and enlightening, but he refers only superficially to the ideological struggles of the period. Like most other observers, he believes that monetary policy was largely negative and that no serious movement could be observed in favor of alternatives to a return to the prewar parity of the gold dollar.[8]

Congressional debates give a very different impression. The problem in 1865 was obvious enough. Issues of government currency after 1860 had tripled the stock of money, while the price level had approximately doubled during the same period. The market price of gold had fallen by this time from its 1864 high point to about 150 percent of its prewar parity value, so it was still 50 percent higher than the mint price. Such circumstances permitted several courses of monetary policy. The most obvious combinations of ends and means were as follows.

1. The general price level could be lowered by contracting the paper-money stock. The market price of gold would then fall. When it was within reach of the mint price, resumption could be declared.

2. The same decline in the price level could be attempted by holding the stock of money constant and letting the increase in production—natural growth—produce a gradual decline in prices until the market price of gold was within reach of the mint price.

3. The mint values of gold and silver could be increased by a statutory decrease in the gold and silver contents of the two metallic dollars legally defined. In other words, simple devaluation could be effected to correspond to the immediate postwar market values of the gold and silver dollars.

4. The specie standard could be completely abandoned in favor of the inconvertible paper-money standard then current. This program, adopted in force by the Greenbackers, implied de facto gold and silver demonetization. It differed from de jure devaluation in that the precise amount of dollar depreciation would not be stipulated by law but would be left to the discipline of the market.

5. Another alternative was to wait for an increase in the output of monetary metals. Their relative prices might then fall enough within the framework of a general price level rise to eliminate the discount on them.

The first policy undertaken after the war was an austere contraction of the money stock. It was initiated by Hugh McCulloch, secretary of the Treasury in the Johnson administration, and was affirmed in December 1865 by an overwhelming congressional majority. Tax revenues abounded in the peacetime climate of trade under a wartime tax framework. At the same time government expenditures declined precipitously, leaving fiscal surpluses in the form of cash balances, which included United States notes and gold coin. Some of the United States notes were retired and destroyed; other notes that remained outstanding were funded, that is, exchanged for long-term interest-bearing bonds.

But people very soon found that price levels come down much more painfully than they go up. McCulloch's "immediate and persistent contraction of the currency" was then subjected to an intensive reappraisal by Congress on account of those "who had incurred pecuniary obligations in the expanded currency."[9] In April 1866, just four or five months after the beginning of the contraction policy it had blessed, Congress limited the monetary decrease to $10 million in the succeeding six months and to $4 million per month thereafter.

Contraction even at this new rate was harsh medicine. As table 7.1 shows, the money stock declined at approximately 7 percent per year. The growth in the monetary obligations of national banks was more than matched by a decline in monetary obligations of the government and of nonnational banks, while the reinclusion of Southern population and production imposed an additional burden on the remaining money stock. During the three years of the contraction period (1865-1868), the price level fell at least 8 percent per year.[10] James M. Blaine, in his *Twenty Years of Congress*, reported public sentiment of the times: "The great host of debtors who did not wish their obligations to be made more onerous, and the great host of creditors who did not desire that their debtors should be embarrassed and possibly rendered unable to liquidate, united on the practical side of the question and aroused public opinion against the course of the Treasury Department. In the end, outside of banking and financial centers, there was a strong and persistent demand for the repeal of the Contraction Act."[11]

McCulloch's use of his discretionary powers found no favor even among members of his own party in Congress. Senator William B. Allison of Iowa claimed that McCulloch had not retired any of the greenbacks in the first four or five months of 1867. However, "when it was necessary to use a large amount of money in the western states for the forwarding of the crops [in September and October of 1867], the Secretary of the Treasury then reduced the greenback circulation $16 million in two months; . . . so that when Congress came together in December 1867, they withdrew from the Secretary of the Treasury the power which they believed he had abused." Senator John Sherman affirmed Allison's interpretation: "I do not differ from the Senator from Iowa."[12]

The act repealing all contraction of the currency was passed by Congress in February 1868. It prohibited the secretary of the Treasury from making "any [further] reduction of the currency by retiring or canceling United States notes." From this time on, the moderate conservative policy of "growing up to the money stock" (the second alternative) was followed officially. Unofficially, procrastination became the norm; and after a few years many were paying only lip service to the resumption ideal.

Ulysses S. Grant was elected president in 1868 following the general disaffection of the Republican party with Andrew Johnson. Grant replaced

TABLE 7.1. Stock of money and components, 1860-1868 (millions of dollars).

Year	Deposits national banks	Deposits nonnational banks[1]	National bank notes	Nonnational bank notes	Government currency	Total[2]	Wholesale prices (1910-1914=100) Warren and Pearson	Wholesale prices (1910-1914=100) Kindahl
1860		310		207	21	538	93	86
1861		319		202	16	537	89	89
1862		357		184	139	680	104	98
1863		494		239	433	1176	133	118
1864	10	233	31	179	612	1202	193	148
1865	147	75	146	143	646	1624	185	200
1866	614	64	276	20	524	1579	174	172
1867	695	58	287	5	476	1511	162	172
1868	685	53	294	3	394	1489	158	158
	745							

Source: Historical Statistics, pp. 624-630, 648-649. Price indexes are Warren and Pearson's from Historical Statistics p. 115; and from James Kindahl, "Economic Factors in Specie Resumption," Journal of Political Economy (1961): 36.

1. The last four or five values in this column certainly understate the total volume of nonnational bank deposits.

2. The total stock of money given here is at best a rough approximation to reality. The total amounts in the hands of the public cannot be found simply by adding the various components because some of the components served as a reserve base for the others. Government currency, for example, was held as a reserve by national banks, against which these same banks issued national bank notes. National bank notes, in turn, were held as reserves by nonnational banks, against which nonnational banks created deposits. The whole problem is made more complex by the division of the Union during 1861-1865. In addition, deposit values include interbank deposits. If interbank deposits are excluded, as they should be for proper measurement, changes in the net money stock would closely approximate changes in prices. (See Friedman and Schwartz, Monetary History, p. 704.)

secretary of the Treasury McCulloch, who had been a supporter of Johnson, with George S. Boutwell of Massachusetts. Boutwell had been a member of Congress in the House of Representatives before his appointment to the Treasury and was asked to serve in the cabinet as a result of his anti-Johnson activity in the House.[13]

Boutwell had been secretary only about six months when the Black Friday incident occurred, on September 24, 1869. This drama was an attempt to "corner" gold by the famous speculators James Fisk and Jay Gould. Prices of all goods and services, including gold, had been falling as a result of the Treasury's contraction policy. Fisk and Gould felt that they could artificially "bull up" the price of gold to their advantage if they could be sure of a temporary do-nothing policy by the government. They undertook aggressive gold-buying policies in the summer of 1869. At the same time they propagandized Grant and Boutwell with the admonition that gold sales by the Treasury Department would adversely affect the impending movement of the crops. By means of adroit financial maneuvers they finally effected a temporary corner in gold, although the Treasury Department quickly broke their scheme with a sale of $4 million in New York's "gold room."[14]

The notoriety accompanying the Black Friday incident led to a congressional investigation in the course of which norms for Treasury policy were advanced. The majority report of the investigating committee recognized that "for all purposes of internal trade, gold is not money, but an article of merchandise; but for all purposes of foreign commerce it is our only currency." Common opinion was that treasury accumulations or disbursements of gold significantly affected both foreign and domestic commerce. The rationale of this view went somewhat as follows. If the Treasury sold gold in the open market and held on balance the currency it received in exchange, the greenback price of gold would fall. Gold would be exported and goods and services imported. Domestic prices would fall and the movement of the crops, especially, would be inhibited. If the Treasury then spent the dollar proceeds from the gold sales, only the price of gold would be lower than initially and movement of the crops would not be impeded. Boutwell's statements before the Garfield committee reflected this argument. To prevent a decline in business after the sale of gold during September 1869, he had ordered an immediate purchase of bonds in the open market. His decision to sell the gold, he said, was "not for the purpose of forcing down the price of gold, . . . but because we thought the business of the country was in danger."[15]

The minority of the investigating committee addressed themselves to the question of "disasters" in general. "It is impossible," they said, "to prevent large amounts of gold from accumulating in the Treasury." They cited McCulloch's policy of countering "speculative combinations," but they alleged critically (and incorrectly) that Boutwell was indifferent to the course of the money market. At the same time they complained of the "aggrandizement of power in the federal government . . . which affects at its will all the values of the country."[16]

They here expressed a common contradiction in popular norms for policy. While blaming the secretary for not properly overseeing the state of the money market, they criticized centralized discretionary control by the government. They concluded with this indefinite prescription: "The amount of coin . . . kept in the Treasury in reserve as a preparation for unforeseen emergencies, and to give steadiness to the convertible value of the legal tender issues, must depend upon contingencies that cannot be anticipated."[17]

This ambivalence emphasized the need for a specific congressional policy. The amount of cash the Treasury should keep, what the Treasury should be permitted and prescribed to do with it, what the long-run currency policy should be—all these questions should have been answered by Congress. Even when resumption was accomplished, some of these issues would still be unsettled.

Congress did nothing at this time to clarify Treasury policy. It did try to do something about the currency. United States notes had been frozen in 1868 at $356 million, and national bank notes had been fixed since the organization of the system at $300 million. Still outstanding were about $45 million of three percent certificates, which were used exclusively as bank reserves. Attention in Congress during early 1870 was directed toward retiring these certificates and extending the permissible issues of national bank notes.

Of the $300 million of national bank notes apportioned to the national banks organized in the states, the first $150 million were to be rationed according to "representative population, and the remainder [at the discretion of] the Secretary of the Treasury . . . having due regard to existing banking capital, resources, and business of such States . . . "[18] Although most of this apportionment was made after the end of the war, the South and the West did not get allotments of national banks or national bank notes anywhere near their pro rata share. By 1868 with the quotas almost complete, national banks in southern states had only 4 percent of the banks and 3 percent of the total notes.[19]

The reason for this misallocation, in apparent disregard of the apportionment provision in the act, is to be found in a section of the Internal Revenue Act of 1864 which states that all existing state banks had preference in converting to a national status over newly organizing banks, and the National Bank Act itself implied as much. The comptroller of the currency and the secretary of the Treasury also acted on the presumption that the primary intent of Congress in framing the National Bank Act was to nationalize the existing system.[20] In practice this principle conflicted with the principle of apportionment.

Secretary McCulloch had expressed in his report for 1865 the idea that the national bank notes would simply substitute for retired state bank notes. He felt, he said, that it was his "duty to discourage, in many instances, the organization of new banks" in order to keep the stock of money under control and on the rigorous path to resumption.[21] McCulloch was well aware that the South and the West were deprived of their share when the national bank notes were allocated. However, he disagreed with the comptroller of the currency, Hiland R. Hulburd, who favored further issues of these notes beyond the original $300 million on the condition that United States notes would be retired simultaneously. But McCulloch, as well as Hulburd, believed the issue of notes could be left unconstrained by quotas once specie resumption was accomplished.[22]

The unfulfilled provision in the National Bank Act calling for rationing half the notes in strict proportion to "representative population," together with retirement of United States notes and the accompanying hardships of the contraction policy, led to some serious reconsiderations of currency questions in Congress. Two related issues appeared in addition to the question of the sheer quantity of money: elasticity of the currency and per capita distribution. Greenbacks were touted as a government debt issued without interest charges. They thus had the advantage of saving the government interest expense. It was a short step for Greenbackers to recommend that *all* remaining interest-bearing bonds likewise be converted into greenbacks. The conservative, Republican, "banking school" spokesmen, however, favored the extension of national banks and national bank note issues because of their greater potential as an elastic medium. United States notes, Comptroller Hulburd stated in 1867, are "an iron currency in [their] utter want of elasticity so essential in a circulating medium."[23]

Elasticity was seen as a seasonal variation in the amount of notes needed to keep business steady. The idea of per capita currency came from the "representative population" phrase in the National Bank Act, and it became a ubiquitous point of congressional discussion. The population figures, by which apportionment of national bank notes was supposed to be decided, were revised as a matter of course by the census of 1870. So bills for new apportionments and reapportionments were duly introduced and discussed during the Forty-first Congress.[24]

The arguments for more money per capita to correct the obvious malproportion in the South were made in conjunction with the idea of retiring the three percent treasury certificates. Since these certificates were "lawful money" as bank reserves and amounted to about $45 million, the bill that went through Congress was a kind of monetary omnibus. It looked to the retirement of the $45 million three percents and the apportionment of an additional $45 million in national bank notes to fill the glaring gaps in the distribution of existing notes.

The absolute deficiencies in the South and in the West amounted to over $94 million, and considerable sentiment was expressed in the House of Representatives for adding this amount to the original apportionment. The Senate insisted on limiting the increase to the value of the three percent certificates about to be retired ($45 million) and on making the new issues of notes contingent on the actual retirement of the three percents.[25]

Opinion in both houses was favorable to a compromise through a conference committee so that the currency would at least be redistributed if not increased. However, some congressmen expressed misgivings about the bill's ability even to maintain the currency. Ebon C. Ingersoll of Illinois thought the bill would provoke a net contraction. The bill, he said, "proposes to increase the present national bank circulation . . . by $45,000,000. It then proposes to withdraw the $45 million [of three percents] that are now held . . . by the banks as a reserve under existing law . . . I hold that this proposition involves a positive contraction."[26]

To this insight James Garfield replied that retiring the $45 million of three percents would not be a contraction because these certificates could not be used as currency, "except as reserves in the banks."[27] This exception, of course, was what made the certificates high-powered money. They provided a base for multiple issues of national bank notes, which in turn could be used as currency by the nonbank public and as reserves by nonnational banks for a further multiplication of deposits.

Garfield also noted that national banks held $55 million excess reserves. He reasoned that the retirement of the three percents would therefore reduce only surplus reserves. He believed that an increase in bank deposits would offset the reduction in hand-to-hand circulation caused by the substitution of greenbacks for the three percents as national bank reserves.[28]

Confusion arising from the retirement of one kind of money while granting permissive increases in another is evident in the debates. Benjamin Butler of Massachusetts was told by one banker that the bill would produce an expansion of the currency, while another said it would provoke contraction.

"Now," he asked Garfield, "if such able and experienced men cannot tell what this bill is, why should we vote for it? [Laughter]."

Garfield answered: "If so, you had better not vote for it." And Butler allowed that indeed he would not.[29]

To stay alive the bill had to go before a conference committee composed of four members, two from the House and two from the Senate. It was reported back to the House, but was rejected, and went to another

conference. In the second conference the anticipated increase of $45 mil-
lion in national bank notes was seen to necessitate about $9 million of
United States notes as national bank reserves.[30] Thus to keep the money
supply constant—the compromise desideratum—another $9 million had
to be added to the $45 million, a total of $54 million. The compromise
bill was agreed to and became law on July 12, 1870.

The act also provided that $25 million of the total $354 million could
be reapportioned, but only after the supplementary $54 million had been
used up. Even then the comptroller of the currency would be required to
give one year's notice to the banks that had an excess. Yet another delay
would result from the provision that the apportionment values be figured
as soon as practicable after the census of 1870. This constraint meant that
at least an additional six months would elapse before any kind of reap-
portionment would or could occur. Thus the general timetable was as
follows:

1. An additional $54 million worth of national bank notes were to be is-
   sued to banks in states that had a deficiency from the original issue.
2. About 80 percent of the new notes were to go to the South and the
   West; but these sections had priority only if banks applied for their
   quotas within one year after the act was passed.
3. The secretary of the Treasury was "to redeem and cancel" the three
   percent certificates in amounts equal to the national bank notes so issued. To enforce the retirement of the certificates, interest payments
   on them and their "lawful money" (bank reserve) function were to
   cease.
4. After the $54 million were all apportioned, the comptroller of the cur-
   rency could reapportion $25 million upon applications by national
   banks in the deficient states. The $25 million were to come first from
   banks having the largest amounts of notes outstanding.[31]

Table 7.2 compares bank note circulation in 1862 and 1873. It also
shows the growth (+ or −) in note circulation, the amount each section
was due by the law of 1870, and the remaining excess or deficiency. The
eastern states were relatively well endowed with bank notes, while the
South and the West had an apparent blight. The Middle West's notes outstanding had a high rate of growth, but these states were due even more
than they had. Since national banks did not form in the South and the
West as anticipated, their quotas of notes had been allocated to new and
existing banks in other sections.[32]

The time series data in table 7.3 show the major monetary variables in
the national banking system between 1870 and 1879. To deflate the intra-
system credit structure, total currency and deposits and total reserves
(columns 1 and 4) are reduced by the deposit reserves ("Due from redemption agents") in reserve city national banks. The residuals (columns

TABLE 7.2. Bank note circulation in 1862 and 1873, with rates of increase and authorized amounts according to the apportionment provisions (all but changes in millions of dollars).

Region	Circulation		Change (%)	Authorized apportionment, 1870	Excess (+) or deficiency (−)
	1862	1873			
East	65.62	110.49	+ 69	39.80	+70.69
Middle	82.37	124.61	+ 52	115.19	+ 9.42
South and West[1]	71.10	38.16	− 47	89.25	−51.09
Middle West	19.68	78.79	+295	100.21	−21.42

Source: *Report of the Comptroller, 1873*, pp. 71, 75.
1. Does not include Mississippi, Arkansas, or Texas.

TABLE 7.3. Selected statistics for all national banks, March 1870 to October 1878 (all but ratios in millions of dollars).

Date	(1) Total currency and deposits[1]	(2) National bank inter-bank balances[2]	(3) = (1) − (2) Net currency and deposits	(4) Legal reserves held	(5) = (4) − (2) Basic reserves held	(6) Legal required reserves	(7) = (4) ÷ (1) Ratio of legal reserves to currency and deposits (%)	(8) = (5) ÷ (3) Ratio of basic reserves to net currency and deposits (%)
Mar. 24, 1870	850 (278)	73	777	236	163	172	27.8	21.0
Oct. 8, 1870	813 (279)	66	747	204	138	163	25.4	18.5
Mar. 18, 1871	891 (289)	84	807	234	150	180	26.3	18.6
Oct. 2, 1871	952 (301)	87	865	233	146	181	24.5	16.9
Feb. 27, 1872	952 (306)	90	862	228	138	190	23.9	16.0
Oct. 3, 1872	947 (318)	81	866	209	128	186	22.1	14.8
Feb. 28, 1873[3]	999 (320)	93	906	228	135	196	22.8	14.9
Sept. 12, 1873	1003 (323)	93	910	225	132	198	22.4	14.5
Oct. 13, 1873[4]	927 (321)	54	873	182	128	188	19.6	14.7
Feb. 27, 1874	1025 (320)	101	924	274[5]	173[5]	205	26.7	18.7
Oct. 2, 1874	713[6] (315)	84	629[6]	244	160	149	34.2	25.4
Mar. 1, 1875	722 (306)	90	632	238	148	150	33.0	23.4
Oct. 1, 1875	731 (300)	86	645	234	148	152	32.0	22.9
Mar. 10, 1876	722 (289)	99	623	251	152	150	34.8	24.4
Oct. 2, 1876	708 (276)	88	620	237	149	148	33.5	24.0
Apr. 14, 1877	697 (277)	85	612	231	146	145	33.1	23.9
Oct. 1, 1877	670 (276)	73	597	211	138	138	31.5	23.1
Mar. 15, 1878	672 (285)	86	586	240	154	139	35.7	26.3
Oct. 1, 1878[7]	678 (285)	85	593	228	143	141	33.6	23.1

Source: Columns 1, 4, 6, and 8 were obtained from *Reports of the Comptroller of the Currency*, 1870–1878. Columns 2, 3, 5, and 7 were derived from these data.

1. Notes outstanding are shown separately in parentheses.

2. Inter-national bank balances were labeled, "Due from redemption (or reserve) agents." Reserve agents were national banks in reserve cities and New York City. So these balances, while classified as a part of the reserve balances of national banks to whom they were due, were also demand liabilities of the national banks that acted as reserve agents and were no more to be considered reserves for the total national banking system than were national bank notes issued by one national bank and held by another. Deleting them from total currency and deposit issues of national banks (column 3) leaves notes and deposits in possession of the nonbank public. Likewise, deleting them from legal reserves (column 5) leaves the basic high-powered money reserves of the total national banking system.

3. Almost all three percent certificates were retired by this date.

4. This date marked the low spot for bank-held reserves during the panic of 1873.

5. By this date United States notes outstanding had been increased to $382 million from $356 million.

6. From this time on, national bank notes were de facto obligations of the Treasury Department (through the 5 percent redemption fund), so only deposits are included in the obligations of national banks requiring reserves. National bank notes outstanding are shown in parentheses.

7. United States notes were frozen forever at $346.7 million on May 31, 1878.

3 and 5) give the net currency and deposits for which the national banking system was responsible, both to the nonbank public and to the nonnational banks, and the net reserves available to support these obligations. Columns 7 and 8 show the ratios of reserves so defined to comparable totals of notes and deposits.

The retirement of the $45 million of three percents that occurred between March 1870 and February 1873 appears in the table as the decline of $28 million in basic reserves held (column 5). Legal reserves held declined by $8 million (column 2) to complete the arithmetic. Reserve city national banks and all other national banks increased their balances with New York City banks.[33]

While Congress was simultaneously reducing government issues of basic money and allowing expansion of bank-created currency, the Treasury Department was struggling to establish norms for its own conduct. Secretary Boutwell's experience with the gold crisis, plus opinions expressed in Congress at the time and the uncertainties generated under a paper money system, seems to have impressed him with the virtual necessity of discretionary monetary policies by the Treasury Department. Since the quantity of national bank notes was fixed by statute just as rigorously as the quantity of greenbacks, he felt that an impartial governing department (the Treasury) was necessary to provide seasonal elasticity to the money stock. Inactive balances that accrued during the summer, he said, could be used "if necessary, in the purchase of bonds in the autumn, thereby meeting the usual demand for currency at that season of the year." After a specie standard was reestablished, the excess of gold receipts over expenditures would permit similar aid to be furnished in coin.[34]

These observations prompted Boutwell to venture a fundamental doctrine for treasury policy. "Where but in the Treasury Department," he asked rhetorically, "can the power for increasing and decreasing the currency be reposed? I form the conclusion that the circulation of the banks should be fixed and limited, and that the power to change the volume of paper in circulation, within limits established by law, should remain in the Treasury Department."[35]

Boutwell had earlier initiated the policy of counterseasonal bond buying. Bonds were constantly being purchased as required by the sinking fund law, as well as in excess of that requirement; but the rate at which they were purchased during the year was left to the discretion of the secretary. During 1870 one-fifth of the total purchases for the year was made in the eight weeks between September 8 and October 27. In 1871 almost one-third of the year's total was purchased during a four-week

period.[36] The amount of bonds purchased in the autumn was usually between $15 million and $20 million. Since the volume of legal tenders in all
national banks was about $100 million, the treasury purchases contrib-
uted a significant seasonal adjustment to national bank reserves.

Whatever his opinions on resumption when he took office, Boutwell's
tenure as secretary witnessed little progress toward this goal. The economy enjoyed a vigorous growth; business and banking suffered no crises;
and the price level stayed relatively stable. Indeed, progress toward resumption could occur only if the price level fell, and most of Boutwell's
actions with respect to monetary policy were taken to counter falling
prices. The bond-buying policy was typical.

Another example occurred in the fall of 1872. At a time when Boutwell
was absent from the department, Assistant Secretary Richardson issued
about $5 million of United States notes from what he and Boutwell eu-
phemistically and presumptuously had labeled "the reserve." The object
of the issue, Boutwell reported later, "was the relief of the business of the
country, then suffering from the large demand for currency employed in
moving the crops from the South and West. The condition of affairs then
existing in the country seems to me to have warranted the issue upon
grounds of public policy."[37] Richardson's action and Boutwell's approbation excited another congressional controversy that showed the sharp
cleavage of opinion between strict constructionism and liberal pragma-
tism in the conduct of Treasury policy, as well as the passive acquiescence
of Congress to any monetary policy that would maintain a semblance of
the status quo.

The "reserve," the kernel of the controversy, was the $44 million of
United States notes that made up the difference between the *maximum*
amount ($400 million) Congress had authorized during the Civil War and
the minimum ($356 million) Congress had prescribed in 1868. The strict
constructionists, who constituted a majority of the Senate Committee on
Finance chaired by Senator John Sherman of Ohio, held that the minimum of 1868 was also a maximum, that Congress would have declared
otherwise if it had intended otherwise, and that reissue of any of the $44
million difference violated the whole policy of contraction—a policy,
they alleged, that was still in force. The reissue powers granted in the
original legal tender acts, they argued, were under different res gestae.
Their conclusion was correspondingly conservative: "In all questions of
. . . the extent of power conferred by law in matters which affect the public credit or public securities, a reasonable doubt as to a grant of power
should be held to exclude it."[38]

Boutwell based the authority for the Treasury's action on the wording
of the legal tender acts, on the precedent set by McCulloch before the act
of 1868, on the fact that the act of 1868 did not stipulate a maximum, and

on formal opinions in the Treasury Department and in the Department of the Attorney General. Before March 4, 1869, he said, large sums of notes were held in the office of the treasurer "as a surplus-fund . . . for the pur-_ pose of meeting any sudden drain upon the Treasury, and that practice has ever since been continued."[39]

The minority of the Senate committee supported Boutwell, declaring that the legal tender acts and the act of 1868 fixing the minimum did not conflict and that "Congress intended to leave the amount of cash balance an open question subject to the decision of the Secretary of the Treasury, in accordance with the 'exigencies of the public service.' " They concluded with a permissive statement very much in contrast to that of the majority: "Where no direct conflict between two different measures of legislation is apparent but the legislative power is silent upon any given question connected with those measures, it may become necessary for the executive power to supply the omission."[40]

In fact, Congress had not intended either to grant discretion to the secretary in the use of the "reserve" or to deny it. The issue had simply been overlooked. The committee was trying to impute law to a vacuum. Congress could have settled the issue with direct legislation, but none was passed at this time. Congressional sanction for the concept of the $44 million "reserve" under secretarial discretion must therefore be presumed.

Almost all analyses of Civil War finance concentrate on the fiscal-monetary experience of the North. Important and revealing as this example is, the similar experience of the South is just as instructive. Only in recent years have economists examined the Southern example in analytical detail.

The first such study was done over twenty years ago by Eugene Lerner as a doctoral dissertation. Lerner's study was then published as two journal articles and as a section in *Studies in the Quantity Theory of Money*, edited by Milton Friedman.[41] Lerner opened much new material, and his work is valuable in many regards, especially with respect to prices and wages. However, his analysis of the growth in the Confederate money supply and of the relationship of the money supply to prices is marred by some understandable errors in accounting the money stock and by a too-general view of the South's institutional arrangements in financing the war. The monetary-fiscal section of Lerner's work has recently been reappraised and modified by John M. Godfrey in his doctoral dissertation.[42]

Godfrey's study significantly revises Lerner's estimates on the growth in the Confederate money stock and therefore on the relationship between money and prices. Most of the errors Godfrey found, both in Lerner's work and in some earlier studies by historians, resulted from insufficient attention to details of accounting and aggregation. (This kind of oversight does not detract from the scholarship of Lerner and the others. It only demonstrates that the monetary analysis itself is worth more intensive investigation than was devoted to it.) Godfrey found that the issues of notes by the Confederate government, while accounting for over 90 percent of the increase in the total stock of money, had been overestimated by 20 to 30 percent because observers had not taken proper account of certain refunding operations.[43]

Bank-issued money was another item subject to error. Especially important was the accounting of bank-held cash and interbank deposits. When these items were correctly accounted, bank note and deposit expansion contributed only about 6 percent to the total growth of the Confederate money stock. State currency issues then contributed about another 3 percent.[44]

Godfrey's new estimates, when aggregated, show that the Confederate money stock fell between January of 1860 and January of 1861. It then rose to about twenty-two times its 1861 value by February of 1864, fell *by one-third in the next two months* due to a currency reform, and then rose by about 20 percent to January of 1865 when data became unavailable.[45]

Increases in Confederate prices were highly correlated with growth of the money stock until the currency reform of February 1864. At this point, prices increased enormously as people tried to get rid of their money in order to escape the burden of the reform, which was a two-for-three exchange of new notes for old. Declines in real output associated with the trauma of defeat aggravated the price picture, so that during 1864 prices doubled even though the money stock was 23 percent lower in January 1865 than it had been in February 1864.[46]

The major differences between Federal and Confederate financing of the Civil War were in the role banks played and in the fiscal practice of government debt issues. Confederate banks, which had less than 20 percent of the capacity of their Northern counterparts, contributed only 6 percent to total monetary growth in the South, while Northern banks were responsible for perhaps 75 percent of monetary growth in the North.[47] Confederate bond issues provided only 21 percent of total government "means" in the Confederacy, while they contributed 65 percent to total revenues of the Northern government's operations.[48] Whether these contrasts of fiscal and monetary policy made any differences in the real sector is a moot question. What they demonstrate is that financial policies in "emergencies" can be diverse.

8. The Panic of 1873 and Resumption

Gold and silver! They are the legal tender of Commerce and the Constitution . . . the legal tender of God Almighty, who has made it precious! (Samuel Cox, House of Representatives, 7 June 1870)

Boutwell resigned his cabinet position early in 1873 to take a seat as United States senator from Massachusetts. His assistant secretary, William Richardson, was then appointed secretary. Richardson had worked very closely with Boutwell; he was a personal friend and had been appointed assistant secretary on Boutwell's urging.[1]

The Treasury's cash balance again increased during the fiscal year 1872-73 (see table 8.1), as practically no open-market purchases of securities were made. "Anticipating the usual autumn stringency," Richardson had the Treasury sell gold in the summer of 1873 and accumulate about $14 million of currency "with the view of using the same . . . in the purchase of bonds for the sinking fund . . . during the autumn and winter."[2]

The reduction of $45 million in the three percent certificates had been matched by an increase in national bank notes outstanding. For this exchange to take place, the reserve ratios of national banks had to fall (see table 8.2), with the result that banks in many states showed deficient legal reserves through the first half of 1873.[3]

In his last annual report Secretary Boutwell had warned: "There is practically no reserve to meet the increased demand for money due occasionally to extraordinary events at home or abroad, and arising periodically with the incoming of the harvest."[4] Boutwell proved to be a prophet in his own time. By September of 1873 the New York banks had insufficient reserves to meet the seasonal demands of the autumn, and on

TABLE 8.1. Current assets and liabilities of the Treasury (millions of dollars as of June 30).

Year	Total cash balance	Coin and coin items	Other lawful money	Currency liabilities outstanding[3]	Ratio of cash balance to current liabilities (%)
1868	131	n.a.	n.a.	444	29.5
1869	159	114[1]	45[2]	392	40.5
1870	150	113[1]	37[2]	398	37.6
1871	113	99[1]	14[2]	398	28.3
1872	108	90[1]	18	399	27.0
1873	132	88	44	402	32.5
1874	156	79	77	429	36.4

Source: *Reports of the Treasurer*, 1868-1875.
1. Labeled "gold and silver" instead of "coin and coin items."
2. Cited as "currency" in other parts of the reports, these items presumably consisted of national bank notes and United States notes on hand, but excluded the "reserve."
3. United States notes and fractional currency.

September 8 the big panic began. As table 8.3 shows, reserves declined dramatically—from almost $34 million on September 6 to just over $5 million by October 18. The extraordinary demand for cash in New York was a demand for both specie and United States notes. Note and specie reserves of national banks fell by $14 million, or over 50 percent, in four weeks, and deposits declined by $50 million, or 28 percent, in the same period. At this point the overall reserve ratio for the entire national banking system was down to 19.6 percent, and the basic ratio was 14.5 percent (table 7.2). These values reflect the decline in high-powered money (the three percents) and the permissive increase of national bank notes outstanding. The $4 million decline in basic reserves held between September 12 and October 13, 1873, was translated into a decrease of $76 million in total currency and deposits.

Secretary Richardson made a pretense of initiating a treasury policy. He began well enough by buying bonds for the sinking fund with the $14 million he had obtained from gold sales in the summer. After a few days he ordered the purchases stopped because "it became evident that the amount offering [*sic*] for purchase was increasing to an extent beyond the power of the Treasury to accept." He had not, he said righteously,

used any part of the forty-four millions of United States notes, generally known as the reserve . . . [General panic conditions] could not

TABLE 8.2. Ratio of Reserves to liabilities on selected dates for national banks in states, redemption cities, and New York City (percent).

	Oct. 5, 1868	Oct. 9, 1869	Oct. 8, 1870	Oct. 2, 1871	Oct. 3, 1872	July 13, 1873[1]	Sept. 12, 1873	Dec. 26, 1873	Oct. 2, 1874
States	22.9	20.5	20.9	21.2	19.2	20.6	20.6	20.8	19.1
Redemption cities	31.6	31.5	29.4	28.7	25.9	28.0	25.2	26.9	25.9
New York City	32.6	34.7	28.5	26.7	24.4	30.1	23.4	29.7	29.7

Source: *Reports of the Comptroller of the Currency,* 1869–1874.
1. Not seasonally adjusted. Values for July would naturally be much higher than those for October.

TABLE 8.3. Average weekly liabilities and reserves of national banks in New York City for September and October 1873

| Week ending | Liabilities (millions of dollars) | | | Reserves | | | Ratio of reserves to liabilities (%) |
	Circu-lation	Deposits	Total	Specie	Legal tenders	Total	
Sept. 6	27.3	183	210	19.90	34.00	53.9	25.7
Sept. 13	26.4	178	204	17.70	32.50	50.2	24.6
Sept. 20	27.4	169	196	16.10	30.10	46.2	23.6
Sept. 27	27.3	150	177	11.50	17.90	29.3	16.5
Oct. 4	27.4	132	159	9.24	9.25	18.5	11.6
Oct. 11	27.4	132	159	10.50	8.05	18.6	11.6
Oct. 18	27.4	130	157	11.70	5.18	16.8	10.7
Oct. 25	27.4	126	153	11.40	7.19	18.6	12.2
Dec. 26	27.0[1]	169[1]	196	19.70	24.50	44.2	29.7

Source: *Report of Comptroller of the Currency*, 1874, p. 170.
1. Approximate.

be avoided by any amount of currency which might be added to the circulation already existing. Confidence was to be entirely restored only by the slow and cautious process of gaining better knowledge of true values . . . and by conducting business on a firmer basis, with less inflation [*sic*] and more regard to real soundness and intrinsic values.[5]

Several proposals for getting United States notes into circulation were broached by interested business groups. Richardson rejected them all because, he said, the Treasury's business did not include dealing in gold or foreign exchange, Congress had not authorized prepayment of the outstanding loan, and the issue of notes from the reserve "for the sole purpose of affecting [the money] market . . . ought not to be the business of the Treasury Department." Since the legal authority of the secretary's discretion over disposition of the reserve was still not clear, Richardson recommended that Congress answer the question "by a distinct enactment."[6]

Congress procrastinated. It was waiting for something to happen. What happened was that fiscal receipts underran fiscal expenditures in November and December of 1873, so that the secretary was forced for fiscal reasons to reissue $26 million of the $44 million reserve. This action relieved the crisis. Comptroller of the Currency John Jay Knox noted that resumption of currency payments—United States notes for national bank notes—occurred November 1, 1873.[7]

Congress had many monetary problems to consider during the session that convened in early 1874: the panic that had just passed, the inelasticity of paper money, the stubborn refusal of national bank notes to apportion themselves "equitably" throughout the country, the relative volumes of national bank notes and United States notes that should be in existence, the Treasury's discretionary control over the currency, and the difficulty of resuming specie payments. John Sherman, assuming the role of cameral critic, indicted his Senate colleagues for favoring the goal of resumption in their speeches while hedging on this principle by promoting devious increases in the money supply. United States notes, fractional currency, and national bank notes had all increased in the past four years, he pointed out, and the premium on gold remained. He gently chastised Boutwell for his part in expanding the money supply and ended by saying that the correct quantity of money was the amount that could be maintained within the framework of a specie standard.[8]

Boutwell answered Sherman's arguments by observing that commercial countries were subject to a perverse elasticity in their bank-issued currencies. Relief might then occur either by suspension of specie payments and the issue of additional (*sic*) bank notes or by central bank intervention to make additional credit available. Suspension and the resulting commercial chaos, he thought, were primitive and obsolete; central banking methods were a contemporary improvement. But relief from the effects of bank panics, he said, had never been attained even in England "without the personal intervention of men possessing power." The use of the "reserve" in four of the last five years was

> in its effect . . . substantially what is done by the Government of Great Britain through the Bank of England. The Secretary furnished temporary relief, not . . . by loans, because the Government of the United States is not engaged in making loans, but by adding to the circulation of the country, diminishing its value, . . . and changing the relations of debtor and creditor. Clothed with authority by law, . . . the Secretary could not sit silent and inactive while ruin was blasting the prospects of many and creating the most serious apprehensions in all parts of the country. It was a great responsibility; but it is a responsibility which must be taken by men who are clothed with the authority.[9]

Further decreases in the price level, Boutwell felt, were uncalled for. "We have no right morally," he argued, "to change the relations of [debtors and creditors]." Government bonds had long since appreciated to par in gold, even though United States notes still circulated at a 12 percent discount to gold. The creditor class could therefore have made up losses on the depreciated dollars of the civil war years "by investing the moneys received in securities of the Government." In short, depreciation losses on paper money had long since been capitalized. Resumption, he suggested, would occur by means of "natural progress . . . in the uses to which currency can be applied." He cited England in 1822 as an example of an economy that grew up to an inflated money stock.[10]

This attitude toward resumption was typical of many conservatives in the Grant administrations. Resumption was always favored, but as a policy that would be implemented sometime in the future by means left unspecified. Some opposition Democrats tried to make political capital of conservative procrastination by arguing vociferously for resumption. Their resumption, however, was always in gold *and* silver coin.[11]

If *a* monetary policy could be assigned to the incumbent administration between 1868 and 1874, it was one of ad hoc means for maintaining the existing stock of money in the economy without allowing increases in the outstanding liquid obligations of the federal government. National bank note policy had been the principal vehicle for effecting these tenuous and unspecified ends, but increases in the circulation of national bank notes had not been matched by the more equitable distribution anticipated by the original national bank act.

The cheap-money-greenback movement was largely a reaction to this maldistribution. It exerted continuous pressure on the national banking system after 1867—to such an extent, in fact, that the national banking system "suffered a precarious existence for the next ten years with strong probabilities of its abandonment."[12]

Southern and western greenback sentiment is seen in an address made in the Senate by John Gordon of Georgia in early 1874. Gordon voiced the antipathy of these regions to resumption. "The evil [of the recent panic]," he said, "is found . . . in the rigidity of volume, the non-elasticity and therefore insufficiency [sic] of the currency." He saw money flowing to New York where it encouraged speculation and then could not be available for crop-moving. After making a comparison of money per capita between the United States and France, England, and Germany, he cited Henry Thornton on the buoyant business effects that resulted from an issue of exchequer bills, the British equivalent of United States treasury notes. He advocated low interest rates to encourage production in the South and argued that increases in the money supply would obtain this end. He pointedly objected to any policy that allowed falling prices: "The people of the South and West are debtors; . . . their obligations were formed . . . when gold was at 110 to 150; and now to force them to pay in a currency equal to gold would be simply to increase their debts by the amount of 10 to 50 percent . . . Cheap money is the one thing needed for the agricultural and productive interests of this country, . . . cheap interest is what we want."[13]

In the House of Representatives John Bright of Tennessee also commented on the inequities of apportionment and what he regarded as a general insufficiency of the currency. He denied that the currency was superabundant just because of the gold premium, and he closed his speech with an acidic attack on the inhumanity of the movement toward resumption: "To an aristocracy, existing on the annual interest of a national debt, the people are only of value in proportion to their docility and power of patiently bleeding golden blood under the tax-gatherer's thumbscrews."[14]

The opposing opinion was expressed by John Scott, a senator from Pennsylvania. "I have no idea," he said, "that we can gratify what seems to be the desire of very many in the land; that is, start a volume of paper currency running past every man's door like the streams that carry him water, so that he can go out with his dipper in hand and take just what he requires to slake his monetary thirst and make him easy and comfortable in his business."[15]

The discussion reflected the resentment over the government's inability to ration currency in a manner that would satisfy anyone, let alone everyone. In such a situation grudging compromise was inevitable. The act of June 20, 1874, and the Resumption Act of January 14, 1875, shared this feature.

The act of June 20, 1874, froze greenbacks again, this time at $382 million. By this measure Congress allowed to stand the increase of $26 million that Secretary Richardson had issued in late 1873, but it also denied thereafter any concept or use of a reserve at the discretion of the secretary of the Treasury. The act also limited the responsibility for redemption of national bank notes to the United States treasurer in Washington, although in practice the subtreasuries also redeemed notes when called on to do so. To redeem its notes each national bank had to keep with the Treasury a redemption fund that amounted to 5 percent of notes outstanding. The redemption fund served as part of the required reserves against deposits. This provision sharply reduced *required* national bank reserves and together with the increase of $26 million in greenbacks promoted a radical change in national bank reserve positions between October 1873 and October 1874. (See table 7.2.)

The last provision of the act of 1874 allowed national banks to retire their own notes by depositing equal amounts of greenbacks with the comptroller of the currency. The comptroller then paid out the greenbacks as he retired national bank notes. This provision did not affect total greenbacks outstanding; the maximum issue was still $382 million. But it allowed a national bank to decide how much of its own notes it wished to circulate within the constraint of a maximum issue of $354 million for all national banks.

The act of June 20, 1874, was an act of monetary ease and temperance. It allowed the first legal increase in high-powered United States notes in over six years. The elections in the fall of 1874 then witnessed the first overthrow of Republican majorities in Congress since the Civil War. Party leaders felt that their election setbacks resulted from soft monetary policies and their procrastination over resumption.[16] They resolved to get a resumption bill through Congress in the lame-duck session of 1874-75 before they lost control over legislation to the incoming Democratic majorities. They had to be sure they did not do too much, for while resumption was desirable, contraction was not. So any resumption bill, in order to pass, had to be phrased in terms that implied no contraction of the currency. The result of this stimulated effort was the Resumption Act of January 14, 1875.[17]

The Resumption Act may appear to be nothing more than a pious and puritanical determination to do the right thing at the right time. However, it resolved the national bank note currency problem by removing the government's regulatory powers completely, and it was ultimately responsible for reducing the outstanding volume of United States notes by an interpretative provision that allowed secretaries of the Treasury to effect a modest contraction of these notes over the next three years.

The administration of national bank note apportionment was beset with complications.[18] The Resumption Act ended these problems simply by cutting the Gordian knot. It stated that any national banking association could increase circulating notes without limit: "The provisions of law for the withdrawal and redistribution of national bank currency among the several states and territories are hereby repealed."[19]

Tied to the provision for the unconstrained issue of national bank notes was the one that turned out to have real impact. It specified that:

> Whenever, and so often, as circulating notes shall be issued to any such banking association, . . . it shall be the duty of the Secretary of the Treasury to redeem the legal-tender United States notes in excess only of $300 million to the amount of 80 per cent of the sum of national bank notes so issued, . . . and to continue such redemption . . . until there shall be outstanding the sum of $300 million of such legal-tender United States notes and no more . . . And to enable the Secretary of the Treasury to prepare and provide for redemptions in this act authorized or required, he is authorized to use any surplus revenues . . . in the Treasury not otherwise appropriated, and to issue, sell, and dispose of, at not less than par, in coin, either of the descriptions of bonds of the United States described in the Act of Congress approved July 14, 1870, entitled, 'An Act to authorize the refunding of the national debt.'[20]

The author of the resumption bill, the guiding hand for its passage, and later the administrator of its successful implementation was Senator John Sherman. He was chairman of the Senate Committee on Finance during the Forty-third Congress and became secretary of the Treasury under Rutherford B. Hayes in March 1877.

Sherman prepared the resumption bill for passage by caucusing with Republican leaders in Congress before the bill's appearance in the Senate.[21] To get concurrence of the still-existing Republican majorities, Sherman had to frame the bill with tact and with no implication of contraction, for contraction had become political anathema. The rationale given by Sherman for the implied currency changes was that national bank notes would expand or contract only "in case the business of the community demands it." The secretary of the Treasury was then to retire United States notes equivalent to 80 percent of the additional national bank notes, in recognition of the fact that 20 percent in United States notes was the average reserve required against national bank demand obligations. Hence the reduction of United States notes from $382 million to $300 million was supposed to be matched by an increase in national bank notes of $100 million, which would be made possible by diverting $20 million of the remaining United States notes from use as hand-to-hand currency to national bank reserves. "This provision of the bill," Sherman stated blandly, "neither provides for a contraction or expansion of the currency, but leaves the amount [outstanding] to be regulated by the business wants of the community."[22]

The ensuing debate on the bill revealed some interesting congressional sentiments about monetary policy. Carl Schurz of Missouri, a thoroughgoing resumptionist, asked Sherman pointedly whether the United States notes that were to be redeemed could then be reissued in the same fashion as the $26 million reserve that had been reissued by the Treasury Department in 1873. Sherman replied that he would leave the word *redeem* to be interpreted by future Congresses when greenbacks were down to the target of $300 million. "Practical men dealing with practical affairs," he said, "cannot introduce into this bill a controversy which will prevent that unity that is necessary to carry out the good that is contained in this bill."[23]

Sherman's refusal to make the bill specify unqualified destruction of United States notes prompted many senators to condemn the bill as inflationary. John Stevenson of Kentucky had perhaps the best characterization of it. "The bill," he said, "is a species of Janus-faced legislation . . . [It is a measure] upon which expansionists and contractionists could temporarily unite." Both groups, he said, could think that they had triumphed.[24]

The real force in the bill was the hidden contraction in high-powered money (United States notes) that it permitted and encouraged. Whenever national bank notes were issued by the comptroller of the currency, the secretary of the Treasury had to use any fiscal means in his power to redeem United States notes, that is, take them out of circulation.

Specific and innocuous as this provision sounded, its use for good or for evil was again subject to the discretion of the secretary of the Treasury who administered it. If he chose to retire United States notes up to 80 percent of the *net* amount of new national bank notes issued, the money supply might have stayed roughly constant.[25] If he chose to retire United States notes on the basis of *gross* national bank notes issued—that is, without counting notes voluntarily retired by the banks themselves as permitted by the act of July 20, 1874—the resulting reduction of greenbacks might have virtually no relation to the net change in national bank notes.[26] Under the "gross" interpretation, the total currency could increase only if the gross decrease in national bank notes was less than the difference between the gross increase in such notes and the net amount of greenbacks retired.[27] In fact, gross issues of national bank notes over the next three years amounted to about $45 million, permitting the retirement of $36 million in greenbacks. *Net* issues of national bank notes, however, declined by about the same amount as United States notes (column 1 in table 7.2).[28] The outstanding currency, therefore, did not stay constant, with national bank notes reciprocally increasing as United States notes declined. Outstanding quantities of both currencies were reduced, and prices continued to fall.

How much guile was there in the Resumption Act when it was passed? To what extent was the decrease in United States notes seen as a leverage factor that would decrease the total money supply? Apparently not much. Several senators thought the act would promote inflation. Carl Schurz observed, for example, that to get resumption the proportion of paper to gold would have to be reduced; "and in this respect," he concluded, "the bill before us is palpably and deplorably inadequate." In addition, an amendment that explicitly proposed contraction of United States notes at the rate of $2 million per month until resumption was achieved was defeated in the Senate by a vote of 44 to 6.[29]

Sherman may have had some intuitions about the contraction that would result from the deflation of United States notes. The 80 percent reduction clause, he remarked, "not only leads us toward specie payment, but lessens the volume which we are bound to redeem when the time comes for final redemption." The general sentiment of the Senate was expressed by Allen Thurman of Ohio: "It is very difficult to find out what is in [the bill] . . . There is a great deal of omission, but the least possible amount of commission that ever I have seen in a great public measure."[30]

The House of Representatives passed the bill without debate just as it came from the Senate, and it became law January 14, 1875. Many who voted for it "in principle" undoubtedly assumed it would never become operational, and others who voted for it determined that it would never be so privileged. It called for fractional silver coinage in place of fractional paper money, and it slightly subsidized gold coinage by repealing the coinage charges of $0.002 per $1,000. Finally, the act permitted free banking.[31] National banks could issue as much or as little currency as they wished so long as they obeyed reserve requirements and other national bank regulations. Apportionment problems of national bank notes became a thing of the past.

The secretaries of the Treasury who served after passage of the Resumption Act were partisan resumptionists who simply carried out the "gross" interpretation of the law. When Rutherford B. Hayes was elected president in 1876, he appointed Sherman secretary of the Treasury. This appointment gave Sherman the opportunity to implement and administer the policy he had authored in the Senate. Since the basic stock of high-powered money was declining slowly but steadily due to the 80 percent provision in the Resumption Act, Sherman could promote a policy of doing nothing and the gold premium would gradually disappear as the general price level fell.

Sherman's opinion on resumption was adamant, but it did not imply that he favored a rigidly metallic monetary system. Far from it. His ideal system called for (1) United States notes, "carefully limited in amount" and "supported by ample reserves of coin in the Treasury," (2) "supplemented by a system of national banks . . . free and open to all, . . . with power to issue circulating notes secured by United States bonds, . . . and redeemable on demand in United States notes or coin," plus (3) the limited coinage of silver as a minor currency. The government, he thought, was "a safer custodian of reserves than a multitude of scattered banks"; but banks were better for handling "the ebb and flow of currency caused by varying crops, productions and seasons." Even Sherman's ideal monetary structure had to allow for periods in which it was "impracticable to maintain actual redemption . . . Every such system," he concluded pragmatically, "must provide for a suspension of specie payments."[32]

The Democratic Congress was not ready to give up so easily. The Resumption Act had been passed in a lame-duck session (Forty-third Congress, second session) just before a legislature much less amenable to resumption convened. Bills for repeal of the Resumption Act were then introduced in the Forty-fourth Congress, but no such bills could get through the Senate, much less past the executive. The elections of 1876 and 1878 likewise resulted in Congresses that were antipathetic to resumption; but Hayes, elected president by a majority of one electoral vote in a bitterly disputed contest, conscientiously supported the resumption ideal. Thus only a bill to repeal that had better than a two-thirds vote in Congress could get past an executive veto.

The hostility of Congress and the public to the resumption medicine became intensive during the years 1876-1878. This hostility was reflected in the free-silver-cheap-money movement that appeared in the mid-1870s. Late in 1876 a silver commission was formed by a joint resolution of Congress to "do something" for silver. It was composed of three senators (Jones, Bogy, and Boutwell), three representatives (Gibson, Willard, and Bland), and two non-political experts (William Groesbeck of Ohio and Professor Francis Bowen of Massachusetts).[33] The duties of the commission were to inquire into (1) the causes and effects of changes in the relative values of gold and silver; (2) the policy of restoration of the double standard and the mint values at which it would be restored; (3) the effects of the policy of continuing legal tender (United States) notes concurrently with the double standard; (4) the best means of "providing for facilitating [sic] the resumption of specie payments."[34]

The commission presented one majority and two minority reports. The majority, five of the eight members, claimed that a double standard was necessary to prevent chronic crisis and business paralysis. They recommended the restoration of the double standard and the unrestricted coinage of both metals, even though they could not agree on the legal relationship between the metals (mint values) that should be established. The place of a convertible paper currency in a metallic system, they thought, was uncertain. Only Great Britain had accomplished a resumption with a mixed-money system, and then after "an unexampled commercial and industrial depression, covering nearly the period of a generation . . . The Commission," the majority report emphasized, "have been able to arrive at only the one single conclusion that resumption in this country is not practicable under the circumstances, until the laws making gold the sole metallic legal-tender are repealed."[35] This point was reiterated and emphasized in the face of disagreement over the precise monetary relation that should be established between gold and silver. The political price of resumption was silver remonetization. Even the minority report of Boutwell disagreed with the principle of silver remonetization only if it did not occur on an international basis.[36]

The minority report, written by Professor Bowen and concurred in by Representative Gibson, stressed stability in a standard of value as opposed to mere facility in a medium of exchange. It argued (without much substantiation) that both legal tender paper and silver gave rise to extremes in price fluctuation. "What we dread," the report states, "is not the *fall*, but the *fluctuation*, in value of the would-be standard, and the feeling of uncertainty thereby produced." It interpreted the price level decline of late 1876 and the corresponding decline in the gold premium on greenbacks as results of decreased issues of national bank notes and United States notes—although it incorrectly contended that the decrease in paper money occurred "spontaneously, and without any aid from legislation."[37]

In general the minority report concluded that (1) silver was too much subject to depreciation to be a suitable standard of value; (2) the use of legal tender paper was "unjust"; (3) resumption was within reach, due to the "spontaneous" contraction of the paper money at the rate of $3 million per month during the previous two years; (4) Congress should authorize coinage of a fiat (subsidiary) silver dollar of 345.6 grains to replace the fiat paper dollar; (5) Congress should also authorize devaluation of the gold dollar by about 2.6 percent (from 23.2 grains to 22.6 grains); and (6) *net* contraction of the paper currency should continue.[38]

The minority's advocacy of gold-dollar devaluation was indeed surprising, even though the proposed percentage was small. Jones, Bogey, and Willard of the majority recommended a legal relationship between the two metals of 15.5 to 1 instead of the old relationship of 15.98 to 1. They could have obtained this new relationship either by reducing the silver content of the silver dollar from 412.5 grains to 399.9 grains or by increasing the gold content of the gold dollar from 25.8 to 26.6 grains (0.9 fine). These alternatives would have had opposite effects. The former would have been inflationary, the latter deflationary. Not unnaturally they recommended the former. They did not imply that easing prices was a desideratum, but their earlier analysis had stressed the evil of falling prices.[39]

Groesbeck and Bland of the majority concurred in recommending the old silver dollar. They disagreed with the rest of the majority that the silver dollar of 412.5 grains was undervalued at the mint. They felt that reviving the question of relative mint values would impede much of the progress already made on silver remonetization.[40]

The comprehensive report of the Silver Commission, while it included diverse views on remonetization and the valuation of both gold and silver, concurred in advocating a cheaper dollar than either of the metallic dollars of 1860. One group was satisfied with the naturally cheaper silver dollar; another group would have devalued even that; while the sound-money group favored a dollar exclusively gold, but one that would be devalued a modest 2.6 percent. Given evidence of such diversity, one can hardly agree with Kindahl's conclusion that "no thought was given to the possibility of resumption through the expedient of devaluation."[41] Even Sherman suggested that "if the financial condition of our country is so grievous that we must at every hazard have a cheaper dollar, . . . it is far better, rather than to adopt the single standard of silver, to boldly reduce the number of grains in the gold dollar, or to abandon and retrace all efforts to make United States notes equal to coin."[42]

The greenback movement itself implied de facto devaluation through demonetization. Had silver not emerged as a more respectable form of cheap money, the greenback movement might have thwarted resumption until late in the century when gold became cheaper to obtain.

The Bland-Allison Act of February 1878 was the legislative result of the Silver Commission's work. It called for the secretary of the Treasury to purchase monthly between $2 million and $4 million worth of silver at market prices. The bullion was to be coined into dollars of 412.5 grains; but these dollars would be issued by the Treasury only if its other revenues were insufficient for ordinary fiscal payments.

The price of greenbacks in terms of gold gradually approached the prewar parity; the discount by the end of 1877 was only 3 percent. This trend corresponded to changes that had taken place in the money stock since 1874.[43] When the premium on gold seemed certain to reach zero, Congress repealed the 80 percent clause in the Resumption Act and on May 31, 1878, froze the volume of United States notes forever at $346 million. Enough was enough.

Sherman had meanwhile negotiated with bankers and foreign investors in order to accumulate a treasury balance of gold that was presumed necessary to cover redemption of paper money. But the gold was not needed; market forces had done their work. Resumption occurred without a tremor on the date set and with virtually no demands for redemption.

Sherman impounded most of the silver coined under the Bland-Allison Act, so silver had little effect on the price level before resumption. His advocacy of a mixed-money system was indeed a compromising position; it earned him the reputation of being a "shifty Secretary."[44] Nonetheless, resumption would probably not have been accomplished without his moderate compromises and the element of deviousness involved in the retirement of United States notes.

Resumption of specie payments in 1879 was a remarkable political and economic accomplishment, but it had precedent—in the United States in 1819 and in England in 1822. As a political achievement, it required a disciplined approach to price-level adjustment, with corresponding hardships to debtors and with depressive effects on business activity and spending. (Paradoxically it had little effect on total production.) That such price-level discipline was obtained several times in political democracies during the nineteenth and once during the early twentieth century following World War I is a tribute to the political character of the era—or possibly to the wisdom of political leaders for not chartering omnipotent central banks that would usurp the functions of metallic standards and make paper-money inflations permanent.

The economics of resumption required that prices fall to about the level prevailing before the paper-money inflation.[45] Such an adjustment could have resulted from various combinations of (1) reduction in the stock of money, (2) growth in output, and (3) reduction in the rate of use of money. The first of these methods could take any one or combination of three variants: (a) reduction of high-powered money, (b) reduction in the deposit-reserve ratio, and (c) reduction in the deposit-currency ratio.

In the immediate postwar period the stock of money was reduced by wholesale destruction of high-powered money, harsh medicine even for Victorians. So from about 1868 accepted policy was to hold the stock of currency (and presumably of all money) constant and allow the growth in output to promote a gentle decline in the price level. This method had the clear consensus of the political center, and nothing could get through Congress that would have violated it.[46]

The Resumption Act, on the face of it, left this political principle undisturbed. However, its wording was imprecise enough to allow a secretary of the Treasury to promote a limited contraction of United States notes. All three secretaries between 1875 and resumption wished to see resumption accomplished, and so they interpreted the Resumption Act in a way that permitted them to reduce greenbacks.[47]

Milton Friedman and Anna J. Schwartz present an accurate and detailed account of monetary developments in this period. They contend that the decline in high-powered money in the last few years before resumption was "an accomplishment of omission, as it were, not of commission . . . The decline . . . owed less . . . to any Treasury action under the influence of the Resumption Act than to the decline in the two deposit ratios, a decline that we have attributed to a rise in bank suspensions."[48] In this part of their analysis Friedman and Schwartz correctly assess the causes and consequences of changes in the two monetary ratios, and they heed the decline in high-powered money. They themselves, however, commit a "sin" of omission in not recognizing the monetary effect that was contrived by treasury interpretation of the Resumption Act. Contrary to what they assert, at least one political factor was of some importance.

What would have happened if the Resumption Act had not been passed? Without a Resumption Act, Rutherford B. Hayes might not have been elected in 1876, and Samuel Tilden, the Democratic candidate, might well have signed a bill increasing the currency enough to make resumption impossible. Even though no new currency bill became law until the Bland-Allison Act in 1878 remonetized silver, more Green-backer success in the elections of 1876 may have led to some kind of easy-money law. However, if the policy of constancy in the high-powered money stock had continued unabated, resumption would probably have occurred anyway within a year or two. Growth in output, so long as it was not inhibited by too restrictive a monetary policy, would ultimately have lowered money prices by the necessary amount.

9. Controversy over Currency Denominations

The possession of a few copper cents [in 1862] meant that the owner could ride [the street car] rather than walk . . . It meant that he could buy a postage stamp without an altercation with the clerk, or a cigar without receiving in change a handful of the dealer's own manufactured currency. (Neil Carothers, *Fractional Money*, 1930)

Nineteenth-century discussions of currency theory and policy almost always included arguments over the undesirability of small notes in the monetary spectrum, and the theoretical admonitions were generally matched by proscriptive laws.[1] This controversy has been largely neglected by contemporary historians or dismissed as inconsequential.[2] Inattention to an issue on which so much energy and resources were expended provokes a sense of uneasiness—a feeling that the present is overlooking an important dilemma or frustration of the past. Some recent developments in monetary theory now lend support to the inclusion of denominational variables in general monetary theory and offer additional evidence that the constant preoccupation with small-note issues found in nineteenth-century monetary discourse should be assessed.[3]

The demand for small denominations could be satisfied in four ways. Gold was one possibility, but it was not a good solution because any gold piece smaller than $5 was too small to be used handily. Silver was a prime candidate, and it was used extensively for small denominations in certain periods. However, silver in the United States was undervalued at the mint from 1834 until 1873; that is, it was valued more in the market as a commodity than it was at the mint as a money. So for fifty years—until silver became cheap enough for general monetary use in the early 1880s—the demand for small denominations was not fulfilled by silver except for coins so worn, clipped, and abraded that their commodity value was no greater than their monetary value.

The third candidate was commercial bank notes; but bank notes were inhibited by the universal campaign of sound-money proponents against their issue. Although the sound-money propaganda might not have been completely effective, the legal constraints against small bank notes and the formation of banking institutions had substantial consequences.

The fourth possibility was bank deposits. Deposit banking was still in its infancy; and deposits were a less popular medium in rural and frontier areas such as the South and the West, where transactions were for small amounts and the bank population necessary to oversee deposit clearings was thin.[4]

Small notes in the United States were commonly understood to include denominations of paper currency for $5 or less issued by banks, corporations, states, or individuals. However, the specification of "small" was in part a function of the price level. If prices rose substantially during an inflation, a nominally valued "larger" note would become smaller in real terms, and small notes could then be defined to include the issues of, say, $10 notes in addition to all those of $5 and less.

A commonly held thesis for the existence of small notes was that under an operational metallic standard, banks preferred to issue notes in small denominations in order to minimize the "reflux of their circulation." Small notes, bankers learned from experience, were more likely to continue circulating in a given local area than an equal value of larger notes. Not only were they more useful as hand-to-hand currency, but if ordinary business purposes led an individual or a firm to demand specie for bank notes, a few of the larger denominations cost less in time and trouble to convert to specie than a mass of small notes. Thus they were regarded as an economizing medium, both by their suppliers (banks) and their demanders (the general public), for small denominational coins. For this reason they were less likely to come back for redemption in specie.[5]

An inflation of paper currency within the framework of a mixed-currency system generally provoked the disappearance of metallic coin because of the appreciated nominal value of the coin as a commodity. Paper notes of smaller denominations then came into general use. This association between inflation and the appearance of small notes "proved" to many observers that the small notes "drove specie out of hand-to-hand circulation, and frequently out of the country as well . . . [thus causing] suspension of specie payments."[6] In fact, the denominational proportions of fiat governmental issues of paper money made little difference. Inflation resulted from the sheer quantity of these issues and from the subsequent burgeoning volume of bank notes and deposits based on the original issues of government paper currency.

The subsequent appearance of notes of small denomination was a symptom. It reflected the common need for a medium of exchange to handle nominal purchases and sales formerly handled by coin—coin that had gone into "the arts" to take advantage of the inflated market price of monetary metal. Nonetheless, the simultaneous disappearance of specie and appearance of small notes endowed the notes with a mischievous influence.[7]

The arguments against small notes were vented in classical economic thought by Adam Smith in the *Wealth of Nations*. He noted that the minimum bank note denomination in London was £10 and that the ordinary customer could use such a bank note only to a limited extent before he had to change it into fractional coin. He advocated a minimum of £15 in general around the country as a means of securing the circulation of gold and silver. He argued for this restriction even though he recognized it as "a manifest violation of that natural liberty which it is the proper business of law, not to infringe, but to support." He thought that the right to issue notes of any denomination would endanger the soundness of the currency; so restricting the issue of small notes was like building fire walls to prevent the spread of fire.[8] Henry Thornton, writing in 1802, also alleged that the issue of small notes payable to bearer caused "a great and permanent diminution in our circulating coin" and increased the danger of inconvertibility between bank paper and coin.[9]

The views of these economists were typical for their time and, indeed, for the whole era in which a mixed currency was the norm. Banking policies corresponded largely to these learned prescriptions. The Bank of England, for example, issued no notes under £20 before 1759, when £15 and £10 notes were introduced.[10] During the restriction period the bank was permitted to issue notes as low as £1 and £2, thus demonstrating the need for small notes to fill the void of the missing coin. As resumption of specie payments became anticipated after 1816, the bank reduced its issues of the £1 and £2 notes from a peak of £9.3 million in 1814 to £900,000 in 1822, or from 30 percent of its total note circulation to 5 percent.[11] After 1826 the bank was limited by law to issuing no notes for less than £5.[12]

The monetary events in the United States provoked by the War of 1812 offer another good example of the small-note policy model. The United States Treasury issued large amounts of interest-bearing treasury notes between 1812 and 1815. Of the some $35 million issued only the final $3.39 million included denominations under $20.[13] Since they could be used to pay all duties, taxes, and debts of the United States, the notes were quasi-legal tender. The larger denominations, which included about 90 percent of the total value of all issues, were much more usable as commercial bank reserves than they were as hand-to-hand currency. On the basis of these new reserves, the banks then expanded bank credit, deposits, and currency ("circulation") in any and all denominations currently popular. Such an expansion provoked the usual paper-money inflation and suspension. All specie, including fractional currency, was driven out of circulation, so the banks had to supply small notes. In his review of this event A. Barton Hepburn alleged that the banks purposely foisted small notes on the public: "In order to increase the volume [of notes] as much as possible, . . . a mass of small denominations, some as low as six cents, were issued . . . Suspension of coin payments *naturally* followed."[14] Thus Hepburn found the issue of small notes by the banks the independent event that caused suspension and inflation. In fact, the issue of treasury notes that gave the banks fresh reserves caused the inflation and subsequent demonetization of metallic money. The issue of small notes was again just an ex post symptom.[15]

Before the Civil War, New York and Pennsylvania led the states in prohibiting notes under $5. A dozen other states followed their example, "one of the objects," Hepburn noted, "being to enforce the use of silver and gold in the small transactions of daily barter."[16] The ubiquitous laws against small-note issues were hard to police,[17] but they had significant if not lasting effects on the denominational texture of the monetary system.

This prejudice against small notes was basically contradictory. If small notes were in demand for transaction purposes, they would be used extensively in place of barter and remain in circulation. They could not simultaneously be demanded for monetary purposes *and* cause embarrassment by being turned in for specie.[18]

Gold and silver coins might have defused the small-note controversy if public policy had been more sophisticated and if the discoveries of precious metals had been more regular. In the early part of the century most of the coins in use were Spanish. By 1820 the United States mint had coined less than one piece below a half dollar for each person in the country, and the value per person of the coins in circulation was less than $0.25.[19] This situation was not improved by the Coinage Act of 1834—a law "inspired by crassly partisan motives." It fixed the gold-silver mint ratio too high at the same time that it devalued the gold dollar. Thus it had the effect of providing "for the cessation of silver coinage."[20]

The discoveries of gold in the western United States and in Australia in the late 1840s reduced the real price of gold and correspondingly aggravated the demonetization of silver and the export of silver coins to Europe. The coinage laws of 1834 and 1853 provided for a gold dollar and a subsidiary silver three-cent piece. These two very small coins, together with underweight and worn Spanish coins, were all that were available for ordinary transactions until 1857. The coinage law of 1857, while deficient and imperfect in some respects, effectively complemented the existing coinage system with coins adequate for large and small transactions.[21] No sooner had this state been reached than it was upset by the monetary events of the Civil War.

The paper-money inflation fostered by the federal government during 1861-1865 had the classic, predictable effect on the monetary system. United States notes were issued in massive amounts and in no denominations below $5. The monetary metals rapidly appreciated in market value as the notes were issued; by 1862 what had been coin currencies became commodities. The inflation occurred so quickly that metallic currency disappeared almost overnight, leaving a paralyzing vacuum in the lower denominations. Neil Carothers's account states: "The country found itself, in the midst of a war boom, virtually without a currency between the 1 cent piece and the $5 note."[22] Private businesses and municipalities tried to fill the vacuum by issuing notes, tickets, and due bills, and the government carried out its ill-conceived expedient of a postage-stamp currency. It also passed the National Bank Act in 1863, which allowed national banks to issue $50 million (of a total of $300 million) in denominations under $5, but only until resumption of specie payments when the $5 lower limit would again apply.[23]

The lack of small notes and fractional currency is seen in several treasury reports of the early 1870s. An amendment in 1865 to the National Bank Act had prohibited *banking* corporations from issuing paper currency without paying the prohibitive 10 percent tax, but it had not specified any restrictions on issues of notes by nonbanks. In 1872 the comptroller of the currency, John Jay Knox, entitled a section of his annual report "Shinplasters." Under this heading, he discussed notes issued by the state of Alabama, which were payable and receivable for all state debts:

> Savings-banks, railroad, municipal, and other corporations in the States of Florida, Georgia and other Southern States have followed the example of the State of Alabama, and have issued, and are still issuing, a large amount of similar circulation, some in the form of receipts and certificates, and others in the form of railroad tickets, but all issued in the form and similitude of bank notes, and intended to circulate as money. There is no law in existence to prevent the circulation and no legislative provision for the enforcement of the constitutional provision [against bills of credit] of such issues.[24]

Knox pointed out the same practice in 1873 by the Central Railroad and Banking Company of Georgia. "I am informed that these issues are redeemed by the railroad company," he said, "and that . . . arrangements are being made by manufacturing companies and corporations to issue similar devices."[25] The problem was not confined to the South, Knox emphasized. Mining corporations around Lake Superior and Zion's

Commercial Cooperative Institution of Salt Lake City also issued such notes.[26]

A group of private merchants and bankers of Columbia, South Carolina, petitioned Congress in December 1873 (after the bank panic) protesting similar action. Numerous corporations issue currency that "are *fac similes* of national bank notes," their memorial stated, "forcing that currency upon their employees." On the notes issued by the South Carolina Railroad Company, the petition continued, "the word 'dollars' does not appear." To escape tax, companies lithographed notes "Good for the fare of one passage ____ miles." The memorial cited other examples of questionable paper currency, including notes issued by a building and loan association and by the city of Columbia itself. It concluded by entreating Congress to "bridle this wild delirium which has seized upon these breakers and evaders of the law."[27]

The treasurer, an official who usually did not analyze current monetary conditions, wrote in 1874 that he had had "personal experience and observation" of unauthorized paper money in the South. Issues of local currency, particularly fractional currency, he said, were "put upon everybody in [as] change, and unless used in the place of issue are worthless to the holder."[28]

These protests emphasized the dearth of money generally and of lower denominations in particular, especially in the South and the West. The arithmetic of the denominational problem is simple. Only two combinations of the usual denominations make three dollars' worth of currency— a one-dollar and a two-dollar bill or three one-dollar bills. Since one- and two-dollar bills were scarce, especially in the South, the difficulty of making change for the more usual five-dollar bill can be readily inferred. Under such circumstances the sheer economic necessity for issues of scrip and trade credit made virtually every merchant a merchant-banker. Why not take trade credit as change for, say, a ten-dollar bill at the general store if you knew the proprietor was reputable? He had a whole store full of goods that you could demand as liquidation of the balance if the occasion required it. Thus the genesis of these commercial moneys was a competitive evolution of an economic good in the presence of scarcity. Making the notes payable to bearer rather than as a bookkeeping credit to the order of a single person was simply a cheaper way of handling this kind of exchange, especially for an institution, such as a municipality, that handled numerous small transactions.

Despite widespread use of "unauthorized paper money," its general condemnation by sound-money spokesmen was not often matched or countered by people who realized its utility. One of the few who did was Charles Moran. He argued outspokenly for free banking and for unconstrained issues of small notes.[29] He correctly stated that the fears and prejudices against the issue of small notes were due to the fallacious theories of English and American bullionists, "who attributing monetary panics and commercial crises to over-issues of bank notes, have always urged legislative restrictions to the issues of bank notes so as to force coin into circulation contrary to the self-interest and desires of the people."[30]

Resumption of specie payments in 1879, the extensive recoinage of silver for smaller denominations during the 1880s, and the rapid development of checkbook banking alleviated most denominational problems. After 1886 virtually all denominational constraints were problems of the past.

Strange as it may seem, the denominational composition of the currency during the nineteenth century may have had a significant bearing on the decline in the measured velocity of money so prominent for that period. Computations of the income velocity of money over the century indicate a decline from about six per year in the early part of the century to a value of about three per year or less around 1900. Velocity values then stabilize until 1929, fall substantially during the Great Depression and World War II, then climb to the early seventies.[31]

The steadily declining velocity during the nineteenth century has been accepted as more or less reasonable by many economists who have then tried to develop plausible explanations for it. One hypothesis is that declining velocity results from the effect of secular increases in real income on desired money balances.[32] According to this view money is a superior good having an income elasticity of demand greater than one. As real incomes increase over time, people build up real balances and velocity declines. This theory does not, however, reconcile the apparent secular decline in velocity during the nineteenth century with no apparent *secular* change during the first three quarters of the twentieth century.[33]

A more likely source of bias in velocity measurement is the compilation of the data used to measure velocity. Two series are necessary, money income and the stock of money. To obtain current income values for some past period, the real volume of goods and services produced is estimated and then priced at current market prices *as if it were all sold in markets for money*. This method does no harm if only comparable real incomes are desired. However, if a significant portion of real income is bartered but still accounted as money income, and if a significant amount of money used to transact real product is not counted or is unaccountable, the velocity quotient obtained by dividing "money income" with the measured stock of money will be proportionally larger. It will imply that accounted money is being exchanged much more frequently than is really the case. If, over time, a higher and higher proportion of real product is then exchanged for accounted money while money-holding habits stay constant, the *computed* value of monetary velocity will decline. This "decline" is really a bias; money-holding habits need not have changed.[34]

Clark Warburton states that national income estimates for the nineteenth century are not sufficiently reliable or well-constituted to show how large a proportion of the product was sold in markets and how much was produced by farm and village families for their own use.[35] Whatever the actual proportions, the amount bartered was significant, while the proportion of nonpecuniary income to total income declined steadily. These facts are themselves sufficient to account for a substantial bias in velocity.[36]

The downward bias in measured velocity found in nineteenth-century estimates is compatible with the supposition that significant denominational constraints were also present during many decades of the century. Denominational hindrances would have encouraged swaps, barter, payment in kind, and the use of uncounted and unaccountable moneys to a much greater degree than has been acknowledged or measured. As denominational constraints lessened late in the century, the cost of bringing more and more product and income into the circuit of monetary transactions also become lower. Then with the virtual disappearance of denominational impediments late in the century and the reduction of barter to a relatively small fraction of income, the decided downward "trend" in velocity ceased.

Even more difficult than measuring velocity accurately is estimating the extent of barter and the use of unaccounted substitute moneys. Nevertheless, some inferences on monetary behavior may be drawn from an examination of the relatively accurate time series on currency denominations in the period following the Civil War. The first few years after 1865 were marked by contraction of the money stock and a general deflation. The period from 1868 to 1879 was a time of fasting and cleansing in preparation for resumption of specie payments, a period marked by sharp monetary controversy and uncertainty. The eleven or twelve years after resumption (1880-1891), while not free of controversy, were characterized by a reduction of the unsettling pressures of government on monetary behavior.

Denominational data for United States currency between 1868 and 1891 are summarized in table 9.1. All currency from $1 to $50 is listed except gold coin.[37] In the first period the total dollar value of the currency, although distinctly variable from year to year, stayed roughly constant over the entire period while prices fell by 43 percent.[38] In the second period the total dollar value of the currency increased by 58 percent, a sharp departure from the low growth of the first period, but prices still fell by 10 percent.[39]

Two additional measures can be derived from the listed denominations and the price index: (1) an average annual money denomination and (2)

TABLE 9.1. Number of pieces of standard currency denominations in the United States, wholesale prices, and average denominations, 1868–1891.

End of fiscal year (June 30)	(1) $1	(2) $2	(3) $5	(4) $10	(5) $20	(6) $50	(7) Total	(8) Total (millions of dollars)	(9) Average money denomina-tion ($)	(10) Prices (1910= 1914=100)	(11) Average real denomina-tion ($)
	(Millions of pieces)										
1868	22.3	10.9	35.2	16.1	5.37	0.85	90.7	530.4	5.85	158	3.70
1869	23.0	12.3	34.8	16.2	5.90	0.71	92.9	537.0	5.78	151	3.83
1870	26.2	16.7	37.0	18.4	6.64	0.97	105.9	609.6	5.76	135	4.27
1871	27.8	15.6	34.7	16.5	5.93	0.82	101.4	557.2	5.50	130	4.23
1872	31.1	16.1	35.3	17.1	6.18	0.87	106.7	578.2	5.42	136	3.99
1873	31.8	15.8	35.0	17.3	6.32	0.91	107.1	583.9	5.45	133	4.10
1874	31.0	15.9	36.3	17.1	6.62	1.03	108.0	598.8	5.54	126	4.40
1875	29.4	14.4	31.1	17.1	6.66	1.13	99.8	574.5	5.76	118	4.88
1876	31.3	14.7	28.7	16.6	6.55	1.18	99.0	559.8	5.66	110	5.15
1877	29.0	13.3	28.6	16.3	6.40	1.17	94.8	547.5	5.78	106	5.45
1878	25.9	11.9	29.7	17.0	6.57	0.98	92.1	548.3	5.95	91	6.54
1879	29.9	10.5	30.0	17.1	6.56	0.94	95.0	550.0	5.79	90	6.43
1880	42.3	11.1	33.2	19.1	7.46	0.96	114.1	618.1	5.42	100	5.42
1881	53.0	11.7	33.9	21.7	8.49	1.00	129.8	682.3	5.26	103	5.11
1882	58.6	12.6	33.0	27.4	8.79	1.02	136.4	698.8	5.12	108	4.74
1883	63.7	13.0	32.9	23.0	9.53	1.22	143.4	735.2	5.13	101	5.08
1884	67.0	12.6	32.6	23.0	10.0	1.23	146.4	746.5	5.10	93	5.48
1885	63.9	12.8	31.5	22.1	9.76	1.26	141.3	725.9	5.14	85	6.05

1886	70.5	9.2	33.8	21.8	9.25	1.19	145.7	720.9	4.95	82	6.04
1887	78.7	9.1	36.2	22.6	9.56	1.03	157.2	746.8	4.75	85	5.59
1888	87.8	11.9	41.0	24.8	10.1	1.02	176.6	816.8	4.63	86	5.38
1889	86.3	11.9	40.6	24.2	9.53	0.96	173.5	794.1	4.58	81	5.65
1890	90.9	12.8	42.4	26.1	9.76	0.88	182.8	829.0	4.54	82	5.54
1891	94.0	13.0	45.1	27.2	10.3	0.85	190.5	865.5	4.54	81	5.60

Sources: Currency data taken from *Report of the Treasurer* for 1892, and *Report of Comptroller* for 1878. Price index taken from *Historical Statistics*, wholesale prices in the United States, 1749 to 1890 and 1890 to 1951, Series E1 and E13, pp. 115 and 117. Currency includes United States notes, treasury notes, gold and silver certificates, certificates of deposits, and national bank notes outstanding at the close of each fiscal year. Values are not adjusted for either bank or government holdings.

an average annual real denomination. The average money denomination is obtained by dividing the annual total money value of the currency by the number of notes in existence. The average real denomination is simply the average money denomination divided by the wholesale price index. Table 9.2 summarizes the most important series in table 9.1 and presents corresponding rates of growth from period to period.

The average money denomination fell slightly in the first period, but the average real denomination increased by 74 percent due largely to the fall in prices. In the second period the situation was reversed. The average money denomination fell by over 20 percent, while the average real denomination declined about 13 percent. This entire decline (and more) came in the first year after resumption. In that one year the average real denomination declined 16 percent. This change is seen primarily in the large growth of one-dollar currency.

The difference in growth in the number of pieces of currency in the two periods is significant. Over the earlier period the number of notes outstanding grew only trivially, despite serious deficiencies in fractional currency and nominal increases in money income. In the later period the number of notes increased over 100 percent, or at a rate of about 6 percent per year, reflecting an extraordinary increase in the use of money.

These results, together with the different growth rates in the total dollar value of the currency in the two periods, suggest that the significant increase in lower denominations in the second period permitted a much greater absorption of money. No doubt part of this phenomenon was due to the growth of real output in the economy; but much of it must have resulted from the extension of monetary transactions into markets that had more recently been limited to barter or to the use of unaccounted moneys.[40] This reaction is compatible with the apparent decline in velocity and is supported by the 58 percent growth in the total dollar value of the currency between 1879 and 1891.

The record of policy proscriptions that controlled denominational proportions of currency in the United States is not commendable. Even less laudable has been the overwhelming support of intellectual opinion. The results of these restrictions and prejudices, imposed by custom and law through much of the nineteenth century, was counterproductive.

Barter, scrip, trade credit, and other unaccounted moneys were devices created by individuals and institutions to offset the inhibitive effects of denominational proscriptions.[41] The significant use of these substitutes can be inferred to have biased measurements in the velocity of money until denominational constraints ceased in the 1880s. The distinct differences in both monetary and real denominations between that decade and the preceding one lend substantial support to this contention.

TABLE 9.2. Total denominations (by dollars and pieces), average money and real denominations, and corresponding rates of growth, 1868-1879 and 1879-1891.

Year	Total ($ millions)	Growth (%)	Total pieces (millions)	Growth (%)	Average money denomination ($)	Growth (%)	Average real denomination	Growth (%)
1868	530	—	90.7	—	5.85	—	3.70	—
1879	550	3.8	95.0	4.8	5.79	− 1.0	6.43	74.0
1891	866	57.5	191.0	101.0	4.54	−20.5	5.60	−12.8

10. The Golden Cloud
with the Silver Lining

Mr. President, if gold does go out of this country by reason of a constant increase in its value, I say let it go, and God speed the day when it starts. (John P. Jones, Senate, 29 July 1886)

The official resumption of specie payments at the prewar parity on January 1, 1879, was thoroughgoing and final. However, the monetary structure of the economy by the time of resumption was appreciably different from the one before the Civil War. Even though the monetary system of 1860 had included metallic and paper currencies and bank deposits subject to check, none of the paper money in use had been legal tender issues of the federal government. From 1862 and continuing indefinitely after 1879 the fully legal tender United States notes, first issued during the Civil War, were kept in circulation. Their quantity had been forever fixed by the statute of 1878 at $346 million. To insure the convertibility of this paper into gold after resumption, the Treasury accumulated gold coin and bullion as a redemption reserve for outstanding United States notes. The amount of this reserve was not specified by law, but the actual amount on hand in the Treasury was $135 million in 1878 and gradually increased to as much as $324 million in 1888 before starting a rapid decline to the low value of $45 million in January 1895.[1]

National bank notes had also become an official obligation of the Treasury because of the government securities that banks had to pledge as collateral in order to issue notes and more positively because of the 5 percent gold redemption fund that national banks had to keep with the United States Treasury.[2] So after resumption the Treasury's gold balance acted as a redemption fund for two paper currencies, United States notes and national bank notes.[3]

These two paper currencies did not remain the only fiat currencies. After the passage of the Bland-Allison Act in 1878 allowed the limited coinage of silver, various kinds and amounts of silver currency were put into circulation. Despite its metallic substance, the silver coin was also fiat.[4] By the provisions of the Bland-Allison Act the Treasury had to buy not less than $2 million and not more than $4 million worth of silver per month at market prices. The silver was then to be coined into silver dollars of 412½ grains each. These dollars were legal tender for all debts public and private "except where otherwise stipulated in the contract." Although the law allowed for discretion in silver purchases by the secretary of the Treasury, no secretary of the period bought more than the minimum amount of $2 million per month.

The Treasury Department did not have to circulate coined silver as long as tax revenues were sufficient to cover the cost of the silver purchases. If, for example, the government realized a fiscal surplus of $24 million per year or more before the required purchases of silver, all the purchased silver could be stored. If the fiscal surplus was between zero and $24 million or if the budget was in deficit, all the coined silver would have to be used, or some combination of silver and new government securities would have to be issued.[5]

These conditions allowed the secretary of the Treasury a certain amount of discretion. Instead of financing a deficit fiscal program with disbursements of silver coin, he could request Congress to authorize additional sales of government securities and by this means pay the deficit and store the coin. Then again, even if a fiscal surplus of $24 million or greater was realized, the silver coin could be forced into circulation by means of open-market purchases of government securities. Thus the silver-purchase program was just as inflationary or noninflationary as Congress and the secretary of the Treasury wanted and as fiscal conditions allowed.

That a monetary metal was being purchased, coined, and to a limited extent put into circulation at a mint value significantly greater than the metal's market value has obscured some of the unique features of this operation. First, as F. W. Taussig pointed out, the Bland-Allison Act was the first deliberate policy intended to provide for a regular and periodic injection of currency into the monetary system.[6] No matter that it was silver; even though silver had charisma and silver-state politicians to recommend it, the substance could have been anything. Second, the connection between the purchases of silver and the fiscal necessities of the Treasury induced the secretary of the Treasury to assume some limited authority over monetary policy. Third, the silver coinage need not have been inflationary nor a future threat to the gold standard. As the market price of silver fell, Congress could have increased the silver content of the silver dollar in approximately the same proportion as the fall in its real price. Thus appropriate and timely attention to the mint value of silver could have prevented both the threat of silver inflation and the outflow of gold.[7]

Not much of the purchased silver was circulated until the latter half of 1880, so a sizable silver balance accumulated in the Treasury. From 1880 to 1886 slightly less than the amount currently purchased was put into circulation; between 1886 and 1891 all the old balance and all the current purchases were circulated. By 1892 all the silver coin and bullion left in the Treasury was committed as reserves for silver certificates in circulation. (See figure 10.1.)

The flexibility that was permitted the Treasury Department in circulating silver was analogous to the discretion that was at times possible with respect to greenbacks during the reconstruction period. In fact, the Bland-Allison Act allowed more policies than the greenback acts, although the rate of silver monetization was much less spectacular than the rate of greenback monetization during the war.

The Treasury was thus in the position of a central bank of issue. The secretary following Sherman, Charles J. Folger, said in 1881 that his policy was to keep a gold reserve of about 40 percent against outstanding United States notes in addition to the balance maintained for all ordinary expenditures. "The Government," he stated, "by the issue of its notes, payable on demand, . . . is in a position analogous to that of banking, and should therefore act upon principles found to be sound and safe in that business."[8] In his report for 1882 Folger observed that the government fiscal policy of retiring outstanding debt worked against a monetary policy that would maintain national bank note circulation. National bank notes required the collateral of government securities; so the net retirement of debt meant also a net decline in national bank notes outstanding. He suggested that national banks be permitted to issue notes up to 90 percent of the *market* value of the bonds, which continued to enjoy a large premium in the market, and that other bonds be permitted the circulation privilege.[9]

The balance that appeared in the Treasury in the early 1880s included much of the silver purchased under the stipulations of the Bland-Allison Act as well as gold coin and bullion, some greenbacks and national bank notes, some fractional currency, and treasury deposits in national banks. Against these reserve assets were outstanding gold and silver certificates, greenbacks, some amount of national bank notes, and some percentage of silver coin. (See table 10.1.)

The Treasury had adopted the custom, which had the implied authorization of Congress, of keeping at least $100 million of gold against the $346 million of outstanding greenbacks, a reserve of about 29 percent. It held additional gold—about $10 million—as part of the 5 percent re-

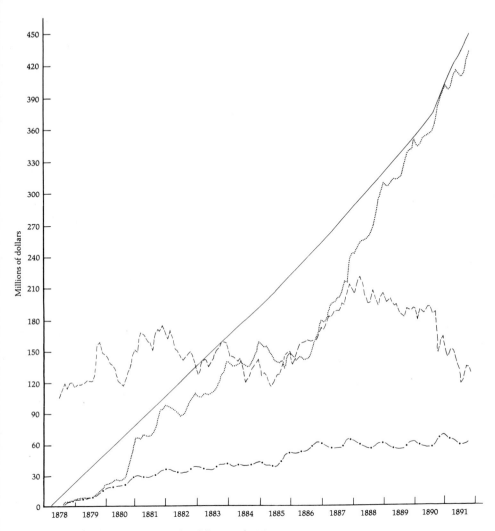

FIGURE 10.1. Components of silver currency and gold in circulation and in the United States Treasury, 1878-1891. From F. W. Taussig, *The Silver Situation in the United States* (New York, 1893), backpiece.

TABLE 10.1. Gold and silver coin and bullion in the United States Treasury, treasury paper currency in circulation, and ratios of gold and silver to currency and gold to currency, 1880-1900 (all but ratios in millions of dollars).

Year	Gold coin and bullion in Treasury	Silver coin and bullion in Treasury[1]	Total gold and silver in Treasury	Notes in circulation[2]	Gold, silver, and currency certificates in circulation[3]	Total currency obligations in circulation	Ratio of Treasury gold and silver to total currency obligations (%)	Ratio of treasury gold to total currency obligations (%)
1880	139	(73) 64	204	659	31	690	30	20
1881	168	(92) 80	249	670	61	731	34	23
1882	159	(106) 93	252	669	82	751	34	21
1883	198	(142) 123	321	660	143	803	40	25
1884	216	(170) 146	362	634	195	829	44	26
1885	247	(194) 163	410	610	244	854	48	29
1886	245	(211) 168	413	609	195	804	51	30
1887	285	(245) 186	471	595	249	844	56	34
1888	320	(278) 205	525	546	337	883	59	36
1889	315	(312) 225	540	515	402	917	59	34
1890	311	(345) 258	569	516	443	959	59	32
1891	267	(397) 327	594	541	462	1003	59	27
1892	259	(446) 324	583	587	487	1074	54	24
1893	189	(489) 319	508	642	437	1079	47	18
1894	145	(510) 288	434	610	450	1060	41	14
1895	126	(508) 286	412	574	425	999	41	13

1896	155	(511)	297	451	554	420	974	46	16
1897	186	(515)	267	454	570	465	1035	44	18
1898	236	(511)	259	495	612	453	1065	46	22
1899	311	(504)	261	572	643	487	1130	51	28
1900	435	(503)	268	703	695	622	1317	53	33

Sources: *Reports of the Treasurer*, 1895 and 1901.

Note: Annual averages of end-of-month figures.

1. Figures in parentheses are monetary values of silver balances. The adjoining figures are the market bullion values of silver at the current market price of silver.

2. Notes include United States notes, national bank notes, and treasury notes of 1890.

3. Currency certificates were large denomination notes used as bank reserves.

demption fund for outstanding national bank notes. National bank notes were also secured by deposit of United States bonds in the Treasury and by the providential reserves held by the national banks themselves. The amount of treasury gold held against silver coin was the total value of the discount between the mint (or monetary) and market (or commodity) value of the silver currency circulating in the economy. Table 10.1 shows the dollar volume of the *net* values of the Treasury's precious metal assets, its paper currency obligations, and the reserve ratios between these two aggregates for the years 1880-1900.

The business boom between 1879 and 1882 effectively silenced the monetary radicals in Congress. Virtually no monetary issues, let alone controversies, appear in the *Congressional Record* during this period. Still, Secretary Folger was forced to heed monetary affairs because of the Treasury's cash balance position. "There is no advisable and lawful mode of disbursing an existing excess of assets," he remarked, "but that of payment of the public debt."[10] This method of relieving the Treasury of cash was somewhat cumbersome because it involved a three-month statutory lag between the call for the debt and its payment by the Treasury, so it could have aggravated any lack of synchronization between receipts and expenditures. Since the outstanding debt was also at a high premium in the market, Folger felt that he needed express authority to purchase it, even though treasury purchases of government securities had been sanctioned by an explicit resolution of Congress. He argued that "reference to the debates in Congress . . . shows that the motive for adoption of [the resolution] was, that the Treasury Department might at any time break a tightness in the money market by putting out money idle in its vaults."[11]

A severe crisis, a sort of capstone to the mild recession of the time, occurred in the New York money market in the spring of 1884. The Treasury Department did nothing unusual to alleviate the situation; the budget continued in surplus and the Treasury's cash balance burgeoned. However, the New York Clearing House Association issued $20 million in clearinghouse certificates in $5,000 and $10,000 denominations to member banks on presentation of suitable collateral, that is, good commercial loans. The certificates were almost all redeemed by July 1, 1884.[12]

This action by the Clearing House Association was an institutional response to an internal liquidity drain. It was, as Redlich states, "the specifically American solution to a problem with which central banks in the other great commercial nations of the world were faced at every crisis throughout the second half of the nineteenth century."[13] It demonstrated that limited central banking functions could be assumed by a private institution and that the actions taken would be beneficial.

The recession, although not severe, seemed to hang on. Daniel Manning, who succeeded Charles Folger as secretary of the Treasury, commented on the "continuing depression universal in varying degrees over the world."[14] He objected to the purchases of silver because they added to the cash balance in the Treasury. Getting rid of this surplus, he said, would "diminish and finally dissipate the objectionable and invidious influence of the Treasury upon the money market and the business of the country." The treasury balance would have been used to purchase government securities, he added, except that the market prices of the securities were "too high" at this time. He concluded his views with a normative and strictly constructionist interpretation of treasury policy. The Treasury's "proper business as a fisc," he wrote, "is to receive the people's revenue from taxes in good money which it has coined for them, and to expend that money as Congress bids, *keeping no surplus* at all beyond what insures punctual payments. A Treasury surplus is standing proof of bad finance—of bad laws, if such have made it necessary."[15]

Manning's reference to the Treasury's surplus was a judgment that embraced not only treasury debt policy, but also silver policy, fiscal policy, and national bank note policy. If taxes were reduced, the balance would lessen; if the Treasury purchased government debt, the balance would also decline. But the outstanding debt to be purchased was collateral security for national bank note issues. A reduction of this debt would therefore reduce outstanding national bank notes. At the same time, since a significant portion of the Treasury's balance was silver, purchase of the debt would put more silver in circulation.

This matrix of monetary combinations was recognized in Congress, particularly during the recession. In late 1884 the Senate debated a resolution against the suspension of silver coinage. Most of the sentiment against silver came from the North and the East and was generally Republican although it crossed party lines. Prosilver opinions were strongest in the South and the West and were usually Democratic and agrarian.

The arguments advanced in favor of the resolution, that is, in favor of silver, were exemplified by the remarks of Nathaniel Hill of Colorado. (Needless to say, representation from Colorado was strongly prosilver.) The trade depression, Hill said, argued against any reduction of silver coinage. In fact, he stated, the Bland-Allison Act was passed because of popular belief that the quantity of gold was inadequate. "There is no inflation of the currency, and it is contraction rather than inflation which is now threatened," he concluded.[16]

John Sherman, back in the Senate after his tenure in the Treasury, answered Hill at length. The expected increase in the commodity value of silver by the act of 1878, he said, had not been realized. At current market prices the silver dollar would have to be increased to 470 or 480 grains (from 412½) to achieve a bullion value equal to the gold dollar. If this change were not made, he warned, the monetary system might revert to a silver basis; and this kind of debilitation, he stated somewhat chauvinistically, would "separate us from the great, powerful, Christian, intelligent, and civilized nations of the world in our financial operations." His own norm for policy would be to stop silver purchases and recoin every silver dollar into a piece weighing 480 grains "by means of a law five lines long."[17]

John Williams of Kentucky responded to Sherman with what might be called the "silver paranoiac" view. "What is there," he asked, "to prevent the bankers and moneyed men of the world, in other words, the goldbugs, from . . . requiring still more silver to be put into the dollar? We believe the fixed purpose of the men who advocate a monometallic system to be to discredit silver altogether and drive it out of the coinage of the world."[18]

Sherman replied as though he were talking to an errant child: "I wish I could cure my friend from Kentucky," he said indulgently, "of the idea that the bankers, or businessmen, or moneyed men of the world have the power to do what he supposes." The values of gold and silver, he explained at some length, were determined in markets. "Market values are mysterious qualities made up by a combination of circumstances, no man can tell how or when . . . The market value of gold and silver will seek its level, . . . and the money kings are as weak as King Canute in resisting the tide."[19]

William B. Allison of Iowa, cosponsor of the Bland-Allison Act of 1878, replied in turn to Sherman that monetary demands and sanctions had a lot to do with "market" value. If the mints of European countries were opened to the free coinage of silver, he claimed, parity between the 25.8-grain gold dollar and the 412½-grain silver dollar would be restored. But if the United States alone embarked on the free coinage of silver, even though the dollar was raised to 480 grains, all the European silver would come to the United States mints and force the United States to a silver standard. The result to foreign countries would be a reduction of their money supplies. Allison held that the governments of these countries would not favor such a result, and therefore any attempt to reach international agreement on an increased silver content of the various silver coins would fail.[20]

Allison was probably correct about international agreement over silver; at least none was ever found. Even if he had been right about a 480-grain silver dollar, *some* weight of silver in a silver dollar would have achieved parity with the gold dollar.

The remainder of this debate centered on the question of why silver coins would not circulate. One faction argued that the Treasury refused to pay them out; the sound-money advocates contended that people simply refused to hold and use them. The evidence suggests that the sound-money men were correct. Some volume of coined dollars, perhaps $50 or $60 million at that time, could be kept in circulation for ordinary coin-currency purposes; but any attempt by the Treasury to augment this volume of coin resulted in redemption of silver at the banks and sub-treasury offices for other kinds of circulating media. If the silver was in the form of silver certificates, that is, just another paper money, it was used to the extent other paper currency was used.

Silver-currency policy was changed in 1886 in a way that verified this pattern. Secretary Manning procured from Congress authority to issue silver certificates of $1, $2, and $5 and to stop issues of greenbacks under $5. This action created a demand for silver certificates. So by 1890 the outstanding volume of silver certificates under $5 was $175 million of a total of $293 million, while coined dollars in circulation remained under $60 million.[21]

Attention in the first session of the Forty-ninth Congress (1885-86) shifted from silver policy, which seemed to be in political equilibrium for the time being, to the Treasury's cash balance and how to disburse it. Several events coincided in bringing this issue into focus. First, the money was there in considerable amounts. Second, this sizable balance was only partially used in ordinary Treasury operations. Third, business activity had not rebounded completely from the recession of 1884. And, finally, several secretaries of the Treasury had requested guidance on its disposition.

On July 13, 1886, a joint resolution was introduced in Congress calling for the Treasury to disburse all the "surplus or balance in the Treasury . . . over $100,000,000 [at a maximum rate of $10 million a month] . . . to the payment of the interest-bearing indebtedness of the United States." William Morrison, a representative from Illinois and chairman of the Committee on Ways and Means, was the sponsor of this resolution. He argued that spending the cash in the Treasury would "tend to make money cheaper, increase the means of exchange, . . . help in the trans-action of business," and inhibit government spending. He noted that the average gold balance in the Treasury since resumption had been $150 million, yet almost no United States notes had been redeemed. Also un-used was the 5 percent redemption fund for national bank notes, which amounted to about $10½ million of the Treasury's balance. In addition, both national bank notes and United States notes were protected by potential sales of United States government securities that could act as a redemption vehicle if necessary.[22] The Treasury balance was therefore largely supercargo.

Most of the prosilver forces, primarily southern, western and agrarian, favored the resolution. The gold-standard people were quick to point out that the Democratic Cleveland administration opposed the resolution. Frank Hiscock, an antisilver Republican from New York, cited a letter from Secretary Manning in which Manning stated rather mildly that reduction of the surplus in the face of current fiscal uncertainties would not be "prudent."[23]

Hiscock was supported by another New Yorker, Abram Hewitt, an antisilver Democrat. Hewitt objected in particular to the discretionary power in the Treasury "to make money easy or to make it tight at its pleasure." The Treasury, he stated, "has now become a great bank, it is a bank of issue, a bank of deposit; it is a member of the [New York] clearing house. It could not disregard if it would the condition of the money market." He felt that if the quantity of paper money fell, Congress would authorize silver certificates until the bullion value of silver in the Treasury was only 35 to 40 percent of outstanding certificates. The Supreme Court's decisions upholding the constitutionality of United States notes, he thought, permitted such an unprincipled increase in paper money.[24]

The prosilver forces, who were generally also advocates of paper money, did not on that account wish to give discretion over the issue of paper currency to the secretary of the Treasury. A. J. Warner of Ohio cited British experience and policy in dealing with a mixed currency and concluded with these revealing words: "In adopting a paper circulation we must unavoidably depend for a maintenance of its due value upon the adoption of a strict and judicious rule for the regulation of its amount." Warner made the obvious point that use of the treasury balance to repurchase outstanding debt would save interest expenditures by the government. Why should a balance of over $200 million, he asked, be kept in the Treasury? "I can understand," he concluded, "how an idolatrous superstition could gather millions of talents in a heathen temple to purchase the favors of the gods; but why should we hoard $228 millions in the Treasury of the United States? Is it to purchase the favor of Wall Street and the banks? If so, it is altogether too dear a price."[25]

Lewis Payson of Illinois was another who spoke in favor of the resolution. He addressed himself at one point to the constitutionality of legal tender issues by the government. He observed that President Cleveland, among others, had questioned the Supreme Court's decisions that had upheld the constitutionality of United States notes. "What can make them believe it?" he exclaimed. "Not [even] one raised from the dead!" The Cleveland administration, he thought, would not abide by the resolution if it passed. "What is needed now, sir," he stated, "is a recognition on the part of the executive officers of the Government that they are not above the law, but subordinate to the will of the people expressed in these Halls in a constitutional manner."[26]

Republicans tried to make political capital of the fact that the resolution revealed a rift between the Democratically controlled House of Representatives and the Democratic administration.[27] The secretary of the Treasury already had the authority "to apply the surplus money in the Treasury not otherwise appropriated, or so much thereof as he may consider proper, to the purchase or redemption of the United States bonds." William McKinley argued that with this authorization already on the statute books the proposed resolution was a vote of "no confidence" in the administration. The Democratically controlled Congresses from 1875 to 1885 had never attempted such a rebuff to the Republican executives who had been in office. Furthermore, McKinley stated, "I would want that discretion [of the secretary of the Treasury] continued, . . . and if [it] is to be taken away from yours [the Democratic secretary] without qualification or condition, it must be your act, not mine."[28]

Nelson Dingley of Maine supported McKinley's position. The resolution, he said, was the "first attempt . . . in the history of this Government to determine by a legislative resolution what should be the working balance of the Treasury . . . No cast-iron rule can be laid down on a matter of this kind." Since the Treasury's working balance was an administrative and not a legislative matter, he said, Congress should not interfere.[29]

The issue was not just administrative. It would have been administrative only if the amount involved were trivial, and trivial it was not.[30] Nor was this instance the first of its kind. Exactly fifty years earlier Congress had directed the Treasury to "deposit" its surplus with the states on the basis of each state's representation in Congress.

All amendments to the resolution were rejected, and it passed the House July 14, 1886, by a vote of 207 to 67.[31] The political division over the resolution involved not only the disposition of the surplus but also the role of the secretary in disbursing it. The prosilver, cheaper-money faction wanted currency put into circulation by means of laws over which Congress had precise control, with no discretion of any consequence at the executive level. The monometallic gold-standard forces, on the other hand, were willing to allow the secretary of the Treasury to retain discretionary powers, but they were opposed to all currency legislation that would make such discretionary powers substantive. In sum, one side wanted power to alter the currency at will, but wanted this power constrained by legislative rules. The other side was willing to give discretionary power to the secretary, but it was power to do almost nothing.

The Morrison resolution, as it was called, came up for debate in the Senate a few weeks after it passed the House. One of the first to speak on the issue was James Beck of Kentucky, who was prosilver and in favor of the resolution. Beck made an excellent presentation of the political utility that the resolution could be expected to yield. At the same time he countered the contention of McKinley and others that the resolution was evidence of a conflict between the Democrats in Congress and the Democratic administration. This resolution, he said, would give the secretary of the Treasury a specific law for his guidance and thus relieve him of a large responsibility. Congress was supposed to have this power, and the secretary was only to be "vested with such discretion as we see fit to give him." The secretary of the Treasury, unlike the other cabinet officers who reported to the president, was required to report directly to Congress: "We with the Secretary of the Treasury manage the purse; the President and the other Secretaries control the sword."[32]

Some of the prosilver senators, as well as some representatives, opposed the resolution because they felt that the contingency reserve of $100 million in gold that the Treasury would still have to keep was unnecessarily large. Henry Teller of Colorado suggested that the economy was experiencing a current scarcity of money and the Treasury was locking up money in the face of it.[33]

One of Teller's silver-state colleagues, John P. Jones of Nevada, presented a detailed account of the demand for money. This variable, he lectured correctly, was "equal to the sum of the demands for all other things and was intimately connected to the quantity of money." Therefore "the regulation of the volume and value of money is one of the highest functions of sovereignty and should under no circumstances be surrendered [to national banks]." Jones would have tied the growth in the economy's stock of money to the growth in population. He was sanguine over the maintenance of gold convertibility. If all the gold were squeezed out of the monetary system by issues of silver, he said, it would "leave the country free to adopt a system of money whose volume and value will be regulated, not as the value of gold is now regulated, by the edicts of blind chance, but by the guidance of human wisdom."[34]

Much of the discussion in the Senate centered on the amount of cash the Treasury ought to have on hand before it repurchased debt. John Sherman of Ohio, now president pro tem of the Senate, distinguished three reserves: (1) the amount kept for redemption of United States notes, (2) a working balance for ordinary treasury payments, and (3) the accumulation needed to purchase bonds when the decision had been made to redeem them. He thought that $140 million was approximately the right amount for ordinary purposes before bonds should be purchased. He compared the Bank of England reserve, which he alleged varied from 41 to 54 percent of Bank of England notes, to the 29 percent that the $100 million gold balance provided against outstanding United States notes.[35] Silver currency also required a gold reserve. "It is maintained at par with gold just like your paper money," he stated, "because it is redeemed, it is received, it is used by the Government in exchange for gold . . . The very fact that the silver dollar is safely stored in the Treasury is the best protection to the value of silver."[36]

The Senate modified the resolution in ways that made its version more conservative than the one passed by the House. First, it added a $20 million supplementary balance, under the discretion of the secretary of the Treasury, to the $100 million already in the resolution. Second, it inserted a contingency amendment allowing the president to proscribe bond repurchases under conditions of "extraordinary emergency." Third, it inserted four amendments to dispose of the so-called trade dollars.[37]

Samuel Maxey of Texas voiced the opinions of several senators when he contended that the effect of the contingency amendment would be to allow an emergency to be declared and purchases halted if the bond purchases involved a disbursement of treasury silver. The payments of silver favored by many congressmen could thus be prevented by executive fiat. The resolution passed by a vote of 42 to 20.[38]

The two versions of the resolution required a conference committee to iron out the differences. Three members from each house of Congress were appointed.[39] This committee agreed that the secretary of the Treasury was a more logical and more appropriate officer than the president to invoke a suspension of the debt repayments due to an extraordinary emergency.[40] This development, together with allowance of a contingency balance of $20 million, emphasized the central position occupied by the secretary. J. B. Weaver of Iowa, who favored cheaper money by an easy currency policy, was therefore against the conference committee's version of the resolution. The secretary, he said, would be the sole judge of an emergency. The resolution in this form was no improvement over the present situation. "Congress is called upon to abdicate and give over its discretion to the Secretary of the Treasury."[41]

Treasury discretion over the cash balance was indeed the focal point of controversy over the resolution. Abram Hewitt of New York, the hard-money Democrat, argued that secretarial discretion was necessary because "the Treasury has in effect become a bank of issue and the place of final redemption for the currency of the country." He felt that this discretion would be necessary as long as the government had United States notes outstanding and a supervisory role over the national banks. Other representatives objected to treasury discretion on constitutional principles and because it violated the spirit of the Independent Treasury Act; still others objected because they felt that the secretary would use this power in undesirable ways, for example as a means of avoiding silver disbursements.[42]

Those legislators who favored discretion were, anomalously enough, the Republican conservative easterners, who for all their conservatism reflected some authoritarian notions. They considered secretarial discretion over the reserve of gold necessary because of its role in redeeming outstanding issues of government currency. They also thought that the reserve balance would have to be used at the "moment when the money markets of the country become unsettled and panicky."[43]

The report of the conference committee was finally adopted 120 to 63 in the House and by a simple voice vote in the Senate. Many of the cheap-money radicals voted against it.

Secretary Fairchild accepted the Morrison resolution as a mandate for policy and retired all the three percent certificates during calendar 1886 and 1887.[44] Since the three percents were authorized collateral for the issue of national bank notes, the quantity of national bank notes in circulation was significantly reduced.[45] (See table 10.2) However, total deposits in national banks increased from $1,117 million in October 1885 to $1,275 million in October 1887, an increase of $158 million, or about 6 percent per year.[46]

The treasury surplus at the end of 1887 was still $55 million over the required $120 million despite retirement of the three percents.[47] The remainder of outstanding government debt was subject to market forces and continued to bear a high premium. All the secretaries of the period commented on this fact and hesitated to purchase more of the marketable debt than was required by the provisions of the sinking fund law—1 percent annually of total debt outstanding. Secretary Fairchild continued this conservatism, if it can be called such, even though Congress had provided for purchases of the debt at the discretion of the secretary by the Appropriation Act of 1881 and by the Morrison resolution in 1886. In lieu of debt retirement, Fairchild formulated a new policy—one that was to have widespread repercussions during the next twenty years: deposit of treasury balances in national banks.

This policy, which appeared to violate both the letter and the spirit of the Independent Treasury Act, was authorized during the Civil War. It was nothing more than an administrative expedient given the Treasury in order to make the business of the Treasury more efficient. It was not supposed to be a grant of power for policy purposes. In fact, Fairchild in his report for 1887 stated that this policy "as a means of keeping the circulating media available for business purposes . . . is very limited under present laws and ought not to be used except in exceptional circumstances such as have existed of late and because there is no better thing to do."[48]

Clearly the deposit was potentially much more volatile than the simple open-market purchases of outstanding debt for which congressional authority had been twice granted. To have excused the deposit policy on the grounds that "there is no better thing to do" thus implied gross administrative ignorance or some sort of deviousness for political purposes. Further in his report for 1887 Fairchild defended the policy on the grounds that the money would be "at once returned to the channels of business through Government payments, [so] no shock would be caused by such withdrawal." If Congress thought the purchase of bonds with the surplus was a better policy, he stated defensively, "specific authority should be given to the Secretary of the Treasury to do so."[49]

This statement is hard to treat charitably in view of the two laws that Congress had already enacted. Fairchild spurned further security purchases and in early 1887 began a systematic policy of depositing treasury balances in selected national banks. These deposits had so far been on the order of $11 million to $13 million with little variation. By April 1888 the amount was just short of $62 million, or about five times the customary balance.[50] (See table 10.3.)

Not only was this volume of treasury deposits unusual, but the method used was highly questionable. Government deposits in national banks required the pledge of government securities by national banks just as did the issue of national bank notes. On his own authority in October 1887 Fairchild determined that national banks depositing 4½ percent bonds might carry the face amount of government deposits on their books; those carrying 4 percent bonds might carry 110 percent of the face amount of the bonds. Since national bank notes could be issued only up to 90 percent of the par value of the bonds and required a 5 percent redemption reserve as well, the banks were easily induced to accept the deposit of public monies.[51] To do so, they were required to reduce outstanding issues of national bank notes still further, since bonds held as collateral for government deposits could not also be pledged as collateral for national bank note currency.

When Congress became cognizant of Secretary Fairchild's policy, another debt-purchase bill was introduced in the House of Representatives February 29, 1888. It called for the secretary "[t]o apply the surplus money now in the Treasury, and such surplus money as may hereafter be in the Treasury, and not otherwise appropriated, or so much thereof as he may consider proper, to the purchase or redemption of United States bonds."[52] This new bill followed almost verbatim the clause in the Appropriation Act of 1881 that had already authorized such purchases. William McKinley pointed out this similarity. He criticized the Cleveland administration for dubbing this authorization "suspicious" and noted that the act of 1881, including the debt-purchase provision, had been passed by unanimous votes in both houses of Congress. McKinley contended that the Cleveland administration had an ulterior motive in not purchasing the debt. The administration, he said, wanted the cash balance in the Treasury to accumulate in order to cause business hardship that would in turn result in more support for its tariff-reduction policy.[53]

Many Democrats in Congress continued to criticize the Cleveland administration's unorthodox monetary policy. J. B. Weaver of Iowa had a

TABLE 10.2. Values for currencies in circulation, excluding gold coin, and absolute changes between March and September, 1880-1900 (millions of dollars).

Year (end of month)	Silver dollars and fractional silver coin	Δ	United States notes[1]	Δ	National bank notes	Δ	Silver certificates and notes of 1890[2]
1880 March	75		323		340		6
Sept.	77	2	320	− 3	340	0	12
1881 March	83	6	325	5	343	3	39
Sept.	86	3	320	− 5	354	11	53
1882 March	87	1	318	− 2	356	2	59
Sept.	87	0	315	− 3	355	− 1	63
1883 March	90	3	317	2	355	0	71
Sept.	93	3	309	− 8	347	− 8	79
1884 March	87	− 3	301	− 8	336	−11	96
Sept.	86	− 1	310	9	324	−12	96
1885 March	84	− 2	300	−10	314	−10	113
Sept.	97	13	296	− 4	310	− 4	94
1886 March	98	1	304	8	312	2	90
Sept.	108	10	302	− 2	301	−11	95
1887 March	105	− 3	318	16	284	−17	132
Sept.	111	6	323	5	270	−14	154
1888 March	110	− 1	314	− 9	255	−15	192
Sept.	110	0	293	−21	238	−17	219
1889 March	108	− 2	307	14	218	−20	251
Sept.	110	2	310	3	200	−18	277
1890 March	112	2	332	22	186	−14	291
Sept.	118	6	334	2	177	− 9	316
1891 March	120	2	334	0	168	− 9	344
Sept.	120	0	327	− 7	166	− 2	379
1892 March	121	1	324	− 3	169	3	404
Sept.	125	4	323	− 1	165	− 4	434
1893 March	126	1	317	− 6	172	7	452
Sept.	123	− 3	332	15	201	29	474
1894 March	113	−10	291	−41	197	− 4	470
Sept.	113	0	267	−24	203	6	452
1895 March	114	1	257	−10	203	0	445
Sept.	117	3	240	−17	207	1	437
1896 March	118	1	232	− 8	214	7	441
Sept.	117	− 1	250	18	221	7	443
1897 March	115	− 2	249	− 1	222	1	454
Sept.	118	3	252	3	226	4	465
1898 March	123	5	267	15	222	−44	488
Sept.	127	4	292	25	232	10	490

Δ	Treasury notes of 1890	Gold certificates	Δ	Currency certificates[1]	Δ	Total currency in circulation	Δ	Percent Δ
		8		8		760		
6		8	0	10	2	767	7	1
27		6	− 2	7	− 3	803	36	5
14		5	− 1	8	1	826	23	3
6		5	0	11	3	836	10	1
4		5	0	11	0	836	00	0
8		43	38	9	− 2	885	49	6
8		55	12	12	3	895	10	1
17		69	14	15	3	904	9	1
0		87	18	16	1	919	15	2
17		116	29	26	10	953	34	4
−19		118	2	23	− 3	938	− 15	−2
− 4		91	−27	12	−11	907	− 31	−3
5		85	− 6	8	− 3	899	− 8	−1
37		94	9	7	− 1	940	41	5
22		98	4	7	0	963	23	2
38		92	− 6	9	2	972	9	1
27		135	43	13	4	1008	36	4
32		129	− 6	14	1	1027	19	2
26		117	−12	15	1	1029	2	0
14		135	18	8	− 7	1064	35	3
25	7	158	23	7	− 1	1110	46	4
28	34	144	−14	11	4	1121	11	1
35	57	113	−31	18	7	1123	2	0
25	78	154	41	30	12	1202	79	7
30	107	121	−33	17	−13	1185	−17	−1
18	129	112	− 9	17	0	1196	11	1
22	149	80	−32	8	− 9	1218	22	2
− 4	141	70	−10	53	45	1194	−24	−2
−18	121	65	− 5	56	3	1156	− 38	−3
− 7	121	49	−16	37	−19	1105	−51	−5
− 8	107	51	2	64	27	1116	11	1
4	104	43	− 8	34	−30	1082	−34	−3
2	89	39	− 4	34	0	1104	22	2
11	90	37	− 2	74	40	1151	47	4
11	90	37	0	53	−21	1151	0	0
23	100	36	− 1	38	−15	1174	23	2
2	97	35	− 1	18	−20	1194	20	2

TABLE 10.2 (cont.)

Year (end of month)	Silver dollars and fractional silver coin	Δ	United States notes[1]	Δ	National bank notes	Δ	Silver certificates and notes of 1890[2]
1899 March	134	7	311	19	240	8	493
Sept.	143	9	315	4	240	0	490
1900 March	143	0	323	8	267	27	488
Sept.	151	8	325	2	319	52	488

Sources: *Reports of the Treasurer*, 1895 and 1901.

1. Currency certificates were simply large denominations ($5,000 and $10,000) of United States notes. This total, including holdings by the Treasury itself, was supposed to be fixed at $346.68 million.

2. This column includes only silver certificates until 1890, at which point it includes treasury notes of 1890. The next column presents treasury notes of 1890 as a datum.

telling argument. "The Secretary of the Treasury," he said, "has serious doubts about his authority . . . to purchase bonds with the money. It is a little singular that some doubt did not arise in his mind as to his power to deposit this amount of money in the national banks." The money had been taxed from the people by the government, deposited in the national banks without interest, he said, and then "loaned back by the banks to the poor wretches from whom it was extorted." Weaver cited the list of 298 banks in which deposits had been made. Many of these banks, he observed, included directors and large stockholders who in the past had been highly placed officers in the Treasury Department. Finally, any attempt to remove the government's deposits would cause serious embarrassment: "The banks, sir, are the masters of the situation, and not the Secretary."[54]

A case was made in support of the administration, but it was not very solid. W. C. P. Breckenridge of Kentucky argued correctly (but irrelevantly) that after the three percents were retired, none of the outstanding debt was callable at the option of the government. He recognized that the remaining debt could be acquired on *market* terms. But, he alleged, the money would then accumulate in the larger cities, where it would cause a "glut" and be delayed "before it could be returned to the places from which it had been drawn and where it was needed." Depositing the money in national banks, he said, scattered it around expediently.[55]

The new debt-purchase bill passed the House of Representatives on

Δ	Treasury notes of 1890	Gold certificates	Δ	Currency certificates[1]	Δ	Total currency in circulation	Δ	Percent Δ
3	94	33	− 2	22	4	1233	39	3
− 3	90	99	66	16	− 6	1303	70	6
− 2	85	174	75	14	− 2	1409	106	8
0	68	209	35	2	−12	1494	85	6

February 29, 1888, without a division, that is, as a routine housekeeping matter. It then went to the Senate and passed there on April 5, 1888. A conference committee was appointed in the Senate to compromise the differences that the two houses had incorporated in their versions of the bill, and the bill itself was returned to the House Committee on Ways and Means for modification. But it was never heard from again.[56] The Cleveland administration, which had simply been procrastinating on the cash-balance issue, accepted the congressional votes on the bill as a mandate for policy and subsequently began systematic purchases of securities under the auspices of a circular issued April 17, 1888. In his report for 1888 Secretary Fairchild stated somewhat pharisaically that "no bonds were bought until there had been an expression of opinion by resolutions [sic] in both Houses of Congress, that it was lawful and proper to invest the surplus in bonds at the premium necessary to obtain them."[57] Of course, the same authorization had been made seven years earlier.

Cleveland's defeat in the election of 1888 resulted in part from the relatively tight money policy his administration had followed. Democratic sentiment in Congress was much looser. Debates in both houses also demonstrated much dissatisfaction with his financial and other policies, such as pension grants.

Benjamin Harrison's secretary, William Windom, in his report for 1889 expressed his disapproval of the deposit policy in the strongest terms. He favored reduction of treasury balances to their former levels "at the earliest day practicable," but he thought the withdrawal of the balances would be difficult and dangerous because "business is adjusted to the increased supply." The policy, he said, was contrary to the spirit of the Independent Treasury Act and "necessarily involves favoritism of the most objectionable character . . . The Secretary of the Treasury . . . may,

TABLE 10.3. Treasury deposits in national banks, 1880-1900 (millions of dollars).

Year	Month	Deposit	Year	Month	Deposit
1880	March	11	1895	March	15
1887	March	19		Sept.	15
	Sept.	25	1896	March	27
1888	March	61		Sept.	17
	Sept.	57	1897	March	17
1889	March	48		Sept.	17
	Sept.	48		Dec.	49
1890	March	32	1898	March	31
	Sept.	31		Sept.	81
1891	March	30		Dec.	95
	Sept.	21	1899	March	89
1892	March	18		Sept.	83
	Sept.	15	1900	March	111
1893	March	15		Sept.	97
	Sept.	16	1901	March	98
1894	March	15		Sept.	109
	Sept.	15			

Sources: *Treasury Reports,* 1895 and 1901.

if so disposed, expand or contract the currency at will, and in the interest of certain favorites whom he may select."[58]

During the year ending October 31, 1889, the Treasury purchased $99 million worth of bonds; and while it continued to pay a market premium for the securities, the premium lessened. Windom had "advised" (warned) the banks to sell their securities back to the Treasury at "liberal rates" in order to avoid any diminution of available reserves.[59] The tightness in the money market and the recession in Europe had similar influences on the dispositions of the banks.

The decade of the 1880s started out auspiciously. The federal government had disengaged itself from discretionary control over the monetary system late in the 1870s by two separate acts. First, it had fixed forever the total stock of government-issued paper currency (United States notes); and, second, it had succeeded in resumption of specie payments. These acts would seem to have reduced significantly the government's mischievous influence. The international gold standard and free markets appeared to be in the ascendancy, and the business boom of the early 1880s emphasized the golden aura of the times.

But the boom turned into a recession, and the fiscal pattern of the period resulted in an accumulating government surplus. A prosperous government side by side with a depressed economy begged for a change in policy that would stimulate the private sector. It took no fiscal-monetary expert to understand that a disbursement of government moneys would have the desired effect.

The accumulation of a federal fiscal surplus meant in practice the impoundment of the silver moneys that were a good part of the surplus. It also brought chagrin to the friends of silver who had expected a general circulation of significant amounts of silver after the passage of the Bland-Allison Act.

The executive branch of the government continued throughout the period to be ruled by presidents and by secretaries of the Treasury who were antipathetic toward easy money in all its guises, while the legislative branch was composed largely of Congresses that favored significant relaxation in the monetary environment. Thus policy during the decade, while not overtly controversial, had much dissent and dissatisfaction running through it.

Disbursement of the government's balances and the thorough circulation of accumulated silver certificates by means of open-market purchases closed the decade. At the same time, the silver bloc was mounting an effective program to increase the circulation of this particular fiat money.

11. The Fall of Silver

> It seems to me that the matter [of the quantity of money] should be referred to statisticians to ascertain the amount necessary, and then we could have some regular rule about reaching the object desired and not be subject to the action of speculators who would devise plans whereby the people would suffer every time. (William P. Stewart, Senate, 8 January 1891)

Economists, historians, and political scientists have devoted much attention to the monetary events and policies of the post-Civil War era in the United States. The gold-standard system, the occasional lapses into paper money, and the emergence of silver as a major monetary metal have been treated at length. The silver story, however, always seems to reach a climax and conclusion around 1896 with the first Bryan campaign—as though the fortunes of Bryan and the free-silver movement peaked simultaneously then declined, unable to meet the political challenge of conservative Republicanism.[1] Perhaps the clearest statement of this chain of events is given by Horace White in his *Money and Banking*. The concerted attempt to restore free silver in the 1880s, he wrote, "culminat[ed] in the famous campaign of Bryan in 1896 . . . The long depression beginning in 1893 gave impetus to the movement, and Bryan took advantage of the widespread discontent in his campaign for the presidency in 1896. Had it not been for the increased production of gold . . . which started the price level upward in 1897, it is barely possible that . . . Bryan might have been successful in 1900."[2] This synchronous view of the economic and political fortunes of the free-silver movement misrepresents what actually happened. Its shortcomings become manifest when the succession of events involving silver is summarized without embellishment.

Significant amounts of silver were coined before 1842 and in the 1850s.

But silver first appeared as a possible vehicle of monetary policy in the mid 1870s, largely because it was being won at lower and lower costs. By 1878 it had supplanted greenbacks as *the* means for promoting cheaper-money policies. In that year Congress passed the Bland-Allison Act, which required the Treasury to buy between $2 million and $4 million of silver a month at the fixed price of $1.29 per ounce to be coined into standard silver dollars.[3] Throughout the 1880s most leading members of the Democratic party as well as a significant number of Republicans from the western silver-producing states agitated for a free-silver law. The rural South and Middle West were composed largely of debtors who sensed correctly that falling prices increased the real burden of their debts, while the silver Republicans of the West wanted support for one of their major commodities. Finally, much sentiment came from groups opposed to national banking and the issue of national bank notes. Many opponents of national banking were also agrarian debtors. Only the opposition of several presidents to the free coinage of silver thwarted several attempts to enact such legislation.

Despite the antisilver administration of Benjamin Harrison, silver proponents won a major battle with the passage of the Treasury Note Act in July 1890. Democratic majorities then swept congressional and presidential offices in 1892, and a permanent silver policy seemed assured. For the first time since 1856 and the administration of James Buchanan, Democrats had won the presidency and had majorities in both houses of Congress. Yet in just a few years politicians representing free silver had lost most of their political capital, and in 1900 gold became the only unqualified legal tender monetary metal. From this time on, silver remained in the coinage and currency system primarily as a subsidiary money.

Nothing in this sequence of events suggests the particular set of circumstances that led to termination of silver monetization. Why did this political-economic force—the free-silver movement—suddenly lose its legislative momentum at just the time (1893-1896) when a cheaper-money doctrine and policy would have seemed most logical and most likely to succeed? In 1896 the free-silver Populist-Democrat Bryan lost to the conservative orthodox Republican McKinley by a larger popular majority than had appeared since 1872. Surely this outcome contradicts every argument that correlates Democratic political success with economic hardship and a doctrine of easy money.

How and why this pattern of events emerged is an intriguing question. Silver's birth and life have been dealt with before, but its crucifixion and death, long neglected, surely occurred before Bryan's Cross-of-Gold speech and campaign in 1896. The result of the subsequent election was anticlimactic to the legislation enacted during the early months of the second Cleveland administration in 1893. The real beginning of the story is the point at which the silver movement achieved its greatest success—the passage of the Treasury Note Act of 1890, sometimes known as the Sherman Silver Purchase Act.

Benjamin Harrison defeated Grover Cleveland in 1888 in a very close election.[4] Without a promise to "do something" for silver, Harrison would not have been elected. The issue was not only doing something *for* silver, but also doing something *with* silver *for* everyone who wanted more currency in the monetary system.

Harrison's secretary of the Treasury, William Windom, was given the task of preparing the administration's silver proposal for congressional consideration. Windom's plan, given in his report for 1889, called for the issue of treasury notes, "against deposits of silver bullion at the market price of silver when deposited."[5] This plan anticipated the deposit of silver bullion at the Treasury and the issue of treasury notes equal in value to the market price of the deposited silver. The price of the silver would be determined at the time of deposit by the secretary of the Treasury.[6] The silver would still be monetized at the historic price of 371.25 grains per dollar, but the given monthly expenditure of $2 million to $4 million would no longer be in force. Furthermore, the secretary would have the right to suspend purchases temporarily and sell silver in the open market.

Both houses of Congress proposed silver bills in the Fifty-first Congress. The original senate bill would have followed the Windom proposal, but purchase at the market price was unacceptable to a large number of prosilver western Republicans because such a plan did not provide government subsidies to stimulate silver production. Edward Wolcott of Colorado remarked that westerners had given "handsome majorities for the Republican ticket." But, he said, "if the Windom recommendation, approved by the President, could have been announced before the election, it is my humble opinion that not a single state west of the Missouri River would have given a Republican majority."[7]

Several more speeches in the Senate argued the merits and demerits of silver. One that was to be significant was given by John Mitchell of Oregon. He suggested the purchase of silver at a limited rate, say 4.5 million ounces a month, in place of free and unlimited coinage—an ideal that could not get past the House.[8]

The Senate, despite the opposition to free coinage in the House, approved a free-silver measure by a vote of 42 to 25.[9] The House rejected the Senate's free-silver provision, 152 to 135. A conference committee made up of three members from the House and three from the Senate was then appointed. The chairman of the committee was Republican John Sherman of Ohio who would steer the committee's recommendations to a conservative middle ground and by his successful intermediation endow the bill with his name.

The conference committee report incorporated Mitchell's proposal for the monthly purchase of 4.5 million ounces of silver at the market price, but the price was not to exceed one dollar for 371.25 grains—the old parity value. Treasury notes issued in payment of the silver so purchased would be redeemable in coin on demand and would be legal tender except "where otherwise stipulated in the contract."[10]

Sherman explained the compromise at length to his senate colleagues. The first order of business, he stated, was to get a bill that would be acceptable to silver proponents while denying free coinage. The silver purchase agreed on was the lower limit that the Senate would accept and the upper limit the House would tolerate.[11]

One free-silver Republican-turned-Populist, Preston Plumb of Kansas, stated that the advantage of free coinage was that it would "release the money supply from the arbitrary control or suggestion of control of anybody. It leaves it subject only to the operation of natural forces."[12] The "anybody" Plumb referred to was the secretary of the Treasury. His statement attests again to the self-regulatory character of a metallic-standard currency. It also provides an interesting contrast to an earlier statement by Senator Jones of Nevada (also a free-silver Republican) on the benefits that would be derived in monetary affairs "by the guidance of human wisdom." Jones had implied that Congress should supply the wisdom. Plumb only objected to such wisdom when it was supplied by the secretary of the Treasury.

The bill of the conference committee passed the Senate 39 to 26 along strictly party lines. It then went to the House and passed there by a vote of 122 to 90, again along party lines. It was signed by President Harrison on July 14, 1890.[13]

Monetization of silver under the Sherman Act did not expand the currency stock appreciably because of the simultaneous outflow of gold and corresponding decline in gold certificates. The monetization of silver in fact stimulated the outflow of gold. National bank notes, which had been declining steadily for ten years, reached a trough in the early 1890s. Still, the total stock of currency grew slowly until September 1893. During the next two and a half years—until March 1896—it declined 12½ percent (table 10.2). Total commercial bank deposits plus currency peaked in late 1892, seesawed downward until mid 1896, and did not regain their 1892 value until mid 1897.[14]

The changes in the growth rates of currency and money are explained by the persistence of United States policy in maintaining gold convertibility in the face of falling prices in terms of gold throughout the trading world. Much of this general price decline reflected the world's increased demand for monetary gold. Between 1867 and 1895 most European countries and India abandoned some form of bimetallism for the single gold standard. The possibility that United States policy might fail to maintain gold convertibility and be forced to accept a silver standard added to the instability of the United States position,[15] and capital outflows aggravated the problem. Ordinarily, when the United States realized large merchandise export balances, gold inflows would have in part reciprocated. "Instead," wrote Comptroller of the Currency Hepburn in 1892, "they sent us our securities [for redemption]."[16]

The decline in world prices and the increased real value of gold reflected the classical adjustment of national money stocks and domestic price levels that had to occur if a gold standard was to be retained. However, no one could foresee how far prices would have to fall before they stabilized; no one could predict when and at what price level world production of gold would again match world demand for gold so that growth in national money stocks of the gold-standard countries might again approximate growth in real output. Nor could anyone predict the role silver might play without jeopardizing the gold standard. If too much silver were monetized, external equilibrium between prices in the United States and prices in the rest of the world (England) could not be maintained. The anticipation of this possibility, encouraged by the continued monetization of silver, made the adjustment even more difficult.

The national elections of 1892 seemed to be an unequivocal victory for the cheaper-money free-silver forces. Democratic candidates for both houses of Congress and the Democratic executive nominee, Grover Cleveland, scored impressive victories. Under such auspices, implementation of Democratic policies would have seemed assured.

Political victory, however, obscured a divisive issue—the monetization of silver. The Congresses and administrations of the previous eighteen years had kept this problem a sectional rather than a party issue. Western Republicans, for example, were adamantly for free silver, while eastern Republicans, as well as Democrats, were against it. The ascendance of Democratic majorities in both houses of Congress took the issue out of Republican hands, where it had been successfully compromised, and allowed it to become an item of controversy within the Democratic party.[17]

Cleveland's generally unfavorable attitude toward silver was well known. What was not certain was how far he would go in opposition to his own party in order to further his penchant for sound money.

This uncertainty was clarified in the early summer of 1893 when Cleveland called a special session of Congress. Business recession was by this time apparent to everyone and was accompanied by the usual external drain of gold and by an accumulation of silver in the Treasury. In his message of instruction to the special session the president noted that business distress was "principally chargeable to Congressional legislation touching the purchase and coinage of silver." The operation of the Silver Purchase Act, he continued,

> leads in the direction of the entire substitution of silver for gold in the Government Treasury, and . . . the payment of all Government obligations in depreciated silver . . . We could [then] no longer claim a place among nations of the first class, nor could our Government provide for the use of the people the best and safest money . . . The Government cannot make its fiat equivalent to intrinsic value, nor keep inferior money on a parity with superior money. [The attempt] has resulted in such a lack of confidence at home in the stability of currency values that capital refuses its aid to new enterprises . . . [Therefore], I earnestly recommend the repeal of [the act of 1890], and that other legislative action may put beyond all doubt . . . the intention and the ability of the Government to fulfill its pecuniary obligations in money universally recognized by all civilized countries. [18]

Cleveland's charge to Congress thus reflected anything but a free-silver philosophy. The only feature that distinguished him from his Republican counterparts was his equally positive attitude toward tariff reduction. On monetary policy he was more conservative—more a gold-standard advocate—than his Republican predecessors.

The division in the Democratic party surfaced when the bill to repeal the entire silver purchase clause in the Sherman Act was presented in the House August 11, 1893, by William Wilson of West Virginia, a "Cleveland Democrat." The free-silver forces, led as usual by Richard P. Bland of Missouri, immediately added amendments calling for the free coinage of silver at 16 to 1 and then for ascending ratios of silver-to-gold up to 20 to 1. If these amendments failed—presumably, each successive ratio would command greater and greater support—the last amendment called for reinstatement of the Bland-Allison Act. [19]

These ratios reflect the statutory mint values of silver to gold. All the ratios were to be achieved by holding constant the mint price of pure gold at one dollar for 23.22 grains, while lowering the mint price of silver successively from one dollar for 371.25 grains (16 to 1) to one dollar for 464.4 grains (20 to 1). [20] The amendments thus gave legislators a multiple choice of policy options: (a) 16 to 1, (b) 17 to 1, (c) 18 to 1, (d) 19 to 1, (e) 20 to 1, (f) revert to Bland-Allison Act with limited coinage of $2 million to $4 million of silver a month. The higher the ratio—that is, the lower the mint price of silver—the smaller the governmental monetary demand for silver, the less silver monetized, and the less silver would jeopardize the ability of the United States Treasury to maintain gold convertibility for other currencies. The market price of silver at this time had gone up to 28 to 1, or about one dollar for 650 grains, but for the previous dozen years it had averaged very near the price that would have implied the 20-to-1 ratio.

Those favoring repeal argued that international agreement on bimetallism was necessary before a two-standard system could succeed. John Pendleton of West Virginia was one of many who made this argument. He had intended, he said, to vote for free coinage of silver at the mint price that would have resulted in the 20-to-1 ratio, but the more he studied the question, the more he believed the same troubles would occur at 20 to 1 that had occurred under limited coinage at 16 to 1. He would agree to a ratio, he said, only in concert with three or four of the leading commercial nations. Otherwise the market value of one of the two metals would constantly diverge from par. Pendleton recommended an issue of $500 million in "good old greenbacks" based on a reserve of $100 million in gold to be obtained from treasury bond sales. He foresaw no calls for redemption of these notes because "[o]ur faith is pledged. The creditor is satisfied with the promise."[21]

Josiah Patterson, another Tennessee Democrat, also discussed the ratio. He pointed out that even a three- or four-cent divergence from par was enough to drive the dearer of the two metals (gold in this case) out of circulation. Even the 20-to-1 ratio would therefore not be large enough in the face of the current market ratio of 28 to 1.[22] "Why advance in the direction of the commercial ratio," he asked, "without going all the way?" A colleague then asked, "At what ratio are you willing to allow silver to be coined freely?" Patterson replied that in view of uncertainties and lack of international agreement, "I am not prepared to vote for any ratio you might name.[Great applause.]" He desired, he said, the free and unlimited coinage of silver but only under international agreement.[23]

Much was made of the monetary planks in the political platforms of all three parties before the elections of 1892. The Democratic platform had argued for the free coinage of both metals under "such safeguards of legislation as will keep the metals at a parity." The Cleveland Democrats first rejected all ratios between the metals, then stated hypocritically that they would vote for free coinage when "proper safeguards" had been assured.[24] Of course, *some* ratio would have provided a proper safeguard, so rejection of all ratios was in effect rejection of any proper safeguard.

Charles Hooker of Mississippi correctly suggested that a change in the ratio would adjust for any change in the relative market prices of gold and silver. "There may have been a change in the relative measuring values of the two metals," he said. "But that change, whatever it may be, can be corrected by a change in the ratio of coinage from the present 16 to 1 to, say, 19 or even 20 to 1. It does not justify the total abolition of silver as a standard monetary metal."[25]

Prestige was another debating point with those opposed to free silver. Cleveland's speech to the special session had emphasized this argument, and Patterson parroted Cleveland. To allow a monometallic silver standard, which would certainly result from free coinage, he said, would align United States policy, "not with the enlightened nations of Christendom, but side by side with China, with the republic of Mexico, with the republics of Central and South America, and every other semicivilized country on the globe."[26]

The relative positions on silver and tariff policy under the Cleveland administration were graphically described by Charles Grosvenor, a Republican from Ohio. The McKinley Tariff Act and the Sherman Silver Purchase Act were Republican measures, he said, and were like the two goats Aaron had as offerings. The McKinley Tariff Act would be a sacrifice to the Lord. But the Sherman Act would be a scapegoat for the business collapse and would be sent into the wilderness with the sins of the Democrats whispered in its ear. This way the president and his cabinet could "disenthrall [themselves] from their allegiance to free silver." The people have been taught, Grosvenor concluded, that the Sherman Act is the root of all evil.[27]

Many free-silver congressmen saw a conspiracy of English moneyed interests who wished to appreciate the value of money at the expense of debtors in the United States. This notion was picturesquely presented in a speech by William Bowers, a Republican from California. "The nation wants more money," said Bowers, "and the head physician [Cleveland] sends us an English prescription telling us that the remedy for scarcity of money is to destroy half of what we have. [Laughter.]"[28]

Most of the prosilver congressmen explicitly specified a proportionality between the quantity of money and prices.[29] Others presented extensive statistics on general prices, using Soetbeer's index of commodities, and compared the movement of the general price level with changes in the price of silver over the previous twenty years.[30] Silver prices had stayed within 4 percent of the prices of all commodities over this period, implying that a silver standard would have been compatible with stability in the general price level. Only one commodity, noted Joseph Sibley of Pennsylvania, had appreciated significantly with respect to silver. That commodity was gold. "Why do you say that silver has gone down," he asked his opponents, "and . . . is debased? Why do you not say that gold has . . . been deified? . . . You do not want an honest dollar . . . You want a scarce dollar." The dishonest dollar, he concluded, was the 150-cent gold dollar.[31]

Sibley's data on the relative prices of gold, silver, and all other commodities were accurate. The only way that the "price" of gold could rise or fall under an operational gold-standard system was by a general fall or rise in the market prices of all other commodities and services. A general decline in all prices was in fact occurring. Silver's value relative to all commodities was meanwhile staying almost constant. This fact seems to argue that the gold dollar should have been devalued so that a smaller quantity of gold would have had a given monetary value. By this means the downward trend in the general price level could have been arrested. But even if the gold standard was to continue on the same terms, some low-enough mint price for silver would have neutralized silver's displacement of gold. Usually, too, monetization of a metal would add enough to the metal's overall demand to raise its price significantly. So silver did not have to be devalued to the 28-to-1 ratio in order to limit its threat to gold convertibility.

The economics of the situation were relatively clear, the politics even more so. Cleveland would certainly have vetoed *any* silver-purchase bill. J. Rogers Hollingsworth in *The Whirligig of Politics* stated: "On the issue of silver repeal, . . . Cleveland assumed that he could lead his party without modifying his views, for the patronage at his disposal would provide the requisite power for repeal."[32] His self-assurance and willfulness in getting his way with Congress were noted time and again, not only in Congress but also in contemporary news accounts. John McLaurin of South Carolina quoted an editorial from the *Boston Traveler* of August 14, 1893, that said in part: "He [Cleveland] had issued instructions to all his cabinet officers that there shall be no more appointments made upon the recommendations of men in Congress about whose vote upon the silver problem there is any doubt. He has gone even further, and has directed that there shall be extended no official courtesy whatever to anyone in Congress until it is known how his vote is to be cast on the silver question."[33]

Cleveland had appointed John G. Carlisle of Kentucky, a former member of the House of Representatives, to be secretary of the Treasury. In Congress Carlisle had been a champion of free silver and had made an oft-quoted speech on the subject in 1878. As a cabinet officer, however, his views changed. His "eloquent tongue," said McLaurin, "is silenced by a Cabinet office."[34] In sharp contrast to the prosilver sentiments voiced by congressional members of his own party, Secretary of the Treasury Carlisle expressed the opinion that "the amount of money in the country is greater than is required for the transaction of the business of the people at this time . . . Money does not create business, but business creates a demand for money, and until there is such a revival of industry and trade as to require the use of the circulating medium now outstanding, it would be hazardous to arbitrarily increase the volume by law."[35] Thus was the secretary able to fashion a monetary theory that fit the politics of repeal.

The repeal bill came to a vote in the House August 28, 1893. The amendment for free coinage at 16 to 1 failed, 125 to 226; at 17 to 1, 101 to 241; at 18 to 1, 103-240; at 19 to 1, 104-238; and at 20 to 1, 122 to 222. Restoration of the Bland-Allison Act failed 136 to 213, and the repeal bill passed without amendments 239 to 108. Achievement of any kind of silver-purchase act in the House would thus have required a "swing" of about forty votes—an astonishing number given the large Democratic majority and the depressed economy.[36]

The repeal bill took only a few weeks to get through the House of Representatives. The rapidity with which the administration achieved its desires without compromising its major tenet raised well-founded alarms in the prosilver wing of the Senate. When the House version of the bill was reported out of the Senate Committee on Finance, debate on it developed into a filibuster.[37]

The Senate Committee on Finance did not change the House version except to tack on a pointless conscience-salving amendment. The added clause was taken from the Democratic platform fashioned at the Chicago convention the year before in anticipation of the general election of 1892. It stated that United States policy would be "to coin both gold and silver into money of equal intrinsic and exchangeable value, such equality to be secured through international agreement, or by such safeguards of legislation as will insure the maintenance of the parity in value of the coins of the two metals, and the equal power of every dollar at all times in the markets and in the payment of debts."[38] This kind of political claptrap had been intended to effect a compromise between the two wings of the Democratic party. The free-silverites could believe that it implied bimetallism, while the antisilver element could use it as a pretext for opposing silver monetization. In fact it had several interpretations. The "parity in value of the two metals" could mean parity at 16 to 1, parity at 20 to 1, parity at 24 to 1, or parity at any other ratio. The "equal power of every dollar at all times in the markets and in the payment of debts" did not specify a benchmark. Did it mean that all dollars were to be kept equal to the gold dollar in purchasing power? or to the silver dollar? Or were all dollars to be kept at a constant purchasing power over time? The amendment begged these questions and offered no decisive plank on the monetary issue for general party support.

The House experience with the repeal bill had shown that a change in the ratio—the simple solution to the problem—was not popular. Many free-silverites felt that it compromised principle too far and that acceptance of a change in ratio implied the operational, practical failure of a double standard.[39]

A standard money metal that could not maintain its value relative to the other metal in a bimetallic-standard system either would displace the other metal or would require devaluation, that is, a reduction in its own mint price. That silver substitute completely for gold was unthinkable. Yet devaluation of silver was also resisted because it seemed an admission that the value of silver was too unstable to justify its continued use as one of the standard metals. Antisilver forces, of course, would not consider any adjustment in the mint prices of the two metals, since they wanted silver demonetized unconditionally.

During the filibuster Senator John P. Jones of Nevada demonstrated the intensity of purpose with which the silver bloc resisted repeal of the silver-purchase clause. His speeches fill almost one hundred pages in the *Congressional Record* and draw on the entire collection of treatises on monetary economics in the Library of Congress.[40] He dwelt at length on the proportionality of the quantity of money and prices and on the automatic functioning of metallic standards. The *level* of prices, he said, was unimportant. "The objection [of free-silverites] is . . . *to the persistence of the lowering process*—the constant and unending fall—which renders it impossible for industry and commerce to find a steady level from which prosperity might begin."[41]

The *New York Times* as early as September 3 predicted how the Senate would divide when the final vote on the bill was tallied. It reported that the faction giving the most trouble was the little group of Republicans from the silver-producing states. "They will oppose any change in the ratio, and they will oppose repeal, and they will oppose it as long as they dare to filibuster. The Democrats can not afford to filibuster. The 'guerillas' can afford anything, for they have little to lose."[42]

True, not enough of the democrats could afford to filibuster. "The [Cleveland] Administration," accused Edward Wolcott of Colorado, one of the "guerillas," "with its petty spoils and patronage, has been able to make . . . many converts [from free silver]." The platform of the Democratic party had "declared in favor of free silver, but the platform meant no more to [President Cleveland] than the wind that blows."[43]

The use of patronage as a "club" to persuade wavering Democratic senators to support repeal was discussed at length by another guerilla, William Stewart of Nevada. Stewart cited an open letter written to Cleveland by T. V. Powderly of Scranton, Pennsylvania. "It has been openly proclaimed," Powderly's letter stated,

> that the Congressman or Senator of Democratic faith who would not act with the Administration in opposition to the expressed sentiments of the platform on which you and they were elected would be

ignored in the distribution of patronage. No denial has ever come from your lips; no friend of yours has ever ventured to contradict the statement to which I allude.

On the contrary, those nearest to you . . . have taken the ground that Federal patronage would be made the club to beat back the tide of popular sentiment.[44]

Cleveland and his congressional supporters did not try to excuse the means that justified their ends. They argued only that the developing depression was due to the adverse effects of the Sherman Act. Repeal of the purchasing clause, they alleged, would act as a "faith cure" and restore confidence.

This argument was one that no logic could either deny or confirm. Confidence could have been used just as easily in support of silver policy as it was used against it. It received its due from William Hatch of Missouri. He cited a facetious bill to restore confidence proposed by the *Washington Post*.

Be it enacted, [editorialized the *Post*], by the Senate and the House of Representatives of the United States in Congress assembled: SECTION 1. That confidence in the financial condition of all business affairs throughout the domain of the Republic is hereby declared to be fully restored. [Laughter.] And all persons are commanded to forthwith conduct their financial and commercial transactions in conformity with this enactment.[45]

As senate discussion of the bill carried on through September into October, Democrats realized that their inability to agree was damaging party prestige and destroying party unity. Efforts to effect a compromise had been sought by Senator Arthur Gorman of Maryland for several weeks, but Cleveland was openly contemptuous of Gorman and his supporters.[46]

On October 4 the *Cincinnati Enquirer* interviewed Sherman on the stalemate. It first asked whether Sherman thought the act that bore his name would be repealed. "I do not," Sherman replied. He predicted that the Democrats would arrange a compromise, such as reduction of the monthly purchase to 2.5 million ounces, and the president would have to agree or "he will destroy his party."[47]

On October 17 Sherman made a crucial speech in which he claimed that Senate Democrats had to pass something or give up. If they could not agree on a measure, he charged, "the people of the United States will take them at their word . . . If they do not agree with the President, let them say so, and formulate their opinions into an act." Otherwise, he said, they must retire, and "we will do the best we can with our silver friends who belong to us, who are blood of our blood and bone of our bone. But yours [addressing the Democrats] is the proper duty . . . You have the supreme honor of being able to settle this question now, and you ought to do it."[48]

The forty-four Senate Democrats, realizing the validity of Sherman's charge, caucused and came to an agreement that was signed by twenty-one free-silver and sixteen administration Democrats, and was opposed by six others.[49] This attempt failed, reported James Pugh of Alabama, when Cleveland "interposed his objections and demanded unconditional repeal at all hazards . . . I am satisfied," Pugh concluded, "that all effort at compromise has failed solely on account of President Cleveland and his Secretary of the Treasury. Their will has been as potential [*sic*] and has served the same purpose as the cloture rule."[50]

The administration was able to preserve its principles intact and refuse the compromise only because it could count on the support of twenty-six Republicans in addition to the twenty or twenty-two Democrats it had bludgeoned into submission. The prosilver forces, said Francis Cockrell of Missouri, had given up more than they wished in the caucus that had initiated the aborted compromise, and now they found Sherman and his "Administration Republicans" arrayed against them.

> Then it was that the incandescent light of nonpartisanism, of the Republican, mug-wump-Democratic coalition was cast athwart our pathway, and the Democratic Administration was revealed in all its nonpartisan perfection, with its unconditional repeal banners still in the hands of Republicans and Mug-wumps and Democrats . . . What does this prove when a Democratic President and Secretary of the Treasury refuse to agree with six-sevenths of the Democratic Senators . . . upon a compromise measure, and prefer to leave the Administration banner in the hands of Republicans and Democrats jointly to placing it in the hands of Democrats only?[51]

What it proved had already been proven. What it forebode was an end to any cooperation between congressional rank and file and the Cleveland administration. Tariff reductions, for example, were doomed by the wounds resulting from the silver conflict.

The battle by this time was over. Voting on amendments began October 27, 1893. William Peffer of Kansas offered an amendment restoring the coinage law of 1837—effectively a free-silver amendment—which lost, 28 to 39. Stewart then did a man-by-man analysis of the Peffer amendment and compared it with the vote taken on a straight free-coinage bill the year before. He found that eight senators had reversed themselves. Had opinions stayed the same, the Peffer amendment would have passed, 36 to 31.[52]

Another amendment offered by James Berry of Arkansas would have revived the Bland-Allison Act. This amendment was rejected 37 to 33.

With this close a division, a three-vote swing would have carried the amendment.[53]

The only amendment that dealt with the ratio was one offered by Stewart calling for a reduction of 25 percent in the gold content of the dollar, with the silver content of the dollar remaining constant. This amendment would have devalued the gold dollar from 23.22 grains to 18.56 grains. It would have adjusted the mint price of gold upward in accordance with market reality—that is, in recognition of the increased real value of gold relative to all other commodities including silver. It would therefore have changed the ratio of value between gold and silver from 16 to 1 to 20 to 1, not by reducing the mint price of silver, but by increasing the mint price of gold. It was a logical proposal in view of the constancy in value between silver and other commodities and in light of the appreciated real value of gold. It was rejected without even a call for the yeas and nays.[54]

As the final vote approached with no concessions, no compromises, and no probabilities for any remedial legislation to ease the monetary situation, Donald Cameron of Pennsylvania observed: "The majority of this Chamber seems determined to act without thinking, for fear that if it stops to think it will not act."[55] George Vest of Missouri, after remarking that repeal meant contraction, stated: "This is the first instance in the history of the human race when men of Anglo-Saxon lineage have been punished because they discovered too much of the precious metals."[56]

The bill passed 43 to 32, then went back to the House for concurrence on the meaningless amendment taken from the Democratic platform of the year before. Bland's motion to recommit the bill for further study lost 109 to 176. The bill then passed 194 to 94 and was signed by President Cleveland the same day.[57]

Repeal of the silver-purchase clause in 1893 has received only perfunctory attention from scholars, primarily because the product of the five months' debate in Congress seemed to be nothing more than deletion of a single simple section of law.[58] But it was the Repeal Act more than the Bryan-McKinley campaign and election of 1896 that marked the end of silver as a major monetary metal and its decline to the status of a subsidiary money. By 1896 mankind had already been crucified on a cross of gold through the concerted actions of a Democratic administration and a Democratic Congress. Why should anyone then have believed that a Democratic vote would have any greater effect in promoting silver monetization than it had had in 1892? Bryan was beaten before he started by the political infection within the Democratic party initiated by the special session of 1893.

The debates over repeal proved that political power in the executive branch even at this time was formidable enough to counteract what would otherwise have been continuation of a silver purchase policy. Whereas the Republican party had successfully compromised within itself to avoid alienating the silver wing from the far West, the Democrats engaged in an internecine conflict that ruined their chances of political success for the next eighteen or twenty years. The anti-silver Republicans —Sherman, Allison, Aldrich, Morrill, and so on—can hardly be blamed for helping the Democrats conclude their fratricide.

The debates revealed much about political concepts of monetary policy. First was the notion that money could be managed; and in the minds of many congressmen was the belief that money should be managed. Some congressmen expressed the more sophisticated principle that the stock of money should be made to grow at the same rate as population and trade—by which, of course, they meant real output. Silver was thought to be the most expedient vehicle for this kind of monetary management. It was cheap, but not too cheap. It was respectable in a way that greenbacks were not. It was substantial and had an appealing ring. It was a precious metal. Its quantitative growth was self-regulating and subject to natural forces. It also had the virtue of being suitable for lower denominational usage.

The so-called bimetallic standard could hardly ever be bimetallic in practice. It required that defined quantities of either of two metals be legal tender for clearing debts written in terms of the unit of account. However, changes in demand and supply for each metal ordinarily tend to change their relative market price. Since their relative mint price must be fixed, the only relief for the disparity between mint and market prices is complete monetization of the metal tending to become cheaper and conversion of the other metal to commodity uses. Thus the cheaper metal always demonetizes the dearer metal unless market conditions for the two metals are essentially constant at the mint price. As Alfred Marshall suggested, bimetallism should be described as "alternative metallism."[59]

This pattern of possible change was not necessarily undesirable. The precious metal industry is extractive and very much subject to diminishing returns in a given state of the arts. Therefore, real values of the monetary metals tend to rise over time, and since mint prices are fixed, such a rise is equivalent to a decline in all other money prices. Use of a bimetallic standard, by shifting the burden of monetization to the relatively cheaper metal, moderates the fall in prices.

This pattern was evident in the United States during the last quarter of the nineteenth century. In the face of increasing world demand for monometallic gold standards and declining production of gold, the real value of gold increased markedly, that is, price levels fell.[60]

Silver was seen by its advocates as a policy vehicle that would temper the chronic decline in prices. But the agitation for free silver, in the presence of a gold standard that would endure, actually had the reverse of the intended effect. The anticipated rise in the price of gold—relative to silver and to all other moneys—which would have been a consequence of the free coinage of silver, generated a capital outflow. Holders of any fixed-dollar claims payable in dollars tried to get rid of them before the quasi devaluation of the gold dollar occurred. This activity further reduced the level of prices in the United States consistent with external equilibrium. As Friedman and Schwartz point out: "Paradoxically, therefore, the monetary damage done by silver agitation [by causing adverse capital movements] . . . kept the money stock from rising as much as it otherwise would have, rather than producing too rapid an increase in the money stock."[61] With a gold standard the price level had to assume a value compatible with the price levels of other countries, and the money stock of the United States had to be a quantity that would produce such a price level. Silver was simply one of the moneys that could respond appropriately to this constraint.

A somewhat different pattern would have emerged if silver had become the monometallic standard. The price of gold would have risen above its mint price, so the price level in the United States would not have fallen as much as it did, and perhaps not at all over the period from, say, 1885 to 1900. With other silver-standard countries, the United States would have had fixed exchange rates; with gold-standard countries, flexible exchange rates.

Acceptance of a de facto silver standard would not have generated a silver inflation, unless the production of silver had realized economies similar to those later experienced in the production of gold. The monetary demand for the standard monetary metal adds significantly to the nonmonetary demand and, in the case of silver, would probably have prevented any inflation.[62] The very fact that the gold price of silver had remained almost constant relative to the gold prices of all other commodities during the time silver was monetized on a limited basis argues that with full silver monetization the silver prices of all commodities would have declined.

Neither monometallic extreme was necessary. The mint value of gold could have been increased (devaluation of the gold dollar), and the mint value of silver could have been reduced (appreciation of the silver dollar). Such a compromise would have had some minor repercussions on foreign trade, but would have had beneficial results on domestic economic activity.[63]

Any metallic or bimetallic standard was bound to be affected by changes in the production of metals, as well as changes in the demands for them, that would on occasion require such official adjustments in their mint values. Since both metals were subsequently obtained at appreciably lower real costs after 1897, lower mint costs for both metals may have been called for some years later. However, mild inflations under metallic standards never seemed to provoke much political agitation for change. Politicians, as well as populations, always seemed willing to suffer gradually increasing prices as long as business remained brisk.

12. Monetary Policy in the Golden Era

> The Treasury has always been the bloody angle of criticism of an administration. (Leslie M. Shaw, Secretary of the Treasury, 1906)

> Most of the practices and projects of the late Secretary [of the Treasury] gave new impetus to the disintegration of that peculiar feature of American finance, the independent treasury system. (A. Piatt Andrew, 1907)

Most price indexes show a minor peak in prices during 1892. Then the struggle over the currency during the next year, the uncertainty it produced, and the elimination of silver as a major currency by the mid 1890s, produced a fall in prices of about 10 percent to the business cycle trough of 1896-97.[1]

The monetary upheaval following repeal of the silver-purchase clause in the Sherman Act was frequently characterized as the "currency famine." The situation was described well by Hepburn, who was himself involved as a policymaker, an advocate of the gold standard, and researcher and reporter on monetary events in that era. During 1893, he reported, interior banks "became impressed with a desire to strengthen their position at home and the withdrawal of a large portion of their New York deposits followed."[2] Reserves of New York banks fell below the legal minimum, and the system suffered all the symptoms of a bank crisis, including suspension of cash payments by banks in many eastern cities.

Clearinghouse certificates were issued during this famine to a greater extent than ever before. Hepburn estimated that at least $100 million of what might be called private-enterprise money was issued—clearinghouse certificates, certified checks, certificates of deposit, cashier's checks, and "due bills from manufacturers and other employers of labor, ... all designed to take the place of currency in the hands of the public." These currencies were subject to the 10 percent tax on state bank notes, but they proved so useful to the economy that "the government, after due deliberation, wisely forebore to prosecute . . . No loss resulted from the use of this makeshift currency."[3]

The private-enterprise money of expediency could not, of course, stay in circulation permanently, but only during the crisis stage of the business decline. More lasting relief came from the world's production of gold, which almost doubled between 1893 and 1897.

The gold boom came none too soon for the advocates of the single gold standard. Even so, the elections of 1896 were in doubt. The monetary issue—the question of the standard—was important in some quarters. But to a sizable group of voters it was too abstract to be of overwhelming importance; they could not identify this issue with the current state of business. Their inability to do so was largely a result of the late struggle over repeal of the silver-purchase clause and the lack of some other dramatic public policy that would bring relief from the depression. By the time of the elections in 1896 repeal was three years old. A new Democratic administration and Democratic Congress could hardly be expected to change radically what the previous coalition after lengthy deliberation had passed; and even if free silver could be achieved, its efficacy as public policy was uncertain. In the end, the "full dinner pail" of the Republicans defeated the free silver of the Democrats by a margin of 53 to 47, and both houses of Congress also returned Republican majorities.[4]

The focus of monetary activity after the election shifted from Congress to the executive administration. The new president, William McKinley, felt obliged to reward dissident Democrats, who had eschewed the free-silver doctrine and openly voted Republican, with a cabinet office. He therefore appointed Lyman J. Gage, a banker and a Cleveland Democrat from Chicago, to be secretary of the Treasury.[5]

John Carlisle, Gage's predecessor under Cleveland, had objected vigorously to the use of the Treasury Department as a supplier of paper money. "The issue and redemption of circulating notes," he wrote in his last report, "is not a proper function of the Treasury Department, or of any other department of the Government." This function, he continued, "ought to be regulated entirely by the business interests of the people and by the laws of trade and the principles which control honest commercial intercourse." All paper currency issued by the government, he concluded, should be permanently retired.[6]

Gage's first report, in 1897, echoed Carlisle's opinions on the dangers of government-issued fiat currencies. The presence of silver moneys subject to gold redemption, he stated, required "the financial wisdom, foresight, and courage of Congress" for safe and proper operation of the monetary system. He urged the creation of a division of issue and redemption, separate from the Treasury Department, that would hold significant stocks of all the major government currencies, as well as the Treasury's gold reserves, so that currency parities with gold would be maintained.[7]

To fill the vacuum that would otherwise be created by taking these currencies out of general circulation, Gage recommended enlargement of the national banking system and additional issues of national bank notes. The National Bank Act would be amended to accommodate the new notes through deposit of government-issued currencies by national banks in the new issue and redemption division. Then the national banks would be permitted to issue new notes to the extent of 25 percent of their deposited reserves. Their issues would be "unsecured by any direct pledge of security but issued against the [commercial] assets of the bank[s]" and would be taxed at the rate of 2 percent per annum.[8]

This scheme was conceived not only to reduce government involvement in the monetary system, but also to provide the monetary system with seasonal elasticity—an ideal that was becoming more and more popular. The current supply of government-issued money was necessarily rigid, but bank-issued currency was "subject to increase at the point where needed, and the needs of the community unite with the motive of the banker in supplying those wants as they find expression."[9]

In his report for 1899 Gage discussed what he considered the two most important monetary issues—the question of the standard and the adaptation of the currency system to the requirements of expanding trade and industry. Although gold was the de facto standard, stability—the main desideratum of policy—could not be maximized unless gold was declared the official standard. "Stability in [bank-issued] currency," he wrote, "should be safely guarded, [but] . . . *flexibility*—the power of needful expansion—must also be provided." As an example of inelasticity in the system, he cited the case of the New York City banks during the preceding autumn. The call for $23 million of currency from the country banks to move the crops had resulted in a decline of $84 million of deposits in New York, and "havoc was wrought in the regular ongoing of our commercial life." This state of affairs, he concluded, suggested a need for the national bank reform, recommended in his earlier report, that would make the supply of bank notes responsive to the needs of trade.[10]

Gage's recommendations were similar to those of the Monetary Commission of 1898. The "Bill Embodying the Commission's Proposals" was introduced in the House of Representatives in January 1898, and many of its provisions finally emerged in the Currency Act of March 14, 1900. This act, sometimes known as the Gold Standard Act, fixed gold as *the* standard legal tender monetary metal. Gage, by occupation a midwestern banker, felt quite comfortable with the conservative, banking-school doctrine of the Indianapolis group.[11]

The Currency Act liberalized the issue of national bank notes, so no stringency appeared in the money market that year when crops were harvested. But Gage pointed out in his report of 1900 that "there is under our present system no assurance whatever that the volume of bank currency will be continuously responsive to the country's needs . . . The supply of currency is related most largely . . . to the price of Government bonds in the market." This relationship, he argued, divorced the supply of money from the needs of trade and commerce, because "there is no discernible relation whatever" between these needs and the prices of government securities.[12]

The greatly increased gold production and the lagged effect of this gold on the monetary systems of the world were changing the Treasury's strategic financial position vis-à-vis the rest of the economy. Between 1894 and 1899 the government's budget was constantly in deficit. But in the fiscal year 1899-1900 the budget swung into surplus and was to stay that way for most of the time up to World War I. In addition to the $150 million gold reserve stipulated by the Currency Act of 1900, the Treasury held additional gold balances of more than $90 million, plus another $230 million of gold against which gold certificates had been issued. The Treasury also had almost $100 million to its account in 444 national bank depositories, and both government deposits and new national banks were being added at rapid rates.[13]

The accumulation of balances of this magnitude in the Treasury created the same problem that had occurred during the gold boom just fifty years earlier: If the gold was in the Treasury, it was not out in markets stimulating trade and commerce. To get the gold out of the Treasury, Gage anticipated payment of interest that was coming due on outstanding debt. Prepayments were timed to coincide with crop moving in the fall of the year. In addition, $19 million worth of the bonds due in 1904 and 1907 was purchased at an average premium to the holders of 12 percent, or 112 percent of par, and another $23 million worth of 2 percent bonds, redeemable at the option of the government, was also purchased.[14]

Purchase of government securities in the open market was a logical means of reducing treasury balances, and many secretaries who had an elementary understanding of the policy implemented such programs. The decision to buy had to be combined with the decision of when and how much to buy. Congress might have made these decisions for the secretary. But legislative awareness of financial conditions significantly lagged the events themselves; and most Congressmen were willing to let the technical experts in the Treasury handle the details as long as no adverse political repercussions developed.

The magnitude of the changes in commerce was demonstrated by the figures for foreign trade. In the four years 1898-1901, Gage reported, the total trade *balance* was $2,354 million, or an average of almost $600 million per year. (The aggregate net surplus for the preceding 108 years had been $357 million.) The Treasury's cash balance increased commensurately and was disbursed again during 1901 by purchase of outstanding government securities.[15]

In his last report, in 1901, Gage discussed at length the imperfections he had observed in the banking and monetary system. Individual banks, he wrote, "stand isolated and apart . . . with no tie of mutuality between them. There is no . . . method of legal association for common protection or defense in periods of adversity and depression." These banks, he said, essentially manufacture or create the medium of exchange in common use. He listed three "causes" for the expansion of bank credit: "a rise in prices of commodities and securities; an increase in the *volume* of these things; [and] an enlarged activity in the sale and transfer of goods and securities."[16]

Gage appeared here to have mistaken symptoms for causes. His next remarks confirm that he was discussing expansion of bank credit within the framework of a given volume of reserves. Ultimately "the diminishing ratio of cash reserves puts a strain on the expanding movement [of business] and impedes further development in that direction." Prosperity follows. But this state of affairs, he continued, is invariably upset by a host of possible random events. The banking system then would face a crisis, and bank credit "is withdrawn at the very moment when support is most needful."[17]

The solution Gage advocated was incorporation of a central bank. He eschewed "a large central bank with branches" because of its lack of general political acceptability. Instead he supported a federated institution. "Can not the principle of federation be applied," he asked, "under which the banks as individual units, preserving their independence of action in local relationship, may yet be united in a great central institution?"[18] This statement exhibits remarkable prescience considering that the passage of the Federal Reserve Act incorporating a federated central banking system along these very lines was still twelve years in the future.

When Theodore Roosevelt became president after the assassination of McKinley, he appointed Leslie M. Shaw secretary of the Treasury. Shaw was from Iowa and, like Gage, was a banker with orthodox and conservative views on finance. His principal political experience had been to champion the gold standard against the attacks of William Jennings Bryan.[19]

Nothing about Shaw's previous professional life could have suggested the policies he was to innovate or appreciably extend during his tenure as secretary. Before he retired early in 1907, he had added the following policies to the Treasury's agenda:

1. Strategic transfers of treasury deposits from the subtreasuries to the national banks.
2. Acceptance of security other than government bonds as collateral for government deposits in national banks, thus freeing the government bonds for use as national bank note collateral.
3. Abolition of the enforcement of a reserve requirement against national bank holdings of government deposit balances.
4. Allowance of the interest-free use of government gold holdings to gold importers as soon as the gold was purchased abroad and until it was delivered in the United States.

Shaw most often used the first policy, augmenting gold reserves in the national banks by transferring subtreasury gold to them, in order to meet the seasonal demand for bank credit. The Treasury for most of this period was in the position of a central bank with varying amounts of free gold reserves. It had outstanding currency obligations of about $1,000 million, two-thirds of which was silver currency, the remaining one-third United States notes. Against these obligations it had to keep $150 million of gold reserves. In addition, it had about $100 million of excess gold and other cash items in the subtreasury offices. This money transferred from subtreasury offices to the national banks in season increased the banks' primary reserves and thus furthered the expansion of bank credit.[20]

Shaw interpreted the laws governing federal moneys to sanctify his actions. One (constitutional) law states: "No money shall be drawn from the Treasury but in consequence of appropriations made by law." Before 1903 internal revenue receipts could be deposited in national bank depositories only as they accumulated, while customs receipts (about 40 percent of total revenues) had to be held by the Treasury.[21] Shaw argued that the depository banks were part of the Treasury. Movement of funds into or out of the banks, from or to the subtreasuries, was not money drawn from the Treasury, but a transfer of the money from one "apartment" to the other. Furthermore, he reasoned, if the bank depositories were part of the Treasury and held legal collateral in the form of government securities against their public deposits, there was little need to require them to hold reserves against these deposits. He thereupon announced that this provision would not be enforced (policy 3).

National banks were required by the National Bank Act to pledge United States bonds as collateral against issues of national bank notes and to hold "United States bonds and otherwise" against deposits of government money. An increase of government deposits in the banks thus generally provoked an increase in the demand for the given stock of government securities, raised security prices, and tended to diminish national bank note circulation. Bank credit could expand only at the expense of bank-issued currency. "We have to bear in mind," Shaw pointed out, "that [national] bank notes are not available for reserve in national banks, but are as good as money in all other banking institutions."[22]

Shaw interpreted *"and* otherwise" to mean *"or* otherwise." He was therefore able to extend public deposit collateral privileges to state and municipal bonds at 75 percent of their face value, on the condition that the federal government bonds thereby released be made the basis of an immediate circulation of national bank notes (policy 2).[23]

Policy 4, undertaken in 1906, was a one-time action. It called for delivery of gold from the Treasury to gold importers before they received gold contracted for shipment from abroad. In effect it subsidized the interest costs of gold in transit, thus decreasing by a few cents the gold import point. It could be viewed as a small, quasi devaluation of the gold dollar.

Shaw used two signals for undertaking monetary action: short-term rates of interest in the money market and the volume of surplus reserves held by the national banks during the summer. He noted that the call loan rate was perhaps only 1 percent in midsummer but might reach 25 percent in November. "Such extremes," he wrote, "can and should be rendered impossible."[24] His concern with short-term interest rates does not imply that Shaw was an incipient Keynesian. It simply shows his need for an index that reflected seasonal variations in the demand for money.

During his first year in office, 1902, he used both novel and traditional monetary policies. In an effort to bolster national bank circulation, the surplus revenues were deposited [in the spring] with national banks upon satisfactory security, but preference was given to such institutions as maintained their limit of circulation. Then, during the months when rates of interest were low, no deposits were made."[25]

The New York money market was more stringent than usual in the fall. Reserve ratios of national banks had fallen below the legal minimum of 25 percent. Shaw then ordered the purchase of government securities in the open market, a policy that had been used frequently during the past fifty years. During the fall of 1902, $70 million of the outstanding government debt was repurchased at 137 percent of par.[26]

The securities that remained commanded a substantial premium in the market. Purchasing such debt with gold would have added gold to national bank reserves and permitted credit expansion. At the same time it would have required the retirement of national bank notes and would have altered the currency-money ratio. Shaw expressed the view that "either the Government debt must be perpetuated as a basis for national bank [note] circulation, and additional bonds issued as occasion may require, or some other system must be provided." The other system he recommended was a "circulation based upon general credits, . . . properly safeguarded."[27] He suggested that national banks be permitted to issue government-guaranteed currency equal to 50 percent of the bond-secured currency already maintained by them, but subject to a 5 or 6 percent tax until redeemed. Not only did he expect this sytem to work automatically; he also argued that it would make "10 percent money well-nigh impossible, and the Treasury Department would be saved a most embarrassing responsibility."[28]

The perverse elasticity of currency with respect to the volume of trade and the paucity of government bonds available to secure bank note circulation encouraged Shaw to attempt what became his primary means of control: the direct deposit of treasury balances in national banks. Cash reserves over $150 million in the Treasury's own offices were excess. When these balances were transferred to national banks, treasury credit with the national bank depositories increased and the cash became primary reserves of the national banks. The banks were thus enabled to expand credit for moving the crops and other seasonal needs. In January and February the reserves returned to the reserve city banks from their country correspondents. Treasury revenues were then deposited in the subtreasuries, and treasury calls to the national banks soaked up what had by then become an out-of-season plethora of reserves.

In 1903 Shaw had $40 million available in treasury offices, but he used only $16 million despite a severe contraction in the securities markets. In 1904 he again had the Treasury buy government securities, this time $19.4 million; and in 1905 the need for crop-moving money once more resulted in treasury monetary operations.[29] The fiscal deficits in 1904 and 1905, which arose principally from construction of the Panama Canal, left the subtreasury reserves too depleted to be used. Treasury deposits in national banks were simply transferred "to the points where seasonal demands were highest." Fiscal requirements necessitated a withdrawal of treasury credits from the national bank depositories; but since these demands were for immediate payment to other sectors of the economy, they were "accomplished without disturbance to business."[30]

In 1906 the gold policy was invoked. At the same time $30 million in Panama Canal bonds had to be floated. To expedite this sale Shaw advertised that any national bank depository purchasing the bonds would have one-third of the money used in the purchase left on its books as a public deposit. He then made sure the banks would have reserves in the fall by withdrawing "$60 million from the channels of trade and locking it up." He dryly observed in retrospect: "Everything seemed serene to everybody [during the summer] except to those who recognize that in this latitude crops mature in the fall . . . The strain inevitable [sic] began to develop. Interior banks called their loans and shipped the proceeds home, but . . . seemed to think it strange that the actual withdrawal of money from financial centers . . . should cause any stringency at these centers."[31] In the last two quarters of 1906 treasury deposits in national banks increased from $66 million to $138 million. This action generated an expansion of over 10 percent in total national bank reserves. The national banks then either expanded credit themselves or shipped the reserves in the form of gold or treasury currency to their country correspondents, who could expand credit even more than the national banks since they maintained lower reserve ratios.

The significance of the $25-$75 million that the Treasury made available as reserves to banks is not overwhelming even when the lower reserve requirement of country banks is included. Specie and legal tender reserves in all banks between 1902 and 1907 varied from $800 to $1,100 million. The national banks held about two-thirds of this amount and the nonnational banks, one-third. The usual treasury deposit, along with equivalent easy-money policies, permitted about a 10 percent seasonal expansion. Such an amount seemed to be sufficient at that time to provide for the seasonal bulge in economic activity.

Policies as unorthodox as Shaw's in the conservative era before World War I were certain to find some disfavor. One would hardly expect, however, such universal criticism. Among his most vociferous critics was the *Nation*, a periodical that regarded his actions in the money market as relief for "a ring of powerful Wall Street speculators." His policies, the *Nation* observed, constituted "meddling by a Government officer in a market where he had no business whatever . . . What is to hinder some benevolent autocrat of the Treasury hereafter," it asked rhetorically, "from . . . buying stocks in support of the stock market?"[32]

Perhaps even more caustic than the *Nation's* criticism was that from such academic conservatives as Eugene Patton and J. Lawrence Laughlin of the University of Chicago, A. Piatt Andrew of Harvard, David Kinley of the University of Illinois, and others, such as O. M. W. Sprague, also of Harvard, who made only incidental references to Shaw's policies.[33]

Patton and Andrew objected to the independent treasury system as a policy institution. The problem of revenues in excess of expenditures, Patton observed, had never been solved satisfactorily. "But this," he avowed, "is an argument for revision of the sub-treasury law, not for granting autocratic power to the secretary of the treasury."[34] Andrew repeated Daniel Webster's sentiments: "The very idea of keeping one's accumulations in carefully guarded idleness pertains to the conditions and habits of the Middle Ages." He deplored the lack of synchronization in government expenditures and receipts, "exaggerated as they are by the absence of a balanced budget."[35]

Patton and Andrew based their primary criticisms of Shaw's policies on his violations of precedent. Andrew pointed out that "deposit of United States bonds *and* otherwise" as collateral for treasury deposits in national banks clearly meant collateral in addition to United States bonds. He admitted that this law had been phrased in 1865 and that it was "doubtless primarily intended to furnish additional inducement for the organization of national banks and the consequent absorption of [government] bonds." He conceded that other secretaries had prepaid interest on the debt, bought securities in the open market, and transferred some deposits to the national banks beyond the $15 million or $20 million usually held in them for fiscal transactive purposes, but he found the degree of Shaw's actions "incredible" and legal only under a "strained interpretation of the law."[36] One might well ask how precedent could ever be established if all actions were based exclusively on previous experiences. The only innovations that could then occur would be due to pure chance. Nothing would be left to imagination or the creative instinct, and little would be left to reason.[37]

To the charge of "unprecedented" Shaw answered: "It has been the fixed policy of the Treasury Department for more than half a century to anticipate monetary stringencies, and so far as possible prevent panics." Panics were, he reasoned, in the same category as pestilences, except that the former caused more hardship. Even though public disasters might result from the avarice of bankers, he continued, "the Treasury Department . . . must to the limit of the authority with which it is clothed, and at the risk of personal reputation [sic], grant relief and prevent disaster."[38]

His detractors were in the contradictory position of criticizing the subtreasury system for being archaic and contributing to monetary inelasticity at the same time that they were railing against Shaw for reversing such infelicities. Their monetary theory also rendered their criticisms invalid. Andrew, for example, argued that "during periods of abounding prosperity, . . . when currency is most in demand, our taxes . . . become unusually prolific." The federal money is then locked up in the independent treasury "at exactly the time when the community in general, and the banks in particular, stand in the greatest need of it." When business is stagnant and idle hoards swell bank reserves, the treasury hoards are dumped on the banks, "although obviously these are the periods when such additions are least needed."[39]

Andrew here expressed the fundamental principle of the commodity theory of money: that the supply of real product generates the supply of money. When used as central banking doctrine, this theory implies that the quantity of money furnished by the central banking institution ought to be geared explicitly to the flow of goods and services. An independent treasury, of course, could not provide this kind of synchronization because it did not deal in the real financial assets that were generated by the output of goods and services. Rather it dealt in government securities, a long-term security that resulted from government fiscal operations at those times when government expenditures had been especially profligate.

The commodity theory of money (without a central bank) has a completeness and thus an appeal not found in other theories of money. For when money is derived from real product, as is the case under an operational metallic standard, the demand for and supply of money are simultaneously determined through market actions involving prices for all goods and services and for the monetary metal. If prices of all goods and services fall, the value of the monetary metal, being reciprocal to the prices of real products, is enhanced. More resources are then devoted to producing the monetary metal, thereby arresting the fall in the price level. The commodity theory of money in this form thus provides mutually interacting demand and supply functions for money.

When this doctrine adopts real bills, as well as real gold, as a supplemental guide to the creation of money, it loses its validity. Real gold is an effective anchor because its supplies are limited and its money price is fixed under the rules of the gold standard. But real bills may have any price that bankers or central bankers attach to them, and their supplies are unlimited. Furthermore, bankers' assessments of their soundness are colored by the current state of business. If business is booming, applications for commercial loans look more eligible, and the generation of new money on the basis of these new bills contributes to the boom. Thus a real-bills doctrine, when used by a central banking institution as a vehicle for policy, tends to be procyclical.

Andrew, as well as most laymen and most congressmen, embraced this doctrine. But Shaw, who was in an official position from which he could foresee an independent injection of high-powered money, simply anticipated from past experience the seasonal increase in the traffic of real commodities and made provision for it. As long as his operations were seasonal or short-run and confined to redistributing the existing stock of high-powered money on the basis of historical precedents, Andrew's norm of needs could not be seriously violated, even though no real bills appeared in the Treasury's operations.

Patton's criticisms also reflected the principles of the commodity theory. He observed that Shaw had asked for power to control the stock of money through the banking system. "To whom should this power be given?" he asked rhetorically. "To an independent irresponsible treasury official, or to the banking institutions of the country, which are in close touch with business conditions? Is not the Treasury *ex natura* in a position where it cannot possibly know the banking needs of the country, since it is not in contact with the world of trade.?"[40]

Banking was to Patton, as it was to Andrew, just another business, but a business that manufactured money complementarily to trade. More important was his willingness to permit the use of private bankers to promote public policy, and monetary policy at that. Only too evident is the bias introduced into policy decisions when an interested private group is allowed to prescribe public policies involving the welfare of that private group as well as the welfare of the community. The discretion of private bankers could not be a satisfactory alternative to a treasury department, properly instructed and constrained by Congress, for carrying out seasonal monetary policies.

Andrew also denied the necessity for public control over the money stock. He felt that Shaw's policies would initiate "among the regular and ordinary functions of the American government the paternal practices of the European central banks." Worst of all, Shaw's policies subsidized banks to some degree and correspondingly discouraged prudent banking. If business crises result "from over-trading and over-speculative propensities of the community," Andrew said, "a stringent market will spontaneously afford the best sort of a remedy by forcing a reduction of bank liabilities." He advocated a laissez faire approach that would emphasize a "law-regarding policy involving the least possible amount of state interference with business." He concluded with an impassioned appeal for legislative relief from treasury meddling "and from all the overnight changes of policy with which the country has been afflicted during the last five years."[41]

Shaw was well aware that his actions gave an air of central banking to the Treasury. He saw the national banks as the branches of this "great government bank." The system he thought, was "not unlike that of European countries, . . . and if properly operated, can be made to accomplish much of what is contemplated by those who advocate the large central bank."[42]

Any monetary policy conducted within the general framework of a metallic standard could have only form-seasonal effects. The secular increase in the stock of gold was enough during Shaw's tenure to provide general buoyance in business. Shaw was aware of the need for a year-to-year increase in the money stock, but his principal concern was seasonal fluctuation in the demand for money. "The average amount of money," he said, "is, in my judgment, abundant."[43]

The subsidization of gold imports should have emphasized the ultimate dominance of the gold-standard system in determining the secular path of monetary activity, but Shaw never recognized this force explicitly. Andrew observed the futility of the gold policy. He imputed to

Shaw a recognition that European central banks might be attracting gold from the United States by an "artful diversion." The gold would have come or gone anyway, Andrew concluded, depending on "deeper lying reasons."[44]

Shaw's gold-import policy and his circular to the national banks advising them that reserve requirements would not be enforced against government deposits were one-time measures that could have only a one-time effect. His acceptance of collateral other than government securities for public deposits and his policy of moving gold reserves into and out of the national banks were long-run, but they would have been limited by a secular drain of gold to other countries. Despite this last possibility he was moved to the following famous observation in 1906:

> "If the Secretary of the Treasury were given $100 million to be deposited with the banks or withdrawn as he might deem expedient, and if in addition he were clothed with authority over the reserves of the several banks, with power to contract the national-bank circulation at pleasure, in my judgment no panic as distinguished from industrial stagnation could threaten either the United States or Europe that he could not avert.[45]

Shaw's statement provided a refreshing positivism. Perhaps one may doubt that any secretary of the Treasury could or should carry out such a policy. But a high-level policymaker, who continually deprecates his own power and who is forever apprehensive about contingencies over which he alleges he has no control, is not appealing.

George Cortelyou, who succeeded Shaw in March 1907, was somewhat of this latter character. He spoke the same words and followed the same policies that had worked so expediently under Shaw; but his measures lacked timing and decisiveness, and his words lacked vigor and conviction. In the first half of 1907 he did not effect enough of a seasonal contraction of treasury deposits in national banks to provide an adequate increase in the fall. Then in May and June he allowed redemption of $61 million of the bonds of 1907, although another $50 million of the same issue was refinanced. During September and October, treasury deposits totaling $28 million were placed week-by-week in the national banks. When the crisis developed in October, another $35 million was deposited within four days. These actions reduced the Treasury's excess balance to $5 million, and no further action could be taken.[46]

By carrying out the refunding operations too early in the summer, Cortelyou depleted the Treasury's reserves so that not enough was available in the fall. Some imagination on his part might have adjusted the timing and method of this ordinary housekeeping operation to have complemented rather than conflicted with seasonal monetary policies.[47] But the failure of treasury policy to stop the panic of 1907 demonstrated that when the monetary reserve in the central agency was exhausted, the specie-flow gold-standard mechanism became dominant. All institutions then had to run with the wind; none could lean into it.

Cortelyou was asked by Congress for a report on the Treasury's actions during the crisis. His response showed that he did not shoulder responsibility lightly. "The present head of the department," he wrote humbly, "has not assumed the obligation [of caretaking the financial condition of the country] willingly and would be glad to be relieved of it at least in part by suitable legislation." The accumulation of currency in the Treasury, he continued, had imposed this unwanted duty on his office. A more desirable monetary framework would "adapt the movement of currency more nearly automatically to the requirements of business . . . and would greatly diminish the sense of responsibility which must weigh heavily upon any occupant of [this] office."[48]

These remarks provided a ready foil for the use of David Kinley, who was perhaps the Treasury's most exhaustive, if not most dramatic, critic. Kinley quoted Cortelyou's "confessional" with approval. "These are wise words," he appended. He then weighed the various pros and cons of the Treasury Department as an agent of monetary policy. While he allowed that treasury actions had been at times proper and acceptable, he concluded that any good effects the Treasury had had in the money market were due almost entirely to fiscal happenstance. If, however, the secretary took positive measures to obviate the ill effects of detrimental fiscal operations on the money market, he was assuming too much power, he was likely to make mistakes, and his interference was arbitrary.[49] Kinley's conclusions permitted no treasury policy. Like other major critics who were also banking-school proponents, he favored a central bank that would work automatically and passively even in its seasonal operations. The Treasury itself should do nothing more than keep a tidy fiscal house.

Shaw was so sensitive to his critics that he made official references to them in his last report. He was confident that his means were reasonable in the light of law and that his ends were justified by their effects on the economy. His critics, he observed, "studied to write articles that would surely be read, and neglected to study actual conditions." Such people "attributed the noticeable tension [in the money market] not to increased business, but to the presence of sudden speculation."[50]

How far a cabinet officer can go in policymaking activities can never be determined to everyone's satisfaction. If he limits himself to the letter of the law in the manner Shaw's critics advocated, the operations of his office may aggravate undesirable events. Government officials, Shaw observed, are only too glad to avoid responsibility. "The rejection of a proposition never causes trouble," he stated. "Affirmative acts only are investigated and censured. Technical objections are as good as valid ones [*sic*] with the average bureau official."[51]

Laws in a free society are written with a knowledge that public servants will have to interpret them with discretion in two senses, with tact and with art. Three questions can then be applied to test whether a policymaker has gone too far: (1) Have the policies been performed in the light of reason and with good intentions? (2) Have the policies had good results? (3) Could a legislative or executive prescription reverse the policies that have been initiated?

The evidence seems to favor Shaw and his policies. The only way to have reduced appreciably the circumstances encouraging discretion would have been to retire all government-issued paper currency. The very existence of this currency in conjunction with an independent treasury argued for seasonal treasury policies similar to those Shaw administered. While he may have overstepped his authority, what was needed was not a central bank that would grow into an omnipotent ogre constantly promoting inflation but simply a resolution from Congress specifying the limits to treasury authority and actions. That such a resolution was not forthcoming is more an indictment of Congress than of Shaw.

Lloyd W. Mints, far from a liberal interventionist or leftist in any respect, once stated that Shaw was the "only good secretary of the Treasury we have ever had."[52] Many years later the nonliberal, nonleftist economist Milton Friedman remarked with his coauthor Anna J. Schwartz that Shaw's policies may well have been an outward and visible sign of typical "bureaucratic megalomania."[53]

These two views are not necessarily contradictory; even a bureaucratic megalomaniac may be an effective policy maker. However, Shaw's writings do not give the impression of megalomania. Rather, he seemed to realize after taking office the pivotal role the Treasury Department could play in ameliorating seasonal hardship in the monetary system. The awareness of this power did not paralyze his ability to think. He simply accepted conditions as he found them and adapted policies to these conditions as practically as he could. Ideally, power should neither choke nor addict its possessor. The evidence is that Shaw stayed within the proper tolerances.

13. Advent of the Federal Reserve System

> Why should we have an emergency currency? . . . The only emergency is the necessity which party leaders imagine confronts them to "do something," even though it be the wrong thing. What the country needs is not a makeshift legislative deformity, . . . but a careful revision and a wise reformation of the entire banking and currency system of the United States whereby panics may be prevented, or, if not prevented, under which their violence may be diminished and the evils consequent greatly abated. (Carter Glass, House of Representatives, 27 May 1908)

One of the least noticed developments in monetary affairs during the early twentieth century was the inclusion of economists in the arguments over economic policy and in the proposals for new legislative measures (invariably called reforms). Many of these economists were highly critical of Shaw's policies. One of them, J. Lawrence Laughlin, was actively associated with the American Bankers Association, and another, H. Parker Willis, was a special advisor to the chairman of the House Banking and Currency Committee, Carter Glass.[1]

Most of the economists who appeared in print, especially Willis and most of Shaw's critics, favored the gold standard, held a commodity theory of money and derived from these doctrines a commercial credit theory of banking. The issue that most concerned them, and many legislators and bankers as well, was the apparent seasonal rigidity of the money stock with respect to the needs of business. The institution they favored for furnishing the elasticity that the monetary system lacked would be endowed with some measure of excess gold reserves, which it would keep on a standby basis. Then expansion and contraction of commercial paper in the interest-earning portfolio of the institution would expand and contract the supply of money as needed.[2]

An important element in this doctrine was the understanding that the central banking institution be immune from political influence. The need for this feature was made acute by the policies of Secretary Shaw. All the schemes for reform included negative reactions to treasury intervention. As J. Lawrence Laughlin stated:

> We must establish some institution wholly free from politics or outside influence—as much respected for character and integrity as the Supreme Court—which shall be able to use government bonds or selected securities, as a basis for the issue of forms of lawful money which could be added to the reserves of the banks . . . It is doubtful if a great central bank—apart from its political impossibility— would accomplish the desired end.[3]

To most economists a great central bank meant a single government-operated institution with a currency monopoly. Such an institution was seen simply as a disguise for a treasury central bank and was unacceptable. Yet the kind of institution that would be desirable was not entirely clear. Laughlin, for example, had government securities as a basis for currency issues; but most economists, bankers, and legislators favored a central bank currency based on the commercial loans generated by the commercial banking system.

In the spring of 1908, the Senate and the House produced fairly similar emergency currency bills under Republican sponsorship. The Senate bill passed 47 to 20, and the House bill 152 to 104. A conference committee was then appointed to compromise the differences. This committee was chaired by Nelson Aldrich from the Senate and Edward Vreeland from the House.[4] The bill finally enacted thus became the Aldrich-Vreeland Act.

The version of the bill agreed to in conference called for the voluntary grouping of ten or more national banks into associations that would act as clearinghouses for the participating banks. They would have approximately the same functions and use the same methods that private clearinghouses had long since established on their own. Notes could be issued on approved city, county, and state securities and on commercial paper, which was "to include only [paper] representing actual commercial transactions, . . . not exceeding four months [to maturity]." Commercial paper up to 75 percent of its face value and local government securities for up to 90 percent of their par value would be the basis for issues of notes. The notes would have the same qualities as national bank notes. They were to be issued "under the direction and control of the Secretary of the Treasury" and were to be assigned to the different sections of the country in proportion to existing banking capital, "except that the Secretary of the Treasury may, in his discretion. . . . assign [any] amount not thus applied for to any applying association or associations in States in the same section of the country."[5] The currency outstanding was to be taxed at the rate of 5 percent the first month and 1 percent each month thereafter. Not only did this act acknowledge and accept clearinghouse central banking, it also reintroduced the discretion of the secretary of the Treasury, whose presence had only recently been found so undesirable!

This idea of a patchwork emergency currency was opposed by Carter Glass. He cited as an authority on the subject a "great banker of the West," Mr. James B. Forgan of Chicago, who was also president of the American Bankers Association. Testifying before the Banking and Currency Committee, Forgan had stated apoplectically that no conditions could ever warrant "the issue of anything that could bear such an infernal name as 'emergency currency.' " The bill, Glass concluded, "puts the Federal Government in the picayune and incongruous business of discounting commercial paper."[6]

Another congressman, John McHenry of Pennsylvania, discussed at length the Wall Street bogeyman. The bill, he said, enables "Wall Street interests" to turn panics on and off at will. The secretary of the Treasury would "become the 'hired man' of Wall Street," and so on. "Shall we close," he concluded, "as a fitting climax to this billion-dollar Republican Congress by crowning our masters, King Morgan and King Rockefeller, the heroes of the last panic, or shall it be King Taft, Wall Street's hired man? [Prolonged applause.]"[7]

Theodore Burton of Ohio, who favored the bill, pointed to the expediency of this measure as well as the necessity for a more comprehensive measure. "The time is coming," he said, "when that general principle [of currency issue commensurate with the volume of business] is going to be adopted," either through a central bank or by other means. The trouble with the emergency currency bill, he thought, was "that it would tend to perpetuate this present system of rigidity, in which there is no flexibility of the currency."[8]

The bill agreed to in conference passed the House 166 to 140. It then went to the Senate where it was met by a filibuster headed by Robert La-Follette of Wisconsin. LaFollette's harangue was more a protest than a serious effort to block ultimate passage. Although he spoke for eighteen hours against the bill and issued thirty-six calls for quorums, he said nothing momentous. His main criticism of the bill was the evil effect of allowing railroad bonds to act indirectly as a basis for the issue of currency.[9]

Thomas Gore of Oklahoma, who also opposed the concept of emergency currency, ridiculed such issues as "electroscoot" currency after an imaginary railway line between New York and San Francisco by which passengers would arrive in San Francisco two hours *before* they embarked in New York. This electroscoot currency, he said, "a carload or two of this 'V and A' panic panacea—will be shipped to San Francisco and will arrive two hours before the panic [initiated in New York] and will prevent the panic."[10]

Gore had some criticism of the distribution of treasury balances to move the crops in 1908. The secretary, he stated, "deposited $34 million in the 'Southern and Western' State of New York, and . . . 62 cents to the great State [of Missouri]."[11] His criticism demonstrated the invidious feelings that could immediately arise over disposition of government largess at the discretion of government officials. It appeared to Gore that treasury policy was confined to helping the wealthy and influential eastern region of the country. The balances so deposited might, of course, have done more financial good for Oklahoma and Missouri by being placed in New York than by being deposited in Kansas City or Tulsa, but this possibility could never be apparent to provincial legislators, however tolerant they otherwise might be of their wealthier neighbors.

The Senate passed the conference version of the bill 43 to 22.[12] The bill was signed by President Taft the same day.

The Aldrich-Vreeland Act also created the National Monetary Commission.[13] This commission was cochaired by Senator Aldrich and Representative Vreeland and was composed of fifteen other congressmen plus a special assistant, A. Piatt Andrew of Harvard University. Various investigations in monetary economics involving both empirical and institutional studies were farmed out to numerous economists in the United States and in Europe. The commission published twenty-four volumes, many of lasting value.

The final volume included a summary of norms that Aldrich had drawn from the commission's work. His principles for a central banking organization included the following:

1. It should not copy the central banking structures of European institutions "without many material modifications."
2. The American institution should mobilize and centralize reserves.
3. The means for maintaining the central bank's reserve should be its rate of discount.
4. In a period of distress the central bank should follow the Bagehot principle of extending "credit liberally to everyone whose solvency and condition entitles him to receive it." At the same time, it should keep its discount rate high to encourage a gold inflow.
5. The gold reserve should be used to the extent necessary.
6. The central bank should have a monopoly of note issue but be constrained by governmental rules.
7. Its operations should be free of political influences.[14]

The immediate result of the commission's recommendations in Congress was a proposal for a national reserve association. A bill to incorporate such an institution was introduced in the Senate by Senator Burton in December of 1911; President Taft recommended it to Congress at the same time. In his discussion of the matter Taft noted that the National Reserve Association (NRA) would eliminate the "troublesome question" of a central bank. The proposed association, he said, "is a logical out-growth of what is best in our present system, and is, in fact, the fulfill-ment of that system." Bankers would devise and operate the new associa-tion, but it would be subject to some form of governmental supervision.[15]

The president's contention that the National Reserve Association was not a central bank was contradicted in the House by Richard Hobson of Alabama. Hobson cited a "critical analysis by Mr. R. C. Milliken, a mon-etary expert in the Bond Building of this city." Milliken stated in his re-port to Hobson that he could find no difference between the NRA and European central banks; nor, he added, "is there any reasonable excuse for not terming [the NRA] a central bank."[16]

Milliken had several objections to the whole scheme. "It teaches the public two fallacies," he argued. First, because it imposed reserve require-ments, it implied that "the ratio of a bank's resources to its total demand liabilities should be uniform throughout the year." Second, "it gives un-due emphasis to [reserves] thereby detracting from the more important factor—the convertibility and character of the whole of [a bank's] as-sets." He argued that the new institution should discount only bills "is-sued for productive credit arising from real commercial transactions to solvent persons furnishing convertible paper payable at short and fixed periods." He felt that a central bank should be divorced from the banking business in the manner of the Bank of England. The British, he com-mented, "have no kindergartens for bank presidents as is our Treasury Department."[17]

The NRA bill was discussed just once in Congress—by Vreeland—and his discussion was allowed only as a courtesy. Vreeland claimed that "practically all the bankers of the United States [and] all the political economists . . . in the colleges of the United States" approved the measure. The present banking system, he thought, was analogous to a faulty rail-road that would cease operations once every ten years. The dispersion of reserves in the present system, he argued, was an invitation to disaster. Five or six of the larger New York banks currently acted as a central bank, but their commercial nature—their profit motivation in particular —meant that they could not "afford to carry great reserves of from 40 to 60 percent when business is good, in order to release them when business is bad . . . We must have an institution to hold our reserves which is not a money-making institution. The idea of profit must be eliminated from its management."[18]

Vreeland very clearly posed the dilemma and the conflict that accom-panies the creation of a central bank in an economy largely operating on principles of private enterprise and in which a metallic standard regulates the monetary system. If the institution were to keep enough gold reserves to be effective in a crisis, it could not operate in the ordinary sense as a private commercial bank and make normal profits. If it was organized as a hybrid, such as the Bank of England, either its income had to be subsidized by some sort of government bounty or it had to have eleemosynary characteristics. If it was then brought into existence as either a subsidized or a nonprofit institution, its rules for procedure would have to be carefully drawn. Otherwise it would find itself in direct conflict with the corrective adjustments forced by the gold standard, or else it would have to operate in violation of sound commercial banking principles.

No one in this era thought of controverting the gold standard as the secular determinant of the money stock. Gold was to be *the* reserve, though it was to be centralized and economized. The NRA, Vreeland observed, would face a 40 percent gold reserve requirement thus enabling it to create two and one-half times as much bank reserves or notes as the gold it held if the need arose.[19]

The structure of the NRA was to include a central administrative and advisory bureau in Washington and fifteen regional or district branches. The commercial banks in each local community would also congregate into local associations, which would be linked to the regional branches. The NRA would be a bank of banks, and commercial banks would be its owners and stockholders. It would set its discount rate as a matter of policy each week, and it would discount bona fide commercial paper having no more than twenty-eight days to maturity. A basic cadre of NRA notes would supplant existing national bank notes; the rest of the institution's issues would develop from the discounts of commercial paper for its participants. It would have forty-six directors who would be recruited from the several districts. Included in this corps of directors would be the secretaries of agriculture, commerce, labor, and the Treasury, and the comptroller of the currency, plus a governor appointed by the president of the United States and two deputy governors. The plan was approved by the American Bankers Association.

Its spokesmen denied that it was a central bank. "Do I mean," Vreeland asked rhetorically, "that we should bring to life the central bank of Andrew Jackson's time? No," he answered; "We should . . . adapt [central bank principles] to American conditions . . . We must let the bankers run the banking business of the country."[20]

The elections in the fall of 1912 significantly modified the political face of the federal government. The Republican party had held the executive office for fifty-two years, with the exception of the two Cleveland administrations. And Cleveland was in many ways at least as conservative as the Republican executives; his role in the demise of silver showed that. The rift within the Republican party split the Republican vote so that the Democratic candidate, Woodrow Wilson, won the presidency. In addition, both houses of Congress went Democratic. This change meant that no monetary measure sponsored by the Republican party could pass. Lame-duck president Taft recommended the NRA again in his annual message to Congress late in 1912, but his effort was futile. If nothing else, the name of the National Reserve Association had to be changed, and its sponsors had to be Democrats. This mutation was to take place in the Sixty-third Congress.

The bill to create the Federal Reserve system was introduced in the House of Representatives in the late summer of 1913 by the chairman of the House Committee on Banking and Currency, Carter Glass of Virginia. Glass emphasized the large popular demand for "reform" of the "barbarous" national bank system then in operation. His committee, he said, had received thousands of letters plus resolutions passed by hundreds of commercial bodies calling for change. He cited the two major deficiencies of the present system. First, no reserve was available to the banking system at critical times. Second, currency outstanding was based on "the Nation's debt," that is, on government securities, rather than on something that would reflect the variable needs of business, such as the short-term paper of commercial banks. The previous Republican-sponsored measures, the Aldrich-Vreeland Act and the National Reserve Association, Glass stated, were dismissed by his committee because they had been denounced by both the Democratic and the Progressive party platforms, "while the platform of the Republican Party was silent on the subject." The principal objection to the NRA (the Aldrich scheme) was that it was "saturated with monopolistic tendencies" and faced an "absolute lack of adequate governmental control." It fell short of being a central bank, Glass said, only because it did not provide for the transaction of business with the public.[21]

Strangely enough, no institution that looked like a central bank could be considered at this time. A central bank was "monopolistic." It was run by bloodsucking bankers who were given special privileges to soak the poor, keep interest rates up, and conspire with Wall Street speculators to cause panics that were profitable to the speculators and themselves. Glass noted that "great pains were observed and much ingenuity exercised" in the Aldrich bill to avoid the appearance of a central bank.[22]

In lieu of such an unacceptable institution, the Democrats conceived of the Federal Reserve system. Instead of one central bank, the Banking and Currency Committee proposed not less than eight nor more than twelve regional banks. The decision-making process by which this number was derived gives an index of the intellectual construction of the system. First, one central bank located in Washington was politically impossible. Well, if not one bank, then how many? The Republican, conservative, northeastern, pronational bank answer was three or four. This number simply carried over into the new institution the three central reserve cities so defined for the national bank system—New York, Chicago, and St. Louis—and added one for the West Coast in San Francisco. The argument was that a minimum number was needed to mobilize and centralize reserves most effectively.[23] The more populist (provincial) rural element of the Congress proposed one bank for each state, plus one, perhaps, for the District of Columbia and Alaska, a total of forty-eight or fifty.

The argument that seemed to carry the most weight in the determination of the right number was one voiced by John Shafroth of Colorado in the senate debate on the bill. He presented the pragmatic parable of a banker pressed for funds because of a run developing on his bank. A bank subject to such adversity, said Shafroth, should be within "one night's [train] ride of a reserve bank." The president of the stricken bank "could then gather the 30, 60, and 90 day commercial paper he wanted cashed, take the train for the city where the Federal reserve bank is situate [sic], and be able to wire he had cashed sufficient securities to meet the demands of all depositors." Shafroth contrasted this expedient relationship with that of "one central bank located several days' run from many of the interior banks." In addition, he argued, a regional system would preserve the personal relationship between the commercial banker and the reserve banker.[24]

Twelve sounded like a good nonmonopolistic compromise between three or four and forty-eight or fifty, and Shafroth's parable expressed very well the reserve-in-emergency nature of what the legislators were looking for. A practical argument was that twelve reserve banks would just about have adequate endowment for their capital structuring if all national banks were enjoined to enter the system.[25]

Acceptance of a regional association concept was one thing; who was to control it and what would be the vehicle for its operations were others. The coordinating agency, of course, was the Federal Reserve Board. Unlike the bankers who would have directed the NRA, the Federal Reserve Board would be nonprofit. "No financial interest," claimed Carter Glass, "can pervert or control [the board]. It is an altruistic institution, a part of the Government itself, representing the American people, with powers such as no man would dare misuse."[26] One of its powers was to permit or require one Federal Reserve bank to rediscount the paper held by another Federal Reserve bank. In this manner it could mobilize reserves for the whole system if need be. Bankers opposed this provision, reported Glass.

They were perfectly willing, under the Aldrich scheme, to confide this power to [themselves], operating for gain, but are unwilling to

lodge it with the Government of the United States to be used for pa-
triotic purposes under a system devised for the good of the country
. . . It is somewhat analogous to the power exercised for years by the
Secretary of the Treasury alone, when, in times of emergency, he has
withdrawn the Government deposits at will from banks in one part
of the country and transferred them to banks in another part of the
country, . . . the difference being that, whereas the transfers have
heretofore been made to the great money centers for the purpose of
arresting stock-gambling panics, the transfers under this bill, if ever
required at all, will be made to promote legitimate commercial transactions.[27]

Glass's apologia is significant because it uses the treasury policies developed under Shaw as a precedent for anticipated Federal Reserve policy. It does not explain how or why the devil in the form of the secretary
of the Treasury would be transformed into St. Michael and all the angels
when in the form of the Federal Reserve Board.

Glass also invoked the fallacious people-control-it-through-the-gov-
ernment doctrine. The Federal Reserve Board, he said, "is strictly a board
of control . . . doing justice to the banks, but fairly and courageously representing the interests of the people . . . The talk of political control [of
the board] is the expression of a groundless conjecture."[28] Yet he cited no
checks and balances that would prevent the abuses he inveighed against.
Under the NRA plan national bankers in reserve cities would at least
have competed with each other for the reserves of the participating
banks.

H. H. Seldomridge of Colorado expressed a similar opinion. "Who
dares to advocate," he asked, "that the Government should not exercise a
controlling and beneficial influence in regulating the volume and distribution of our currency? The great outstanding merit of this bill is that it
places this great power in the hands of the people."[29]

In another exchange between Alben Barkley of Kentucky and William
Baltz of Illinois, this same relationship between people and government
was assumed.

> MR. BALTZ: If this bill is enacted into law, will it not give the Gov-
> ernment control of the finances?
> MR. BARKLEY: It will, and the Government ought to have the con-
> trol.
> MR. BALTZ: Who is the Government?
> MR. BARKLEY: The Government is the people, and the people act
> through their authorized agents, the chief of whom is the President
> of the United States. [Applause on the Democratic side.][30]

Such bland naiveté demonstrated the strong grip that Populist doctrine
exercised at this time. To defend his point Barkley would have had to

show how the people communicated with the president and by what means the president would then control the finances. Any attempt to define and describe such a process immediately reveals its ludicrous character.

One dissenter from this doctrine was John Shafroth of Colorado, who had also given the rationale for locating regional banks "one night's train ride" from every commercial bank. "Our bill," Shafroth declared, speaking of the Glass-Owen bill, "is framed upon the theory that this is a bank of banks for the purpose of preventing runs on banks . . . We have 25,000 people's banks now. What is the use of turning this into another people's bank? Every national bank in the United States is a people's bank . . . You do not want to mix a bank of banks with a people's bank."[31]

Frank Mondell of Wyoming also threw some cold water on the people-government fallacy. "The people pretty clearly understand nowadays that control through a Government bureau, by political appointees, is not synonymous with control by the people and for the people," he said.[32]

George Norris argued that the Federal Reserve Board consisting of four persons appointed by the president, plus two cabinet officers and the comptroller of the currency, "is made at once a football of partisan politics . . . Our banking and financial system [will] be on edge at every presidential campaign."[33]

Glass was anxious to emphasize the nonpolitical character of the new system even though it was to be people-controlled through the government. "There is no politics in this matter; there can be none," he stated. "[No one] has yet pointed out how any part of this system can be perverted to political uses."[34]

A few months later when the bill was on its final passage through the Senate, some congressmen were still complaining that it was a political bill. James Lewis of Illinois took the bull by the horns. "What does my distinguished friend expect in a political government?" he asked, addressing his rhetorical question to one of the complainers. "The senator is right. The bill is political, political to the extent that it voices the political ideas of the people of this country, political in that it expresses in legislation the platform of the [Democratic party] . . . All things must be guided, honorable sir. To some men each system must be intrusted."[35]

All sides seemed to understand that some group of mortals had to control the banking and monetary system. In practice only two groups could possibly exercise this control—the banks or the government—and the sentiment was overwhelmingly in favor of the government. Bankers could not be trusted, neither their competence nor their integrity, claimed Rufus Hardy of Texas. The very fact that the government deposited its fiscal revenues in banks, he continued, argued for government control.[36] "It is the business of Government," added William E. Borah of Idaho in the Senate, "to provide a sound and sufficient volume of currency and money upon which to do the business of the country."[37]

Hardy minimized the powers of the Federal Reserve Board. "A central bank, so much desired by Wall Street," he said, [would have] powers for evil which the Board does not have." He then enumerated the powers the board did not have. It could not loan, earn, own, or borrow one dollar. It could not finance an enterprise. It could not finance a candidate or a campaign.[38] He did not say that the board could not create money or control the money supply.

The opinion of Frank Mondell of Wyoming was not so sanguine.

> The Federal Reserve Board under this bill is an organization of vastly wider power, authority, and control over currency [and] banks . . . than the reserve associations contemplated by the National Monetary Commission . . . It is of a character which in practical operation would tend to increase and centralize . . . It will be the most powerful banking institution in all the world . . . In your frantic efforts to escape the bogey man of a central bank, . . . you have come perilously near establishing in the office of the Comptroller of the Currency, under the Secretary of the Treasury, the most powerful banking institution in the world.[39]

In place of undesirable political control, several Congressmen suggested that the reserve system should feature scientific management. This institution, said Everis Hayes of California, should not become "the football of politics. A banking and currency system is a great, complex, scientific, and business proposition." The science in the management of money was to be obtained by the objective discounting of commercial paper. "The only limit to a commercial bank's ability to discount," said Charles Korbly of Indiana, "is the limit to good commercial paper . . . Such paper springs from self-clearing transactions . . . It is the duty [sic] of the banker to discount freely for his customer in a crisis or panic. The only limit . . . is the limit to good commercial paper."[40]

The notion that production creates money is apparent in Korbly's speech. "The possession of reserves in greater or lesser amount does not in the slightest degree increase the ability of the bank to lend," he argued. "It is what is happening to goods and merchandise . . . that causes high discounts . . . The banker no more deals in money because he handles money," he continued, "than grocers or druggists . . . A bank deals in debts, . . . notes and bills of exchange." Once a banker knew that the rediscounting privilege would be refused on illiquid paper, he would be anxious to confine his loans to paper that he would have no difficulty rediscounting in time of trouble. "The whole purpose of the Federal Reserve Act," he concluded, "is to enforce this practice."[41]

The scientific rationale of federal Reserve policy centered on this

theory of money and credit. To get the necessary elasticity in the monetary system, commercial banks would bring their eligible paper to the
regional reserve banks for rediscount. This paper, if truly eligible, would
have arisen by loans that were the basis for the generation or marketing
of new goods and services. Thus new products would indirectly create
new money. So long as commercial and reserve banks discounted or re-
discounted only eligible paper, any increase in the quantity of credit
would be matched by an increase in the quantity of goods, and no danger
of too much money could arise. The necessity for bankers to extend
credit on good loans would likewise prevent too little money in the system.

The only theoretical question remaining concerned the definition of
eligible. It meant short-term, but how short? It excluded investment
(long-term) loans and certainly speculative loans (those without real collateral). But what did it include? Not until late in the debates did Congress face this question, probably because a definition seemed so intuitively obvious. When its real meaning was finally scrutinized, the term
seemed to imply the need for a scientific authority that was not presently
available in the banking system or Congress, but would spring fully qualified from the Federal Reserve Board after it was appointed. The possibility of such a discovery seemed remote after John Weeks of Massachusetts
pointed out that he had "tried to get 12 or 15 banking men" to define
commercial paper and not one of them could do it.[42] How the board
would obtain the expertise to handle this matter later was a question no
one tried to answer.

Because of doubt about the definition of *eligible* and the discretion necessarily implied by its interpretation, legislators favoring the Hitchcock
bill over the Glass-Owen version wanted to make discounting by the reserve banks a right rather than a privilege. To prevent "gross discrimina-
tion . . . and great favoritism," said Hitchcock in his rebuttal to Owen,
every member bank should "as a matter of right . . . have the privilege of
discounting eligible paper." This right was to be limited to twice a member bank's capital stock.[43] A similar view was given by Knute Nelson of
Minnesota. Nelson believed that eligibility was capable of rigorous definition. If so, then no excuse could be made for not discounting all eligible
paper; and discounting should be a routine right rather than a privilege
subject to the discretion of a board. Discretion by the board and the reserve banks, Nelson added, was unnecessary and undesirable.[44] The eligibility doctrine, as he conceived it, was intimately tied to the elasticity
principle. Only short-term paper, generated by the production of real
goods and services, was eligible, and it was this paper that would give
elasticity to the system. "Short-time commercial paper, which is liquid
and collects itself [provides] a natural system of elasticity," he concluded.[45]

Another senator, Porter McCumber of North Dakota, warned that the currency might be "stretched out three feet and come back only one foot," implying the possibility of chronic inflation. How, he asked, was currency to be contracted after it had been expanded?[46] Robert Owen, the manager of the bill in the Senate, answered. The currency would have been expanded by the discounting of bona fide commercial paper, he said. When the bills were liquidated, the currency would be contracted automatically as the Federal Reserve notes went out of circulation. This argument again implied that physical output generated money.[47]

The concept of the new system most legislators wanted to see embodied in law was the Federal Reserve as a public utility. Everis Hayes of California said that the new institution would provide "public control over the finances . . . similar to the control that is now exercised over the interstate commerce of the country through the Interstate Commerce Commission. [Applause on the Democratic side.]"[48] Some Congressmen extended the idea of public utility and argued that the Federal Reserve should "give the borrowing public a stable and uniform low rate of interest," in the same way that the ICC established low freight rates.[49]

This norm was clearly at odds with the Bagehot principle, which was invoked by name as a guide for policy in the new system by Theodore Burton of Ohio. The Bagehot doctrine argued that the central bank should lend freely in a crisis at a high rate of interest in order to stay the panic and to prevent depletion of the central bank's gold reserve.[50] The high-rate-of-interest doctrine implied the traditional wisdom of the time: that the central bank rate of interest should be kept higher than the market rate.[51] The Federal Reserve Board in Washington, Hitchcock observed, could also order the reserve banks to raise discount rates in order to "check the excessive inflation of bank credit."[52]

Complementary to the public-utility notion was the idea that the board of governors could operate as a "supreme court of American finance."[53] The men chosen for the board, said John Weeks of Massachusetts, should be "as representative and of general recognized capacity in the business world as are appointees to the Supreme Court in the legal world."[54]

L. C. Dyer of Missouri disputed this idealized view of the new system. In doing so he cited a lengthy report from the St. Louis Clearing House Association of bankers. This report noted that appointees to the Federal Reserve Board would not be like judges on the Supreme Court. Justices were appointed for life and therefore were not subject (supposedly) to political whims. Justices had been trained specifically for a profession that was compatible with a judgeship, whereas the new board was proscribed from including a stockholder or an officer of any banking institution. Nor would the Federal Reserve system be similar to the ICC, the report stated, because the ICC had no power to divert assets from one railroad company to another in the fashion that one reserve bank might be commanded to discount the paper of another reserve bank.[55]

Congressmen seemed to want an objective, scientific, disinterested, nonpolitical organization. They wanted the Treasury Department out of policymaking, even if the secretary would have to serve as an ex officio member of the board.[56] And they did not want commercial bankers running the new system, since such a liason would involve a conflict of interests. Too lenient a discounting policy would amount to nothing more than a special interest subsidy for member banks. "Banks should have no more to do with the issue and control of public currency," said Finley Gray of Indiana, "than an elevator company should have to control the supply and distribution of grain . . . [Bankers] are not better nor more to be trusted in serving the public welfare as against their own private interests than other men. Bankers should be prohibited from any association at all with the Board."[57] While most congressmen agreed with this view, they believed that appointees to the board should have had banking experience.[58]

With all the constraints offered by the legislators, the only eligible appointees would have been a group of vestal virgins. It was a lot easier to imagine goals to which the institution could aspire than it was to fashion politically a machine that would function within the desired bounds and accomplish everyone's well-understood objectives.

The House bill passed September 18, 1913, by a vote of 299 to 68. One of the last issues discussed before passage was the propriety of the clause that stated, "Nothing in this act . . . shall be considered to repeal the parity provisions contained in an act approved March 14, 1900," that is, the Gold Standard Act of 1900. Necessary or not, it was left in as a precaution to affirm the priority of the gold standard in determining the money supply. The Federal Reserve system was not to serve as a substitute or surrogate for gold.[59]

The House bill went to the Senate, where it was worked over in the Committee on Banking and Currency for several weeks and reported out on October 8. The manager of the Senate bill was Robert Owen of Oklahoma, while the leader of the opposition was Gilbert Hitchcock of Nebraska. Owen was a Democrat and chairman of the committee that reported out the bill. Hitchcock was also a Democrat and a member of the committee; but he clustered around himself the conservative Republican contingent that wanted a central bank in the mode of the aborted NRA or Aldrich scheme. The bill that was reported out of committee was printed in three columns: the Glass (House) version, the Owen (Senate majority) version, and the Hitchcock version.[60]

The early stages of the Senate debate included discussions of the same issues that had been so tediously worked over in the House. One issue largely neglected by the House was the reserve requirement for Federal Reserve banks. Both the Glass and Owen bills called for reserves of 33⅓ percent against all demand obligations—Federal Reserve notes outstanding and member bank reserves or deposit accounts. Hitchcock's group wanted 45 percent against notes and 35 percent against member bank deposits.[61]

With his higher reserve requirements and 100 percent collateral of "good commercial paper," Hitchcock felt secure in arguing again for the right of member banks to discount. "We have given the right to each [member] bank to secure a discount of paper to a certain extent," he stated. "Each reserve bank is a public utility and responding to the natural demands of business." He repeatedly emphasized that the right to discount denied the necessity for any discretion by the board or reserve banks. To allow such discretion, he cautioned, "is to provide for possible inflation."[62]

The 45 percent gold reserve against Federal Reserve notes was derived from the statutory requirement that the Treasury maintain a gold reserve of $150 million against outstanding United States notes, which had been frozen at $346.7 million.[63] These figures imply a ratio of 43.3 percent. The reserve against notes was to be a gold reserve, not other "lawful money," for example, silver. Hitchcock expressed the prevailing feelings of all sides: "We do not think that the Government of the United States in issuing its obligations, its promises to pay, should reserve the right to pay their [sic] obligations in other obligations."[64]

This same sentiment prevented Federal Reserve notes from becoming legal reserves of member banks. The Owen bill at first incorporated this indulgence on the grounds that all the state banks used national bank notes as reserves. Senator Burton, however, protested vehemently. National banks and Federal Reserve banks, he pointed out, would be "in the same system," a relationship unlike that between national and state banks. The new federal combination of national banks and Federal Reserve banks would therefore be using their own debts as reserves, a highly inflationary arrangement.[65]

The proscription of Federal Reserve notes as reserves for member banks found more arguments and many more supporters. Already accepted was the provision that one Federal Reserve bank could not pay out the notes of another Federal Reserve bank but had to return them to the bank of issue. Hitchcock made the nonsequitur argument that if a reserve bank had to return a Federal Reserve note to its source, "it is ten thousand times more important to require the member banks to do so." The use of Federal Reserve notes as reserves, he continued, would encourage the displacement of gold to foreign countries.[66] He could argue this way only by conceiving of Federal Reserve banks as banks rather than as parts of a central banking system. If currency outstanding was that volatile, reserve accounts at regional reserve banks would be even more inflammatory.

A similar argument was presented by Albert Cummins of Iowa in response to a question on the difference between reserve requirements for currency and demand deposits. A check, Cummins observed, stays in existence only two or three days before redemption, while currency may have a tenure of five years. Therefore (non sequitur again) currency requires a larger reserve.[67] No one asked Cummins why the checkbook balance against which the check was drawn would necessarily be liquidated instead of being transferred to another account.

Several people argued that the commercial paper that gave rise to the issue of Federal Reserve notes was the redeeming medium. The member bank, said John Williams of Mississippi, would get lawful money—gold, greenbacks, or Federal Reserve notes—and pay off its debt to the Federal Reserve bank. So the note lived and died as commercial paper was created and then paid off.[68]

The issue of Federal Reserve notes as reserves triggered the question of potential inflation by the new institution. The appearance of this question so late in the debate may seem odd, but it is largely explained by the wide acceptance of the commodity theory of money: the belief that the money supply was generated in reaction to the supply of products and could not be oversupplied if issued on the basis of real bills in response to legitimate demands by responsible businessmen and bankers. "How do checks and bills come into existence?" asked Charles Korbly of Indiana. "They are the offspring of sales."[69]

Once the question of reserve requirements for Federal Reserve banks and the discounting machinery by which Federal Reserve notes would be issued came under detailed scrutiny, some congressmen had doubts about the objective automaticity of the new system. Elihu Root of New York, for example, observed that the Federal Reserve Board faced "no limit whatever upon the quantity of notes that may be issued," and the reserve banks were similarly unconstrained in their discounting procedures.[70]

Root complemented this criticism with a sophisticated insight into the instability that could be generated by a central bank during a business boom. He warned against loans made "upon security that is good until the time comes when, through a process of inflation, we reach a situation in which no security is good." Then "the standards which are applied in the exercise of that kind of judgment [for discounting] become modified by the optimism of the hour and grow less and less effective in checking the expansion of business."[71]

This statement exposes the instability inherent in real-bills policy. Although Root discussed only the potential magnification of a boom into an inflation, the same argument holds for a downturn and its development into a depression. Once business turns sour—for whatever reason —all loans begin to look bad. Monetary experience between 1929 and 1933 can largely be accounted for by the chameleonlike nature of commercial paper and the orthodox commercial banker views harbored by Federal Reserve authorities.

Another critic in the Senate, Porter McCumber of North Dakota, remarked that only since Root's speech on December 13, two months after the bill was first debated in the House, did the possibility of inflation by the new institution become an issue. "Inflation," he said, "is not elasticity . . . A currency whose expansion is not limited by the act of law creating it, but by the will or discretion of a board, will always result in general inflation." Political pressure on the Federal Reserve Board after notes had been expanded would prevent contraction, McCumber explained; and so, he argued, all Federal Reserve notes should be taxed.[72]

The Democratic sponsors of the bill were quick to defend it against the charges of inflation. Owen argued that the reserve board could set the discount rate at a level that would discourage borrowing.[73] Furthermore, he said, Federal Reserve notes are not a fiat currency because they "are secured by commercial bills of a highly qualified class."[74]

John Williams of Mississippi supplemented Owen's arguments. The board has "no power to initiate, to compel or to consummate any inflation whatsoever. [It has] a power . . . to compel contraction . . . either by raising the interest rate or by refusing its approval to issue of the paper currency by the reserve banks."[75] Williams claimed that the character of appointees to the Federal Reserve Board would prevent the fiat issue of paper currency (sic).[76] He thus accepted the vestal virgin image for the reserve board.

Although no one doubted that the Federal Reserve Act would pass, many controversial features could have been resolved either way, especially if the Democratic caucus had not been so cohesive. As it was, the Glass-Owen bill commanded only a marginal majority on most points. The "right" to discount, for example, which was presented as an amendment by Benjamin Bristow in lieu of "privilege," lost only 31 to 37.[77]

The opposition tried to increase the Federal Reserve banks' reserve requirements to 45 percent against notes and 35 percent against deposits of member banks from a flat 33⅓ percent overall. This amendment lost by a narrow margin, 39 to 42.[78] In the conference to reconcile House and Senate versions of the bill, the majority yielded on this point; so the final reserve requirements became 40 percent and 35 percent, respectively.

The bill included a provision allowing Federal Reserve banks to incur deficient reserves with the penalty of a graduated tax on the deficiency.

This issue was subjected to much discussion in both houses of Congress, because it was seen as a means for obtaining flexibility in a crisis. In defending this provision, Owen observed that Parliament had permitted the Bank of England a similar indulgence on three occasions so that the Bank could issue notes which would stop panics.[79] Without such an escape route, the gold reserve exerted a rigid legal limit on the issue of notes and the expansion of bank credit. With it, the gold reserve could be used to provide some flexibility to currency and reserve accounts. So it stayed in, but the reserve board never used this power.

Theodore Burton then moved to strike out the use of Federal Reserve notes as legal reserves for member banks on the grounds that it posed the threat of inflation. His amendment lost by another close vote, 37 to 40; a two-vote swing would have carried it.[80] This proposal was taken into account in the House-Senate conference; the final bill in fact prohibited the use of Federal Reserve notes as eligible reserves for member banks.[81]

The bill passed in the Senate 54 to 34.[82] It then went back to the House where the Senate amendments were disagreed to 295 to 59. Both houses agreed on a conference, and conferees were duly appointed.

At first the conferees seemed to face a long negotiation in order to get an acceptable bill. As late as December 20 Carter Glass stated flatly, "There is no prospect at all of an immediate agreement." However, the conferees worked hard over the ensuing weekend and came up with a conference report on December 22. The compromise removed the secretary of agriculture from the board and stated that in any conflict of powers with the Treasury Department, "such powers shall be exercised subject to the supervision and control of the Secretary."[83] Somehow, the secretary of the Treasury could never be finessed in the practical conduct of monetary policy.

The minority against the bill in the Senate complained that they had received little satisfaction in the committee's deliberations, but as Shafroth observed, irreconcilable differences existed over certain provisions. The Democrats had condemned the whole concept of a central bank, while every Republican member of the committee had announced his support for it. These Republican views could not be tolerated, for the Democrats were not about to create a central bank![84]

One provision often discussed but not included in the final bill was a deposit insurance plan whereby part of the profits of the reserve banks would be put into a fund to guarantee deposits of member banks. It was thrown out in the conference, reported Carter Glass, because "if bank depositors are to be guaranteed, it should be at the expense of banks not of the United States Government. [Applause.]"[85]

In his benediction on the passage of the bill, Glass recounted the means by which inflation would be checked or guarded against: "First, by the limited supply of gold; second, by the limited amount of short-time commercial paper; third, by the banking discretion of the individual bank; fourth, by the banking discretion of the regional reserve bank; fifth, by the banking discretion of the Federal Reserve Board."[86] This list of safeguards seems to prove too much as well as to include a lot of discretion. It even implies a bias toward contraction. But it does not include scientific objectivity to determine the system's money supply.

The compromise bill passed the House 298 to 60 and the Senate 43 to 25. Many of the Republicans and other dissenters who had objected to specific provisions voted for the final bill.[87]

What kind of institution did Congress think it had created? What kind of institution did it create? Opinions on the first question were as diverse as the makeup of Congress itself; data bearing on the second question may be obtained only from empirical evidence of the period from 1913 to the present, a time span not covered in this study.

One conclusion is certain: The coalition majority that wrote the bill for the new system claimed it was not creating a central bank. It argued that it was creating a group of autonomous regional reserve banks. No matter what was claimed, the Federal Reserve banks compose a central banking system. Gilbert Hitchcock, not a member of the majority, emphasized this fact in the Senate. "The central bank," he said, "does not consist of a vault. The central bank does not consist of a mass of money . . . The central bank consists of central control, and that is provided in this bill. The control is central [in the Federal Reserve Board]; and when you get your control centralized you have a central bank."[88]

A second feature of the new institution on which both its promoters and its opponents implicitly agreed was its scope. The Federal Reserve system was certainly not intended to usurp the functions of the gold standard and become the omnipotent central bank that it now is. It was constructed only to promote form-seasonal elasticity in the economy's money supply, and it was to do so on the basis of bona fide, self-liquidating, short-term commercial loans, what have come to be called real bills.[89] In general, most congressmen saw the economy's real product generating appropriate changes in the money supply through this medium. The Federal Reserve system was simply a formalized scheme for carrying out the process.

The new institution was seen as a regulatory public utility. It was to regulate interest rates and to supervise banking. The statutory 6 percent return paid to the commercial bank members who held stock in the twelve reserve banks reflected this idea. This arrangement, however, is contradictory. Since the commercial banks received the dividends, the twelve reserve banks should have been regarded as the public utility and the Federal Reserve Board as the regulatory body. But the twelve banks were supposed to be the autonomous regulators as well, and they could not be both the income-earning utility and the regulators of the commercial banking system.

The reserve banks were intended to act as a clearinghouse system for their members. Robert Owen confirmed in the Senate that the new system evolved from the "clearance-house associations of the United States. This bill, for the most part, is merely putting into legal shape that which hitherto has been illegally done."[90] Everis Hayes of California remarked that he would have preferred to see "the present clearing-house associations [enlarged and controlled] under proper governmental regulation so as to embrace all the banks, and intrust to such associations the duty of supplying to the people and business interests the elastic currency which is needed."[91]

The issue of clearinghouse certificates during past crises had been the response of private enterprise to an increased demand for high-powered money when some of the real high-powered money was either exported or hoarded. The Federal Reserve system was an attempt to put this practice on an official basis and to insure that the high-powered money was forthcoming by a deliberate and conscious act of policy. Congressmen believed that contrived policy of this sort implied greater certainty than similar results that might be obtained from the profit-seeking actions of commercial bankers.

While policy decisions of government may be more decisive than banker or business decisions based on somebody's bread and butter, they are not more certain to be the right decisions. Other factors determine the propriety and correctness of policy: the validity of the theory supporting the policy; political factors that may have nothing to do with the technical correctness of policy; and the self-interest of policymakers. When these factors are taken into account, discretionary policy does not show a better record than profit-seeking market actions.

Much congressional debate dwelt on the exercise of power in the new system. Those who thought the reserve board would be in control, as Hitchcock did, saw the new institution as a central bank. Others, such as Owen and Shafroth, believed that they had created a bank of banks, one in which the reserve banks (within limits) would be servants of the member banks, while government regulation would be minimal. "Dealing with the amount of money, the paper to be discounted," Shafroth said, "is not a matter in which the Government can be interested." He maintained that the self-interest of bankers would be paramount in a system owned by them, and he argued that bankers should be directors of the reserve banks, but should not be on the reserve board.[92]

Some congressmen believed the new system would create the kind of organization that the antitrust laws were supposed to prevent. "This act," said Charles A. Lindbergh, Sr., of Minnesota, "establishes the most gigantic trust on earth, such as the Sherman Antitrust Act would dissolve if Congress did not by this act expressly create what by that act it prohibited."[93] This view contradicted the belief that the new institution was analogous to the Interstate Commerce Commission.

Benjamin Bristow voiced a criticism similar to Lindbergh's. The bill, he said, "creates a great, top-heavy, organization . . . to provide a flexible currency. A few simple amendments to the Aldrich-Vreeland bill would have accomplished that purpose."[94]

Finally, was creation of the Federal Reserve system the result of a great popular democratic movement? No, answered George McLean of Connecticut. "The present haste to organize the banking system of the country is purely political. There is not one man in ten thousand who cares anything about the subject . . . There is not one man in ten thousand who knows anything about principles or details of banking, and his ignorance in this regard is as natural and excusable as his ignorance of the Chinese language. If I am not mistaken, the alleged popular demand and need for this bill . . . are born of wishes, earnest, deep, and laudable, but purely political in their nature and of very doubtful fulfillment."[95]

McLean's statement, though true, is not the whole truth. Bankers wanted such an institution, particularly one that would subsidize some of their risks by standing ready to discount their commercial paper. But they wanted such an agency only if they could control it; they did not want a system set up by a hostile Congress that would proscribe their activities. Since banking involves technical matters familiar only to bankers, it was natural for bankers to be in charge of the central bank's operations even though central banking and commercial banking are based on some fundamentally contrary doctrines.[96]

The blind men touched the elephant and each one received a different impression of the animal's physical structure. In the case of the Federal Reserve system the blind men constructed a machine. Their views of what they had created were as diverse as the impressions of the men who touched the elephant. They did not know what they had done. As Lindbergh concluded when he voted nay on final passage: "Congress is the greatest of humbugs."[97]

14 Emergence of Central Banking Doctrine: Recapitulation

You set up a National Bank to watch the other banks; but who is to watch the watcher? Where there is but one watchman in a city, albeit the same be a most "grave and ancient watchman," yet does it generally happen, that he betaketh himself soon after twilight to the watch-house, and there most quietly and securely sleepeth out his watch, till his coat be stolen, or the city is set on fire with the candle from his own lanthorn. When it is well burning, and the engines are already at work, he opens his eyes at last, and bawls fire! as lustily as though he had been the first to make the discovery.

Is it not far better to dismiss the watchman, and so to arrange things that it shall be for the interest of the rogues to watch and betray each other's roguery. (Richard Hildreth, *History of Banks*, 1837)

A pecuniary economy may realize four stages of monetary control: (1) No control at all; that is, a policy of complete laissez faire with respect to money. (2) A metallic standard system in which the government fixes the value of the unit of account in terms of a precious metal and then does nothing more. (3) A metallic standard system on which is superimposed a central banking institution that is strictly limited to short-run, seasonal policies so that it can in no way usurp the functions of the metallic standard. (4) A central banking institution standing by itself with complete control over the supply of money entering the economic system.

In the first stage money is created by the decisions of private individuals, whether bankers, barbers, or blacksmiths. The money created may be derived from precious metals or other appropriate commodities, or it may be a token and ledger-credit system. Precious metal currency is simple because the unit of money is itself the redeeming agent; that is, the currency does not require an act of redemption to secure its value, and it thus avoids some of the costs of token and ledger-credit moneys. Metallic currency has other drawbacks—its unit cost as money, the cost of transporting it for redemption, depreciation due to wear and tear—that may be greater than the redemption costs of fiduciary money. Token and ledger-credit moneys must be redeemable if they are to remain acceptable as money. The redeeming agent can be any medium that is mutually agreeable to both the issuer and the acceptor of the money. It need not be a precious metal; it may be anything that has commonly recognized market value.[1]

A monetary system of some sort would surely evolve in a completely free economy for the same reason that round wheels would appear in the industrial system. Both money and wheels greatly reduce the real costs that would be incurred without them. Since everyone's self-interest is better served by a good monetary system than by a bad one, the chances are also very high that repudiation and fraud, as well as depression and inflation, would be minimized under a completely free system.[2] Examples of this kind of system tried strictly on libertarian terms are rare, although the monetary system in the prisoner-of-war camp described by Radford may qualify.[3]

Most political systems never experience this first stage but begin with the second. In the second stage the government specifies that a certain item shall be legal tender, but it takes no further active part either as a supplier or as a demander of the designated money.[4] Determination of the legal tender commodity is itself a major intervention of government. It necessarily implies that private persons must accept the specified item as payment for debt. It thus subjects the monetary system to the coercive power of government, and it implies specification of the unit of account in terms of the quantity of the legal tender medium. A system in which a legal tender medium is imposed without some legal definition of the monetary value of the medium is conceptually possible but unrealistic.

Probably any monetary system operating under a specie standard would enter the third stage of control more or less naturally. In this stage a governmental or quasi-governmental institution issues media of exchange other than the items designated as legal tender; that is, the monetary system becomes mixed. Nineteenth-century systems in the United States and England are good examples of this development. In both countries gold and silver originally provided the monetary base for ordinary bank currency and deposits. Then, in the United States, Treasury currency appeared. It was at first a temporary, partial legal tender, interest-bearing claim on the federal government; after the Civil War it became a permanent, full legal tender, non-interest-bearing currency.

England's experience was slightly different. The crown issued exchequer bills similar to United States treasury notes, but the Bank of England also issued Bank of England notes that became a much more conventional item in the monetary fabric. These notes were used as currency and as reserves by English commercial banks. The Bank of England thus assumed the characteristics of a central bank somewhat earlier than any of the quasi-central banking institutions in the United States. But by 1914 the monetary systems of both countries included currency-issuing central banks whose policies, while deliberate and purposeful, were rigorously constrained by the rules of the operational gold standard.

The fourth stage of monetary control appears when the rules of the self-regulating metallic standard are abandoned so that the central bank has complete discretion over the quantity of money entering the monetary system. This stage may include several substages; abandonment of metallic standard rules may be piecemeal. Since central bank dominance was not reached in England or the United States until long after 1914, I refer to it here only to indicate its existence. The ultimate metamorphosis of central banking has little to do with its origins.

Metallic standards do not require central banks or other forms of governmental intervention. Because such systems are self-regulating, intellectual resources devoted to the behavior of money and to the norms for monetary policy are usually minimal. The system requires attention only when it has been rendered inoperative by an excess issue of some kind of governmental paper money. The paper money raises all prices and tends to raise the market price of the monetary metal—say, gold—as well. Ultimately, the market price of gold separates from the mint price and a gold premium appears.

The most notorious and long-tenured departure of the English monetary system from its specie base occurred during the Napoleonic Wars when bullion payments by the Bank of England were restricted (1797-1821) by act of Parliament. The paper currency of the bank was not at first unduly overissued; the government adopted the restriction policy in 1797 in anticipation of trouble. Once freed from the discipline of having to convert its notes into specie and having only the real-bills doctrine to govern its actions, even as staid an organization as the Bank of England eventually issued enough paper currency to increase prices substantially.[5]

The displacement of specie with paper money in England after 1797 did not provoke any great theories of policy control for some years. One reason was that the Bank of England did not abuse the largess granted it by Parliament. Its new powers appeared temporary both to the bank and to government officials—an expedient to be endured (or enjoyed) only for a limited time. But when the tenure of indulgence was extended, the sense of inhibition waned, and so did the anticipation of an early return to specie payments. Contemporary inquiry then turned to fundamental monetary questions. How could the inflation have occurred in the first place? How should an inconvertible paper currency be managed? It was to this latter question that Henry Thornton made a significant intellectual contribution in the early nineteenth century.[6]

By the time Thornton wrote, the Bank of England was the prototype of hybrid central banks. It carried on a private banking business for profit, and it acted as a bank for the government. Its public feature—its responsibility to make payments for the English government on demand—meant that it had to maintain a sizable coin reserve. It had become, in Thornton's words, "a reservoir of gold to which private banks [could]

resort with little difficulty . . . for the supply of their several necessities."
But it had no other source to which it could turn "for a supply of guineas
proportioned to its wants in the same manner."[7] It was a reserve-holding
institution, and this inadvertently attained role gave it its central banking
potential.

Thornton did not apply the label *central bank* to the Bank of England.
He first defined it as a public bank, a public servant, "completely subject
to [the public] interest." In another context he noted its commercial character. "The Bank of England," he wrote, "like every other mercantile
establishment, carries on its business on such principles as will produce a
profit."[8] Its public character, he thought, should expand at a time of
alarm or panic into a policymaking role. It should become what is now
known as a central bank.

A public bank—one that acted as a fiscal agent for the government—
could also function as a commercial bank; but a central bank that was
also a profit-seeking mercantile corporation would have difficulty. A
central bank must expand loans and discounts—extend its accommodation—even in the face of declining commercial confidence and business
activity, while a commercial bank does just the opposite. The conflict between these two roles was made apparent in Thornton's comment about
the bank's activities during one of "the late seasons of alarm." By restricting its notes during the panic, Thornton wrote, the bank "aggravated,
perhaps, rather than lessened, the demand upon itself for guineas . . . It is
clear, at least, that it did not . . . succeed by the diminution of its notes in
curing the evil which it thus aimed to remedy."[9]

The directors of the Bank of England talked and behaved as though the
bank were exclusively commercial and public. When a crisis threatened,
they could then justify reductions of their paper currency liabilities according to established commercial banking tradition.

As a detached and disinterested observer, Thornton could suggest that
they should expand rather than contract their outstanding paper currency at such times. That "the paramount duty of the Bank of England
[is] to diminish its notes, in some sort of regular proportion to that diminution which it experiences in gold," he advised, "is . . . an idea which is
merely rhetoric." He admitted the necessity for long-run restriction of
notes outstanding to protect the coin reserve. But in the short run, when
the panic itself was the immediate problem, he found several reasons for
increasing paper money issues. The first reason was to check the alarm.
Since Bank of England notes acted as reserves for the London banks,
their maintenance was essential to promote confidence. Once a panic
gained headway, restriction of Bank notes by the bank would lead to an
insatiable demand for gold.[10]

The second reason for maintaining moderate note issues was to prevent a contraction that might hurt production and income more than it would inhibit spending. If output fell more than prices, the crisis would be aggravated. Lags in the effects of policy would also contribute to this undesirable consequence.[11]

At this stage in his argument Thornton specified explicitly the norm that defines a central bank. Gold, he observed, might well be drawn out of the country due to an unfavorable balance of trade. But the Bank of England for a time and to a certain extent, he thought, should permit this condition to continue even though the gold leaving the country would be "drawn out of its own coffers: and it must, in that case, necessarily increase its loans [and notes] to the same extent to which its gold is diminished."[12] Only a central bank could act this way; a commercial bank would have to do just the opposite.

Thornton's summary of central bank doctrine specified five principles for Bank of England policy:

1. Limit the total amount of paper issued by credit rationing, or by what could be called the "hard look" loan. (Here it is *this* time; but watch your accounts closely for there might not be enough to go around next time.)
2. Let the sum of bank notes in circulation "vibrate only within certain limits."
3. Allow a slow and cautious extension of paper currency as the general trade of the kingdom increases.
4. Allow a temporary increase in currency "in the event of any extraordinary alarm or difficulty, as the best means of preventing a great *demand* at home for guineas."
5. However, "lean to the side of diminution, in the case of gold going abroad, and of the general exchanges continuing long unfavorable."[13]

Thornton's extensive prescriptions did something that had not been done up to this time. They answered in some detail the question: What could be the role of a central bank operating within the framework of a specie standard? Any answer except "nothing" had to modify the notion of exclusive control by a self-regulating specie standard. Thornton's principles centered around the desirable results that could be expected from issues of paper money to alleviate short-term stress in financial markets, even though he recognized the traditional wisdom and practical necessity of following the rule of the gold standard in the long run.

The United States was subjected during the War of 1812 to the same kind of paper money inflation that England experienced throughout the Napoleonic Wars. The paper money in the United States was issued by the federal government rather than by a public bank; but both English and

American notes were tenders for all debts and payments to and from the government. The American experience covered a shorter period of time; all the paper money was issued before 1815, and all of it was withdrawn by 1817. During the contraction that followed the inflation, the economy went through all the usual withdrawal symptoms—falling prices, general liquidation, and unemployment.[14]

Resumption of specie payments in the United States occurred in 1819. Just when it was all but accomplished, Congress sent a resolution to the secretary of the Treasury, William H. Crawford, asking for his opinions on norms for the monetary system. Crawford, like most nineteenth-century policymakers, regarded a mixed currency as a pragmatic necessity. The paper money, he noted, was very much in existence and could only be replaced by "the delivery [from foreign countries] of an equal amount of gold or silver." Such an event was not likely. But if the banks judiciously extended paper money based on specie, a workable mixed-currency system could be maintained. Government issues of paper money, Crawford thought, had to be rejected because he doubted "whether a sovereign power over the coinage necessarily gives the right to establish a paper currency." A reasonable doubt of its constitutionality would mar the most ingenious paper-money system. Specie, he stated, tended to preserve a greater uniformity of value than any other commodity and was recommended by "the facility with which it returns to that value, whenever, by temporary causes, that uniformity has been interrupted."[15]

Crawford had read Thornton and was well informed on the monetary experience of England. He attributed England's inflation to the "will of nearly four hundred banks . . . when released from all restraint against excessive issues." He dismissed the excessive issues of treasury notes in the United States by means of outrageous taxonomy: "By the term currency," he wrote, meaning to imply metallic money, "the issue of paper by Government, as a financial resource, is excluded [sic]."[16] In other words, the late issues of treasury notes had not been currency nor contributed to the inflation just ended! Despite his unwillingness to recognize the fundamental role the Treasury had played in the inflation, Crawford did not make the mistake of casting the new Second Bank of the United States into any kind of regulatory role. A bank-generated inflation had occurred. It had been whipped by an austere fiscal policy. The gold standard was once again operational. And that was that.

Central banking practices of the First and Second Banks of the United States differed somewhat in detail from the operations of the Bank of England, but otherwise the institutions were similar. Whereas the Bank of England regulated the monetary system by extending or contracting accommodation directly to the London bill brokers, the Second Bank of the United States adopted as its primary method of control deliberate regulation over the flow of commercial bank notes that came through its offices. If it wished to retard the progress of loans and investments by the state banks, it presented state bank notes to the banks that had issued them for redemption in specie. If it felt that the pace of business activity was satisfactory, it paid out the state bank notes routinely. If it wanted to speed up financial activity, it encouraged the state banks to go into debt to it. By this last means it actively increased the general stock of money, for its own notes were legal tender for all debts due to and claims on the government and were widely used as bank reserves.[17]

A special feature of Second Bank policy was the means by which it ameliorated the shock of an external gold drain. A change in the exchange rate was its signal for action. When the rate changed, the bank intervened to modify the change by using its own gold, by enlarging its credit with its English correspondents (Baring Brothers), and by tightening accommodations to its customers.[18]

The central banking character of the Second Bank has been well documented by Bray Hammond. "The Bank," he wrote, "performed these functions deliberately and avowedly—with a consciousness of quasi-governmental responsibility and of the need to subordinate profit and private interest to that responsibility."[19] Clearly, Hammond's description fits the necessary condition for central banking—that a regulatory function be conducted consciously and purposefully.

The evidence is conclusive that the Bank of England and the Banks of the United States performed as central banks. But to allow this much is not to confirm or admit that a "quasi-governmental responsibility" was vested in either institution. Indeed, the available evidence suggests that these institutions at their inception were specifically discouraged, if not prohibited, from such activity. They nonetheless became active central banks; and this well-recognized development inspired Jacob Viner in his analysis of Bank of England policy and Hammond in his treatment of Second Bank policy to make the fundamental error of imputing to both institutions central banking charges that were not theirs. Both writers seemed to assume that because these institutions initiated certain central banking activities, some sort of implicit sanction must have been given. Viner, for example, furnished the following judgment: "From about 1800 to about 1860 the Bank of England almost continuously displayed an inexcusable degree of incompetence or unwillingness to fulfill the requirements *which could reasonably be demanded of a central bank.*" Hammond, after quoting Viner's passage approvingly, reviewed the sophisticated policies of the Second Bank after 1825 and observed how crude the Jacksonian program was that destroyed the bank. Without elaboration or substantiation he asserted that the Second Bank faced a central banking responsibility, that Nicholas Biddle, the bank's most famous president, accepted this charge explicitly, and that this duty "was not stumbled upon as in England." Later he provided his only justification for this position. "The Bank," he wrote, "[was] the one effective means of meeting the federal government's responsibility, under the Constitution, for the circulating medium." In other words, if the federal government was going to regulate the value of coin, it had to have a central bank as an enabling agency: "The idea that the Federal Bank regulated the monetary supply in accordance with the Constitution's assignment of powers made no appeal to people who did not see that bank credit was part of the monetary supply, or, if they did see, were unwilling to have it regulated."[20]

Hammond's statement and Viner's similar implication about the Bank of England are subtle misinterpretations. The Constitution says nothing about deliberate regulation of the money supply by any institution; it says nothing at all about money, except that Congress shall have the power to regulate the monetary value of the metallic commodity designated to be legal tender coin. Nor do the charters of the First and the Second Banks of the United States imply or assert any such conscious and deliberate regulation. The constitutional basis for allowing Congress to establish the First and the Second Banks was the provision calling for Congress to lay and collect taxes.[21] The central banking activities and powers subsequently seen in the policies of the banks were assumed on occasion by their directors and urged on them by those who might benefit from such actions. They grew naturally from the public fiscal functions with which the institutions were vested when chartered. To allege that these banks were created in the image of control that they came to assume when no explicit evidence can be adduced to support such an argument is an obvious fallacy of *post hoc ergo propter hoc.*

Frank W. Fetter makes a similar observation about the Bank of England. Its central banking qualities, he notes, were unbestowed and unanticipated. It was not established in 1694

> to perform 'central banking functions' . . . [The] development of the note issues of the Bank of England into an important part of the total currency supply, and the use of their notes and deposits as the form in which other banks held reserves took place so surely, but so gradually, that by 1797 institutional realities no longer squared with legal provisions or expressed beliefs. The events of 1793 and 1797 had made clear . . . that with a system of fractional reserve banking some agency—either the Bank [of England] or the Government— must assume responsibility in time of crisis.[22]

Though this argument either justifies or excuses the societal use of the central banking function on the grounds of necessity, it also denies its deliberate creation.

One notable difference is recorded between the fates of the American and English banks. The Bank of the United States was defrocked, but the Bank of England survived. Hammond conjectured that the Second Bank did not try "to avoid acknowledgement of its principal purposes and *raison d'être* or pretend that its accomplishments in the public interest were incidental to the conduct of its private business . . . Perhaps, the Bank of England owed its survival somewhat to its shirking [sic] the responsibility and to its reticence, for the interests that wished to annihilate it differed little from their American counterparts."[23]

When Biddle realized the antipathy of the Jacksonian forces to regulation, he tried to compromise. But he was too late. The movement against the Second Bank did not distinguish between the regulatory function that the bank had assumed and the ordinary and innocuous commercial function it had been granted. The Jacksonians did not have the sophistication to understand this difference, so they simply obliterated the whole institution. The Bank of England, although subjected to many investigations and some of the same hostile sentiment, was much more diplomatic. By insisting that it filled the central banking role gratuitously, it avoided most of the political chastisement that acceptance of central banking norms would have unleashed on it.[24] It is well written: "Whosoever exalteth himself shall be abased; and he that humbleth himself shall be exalted."[25]

The formation of the independent treasury system in the United States in 1846 seemed to mark a departure from previous financial frameworks in both the United States and England. It was clearly a reaction to and a rejection of the Second Bank-Bank of England type of regulatory control. It called on the Treasury Department to keep its own revenue balances and to use only specie or its own notes for government disbursements. The act was frequently referred to as the divorce of bank and state.

The Bank of England was similarly constrained. Palmer's Rule of 1832, which required the bank to change its issues of paper notes in accordance with external specie movements, was a rejection of discretionary regulatory control. The Act of 1844 (Peel's Act), which separated the bank into the Issue and Banking Departments, was another step in the same direction.[26]

The independent treasury kept its own cash and made its own payments through subtreasury offices. As long as its expenditures were greater than or equal to its receipts, it could not build up a cash balance with which to nudge the monetary system. During the gold-inspired commercial boom of the 1850s, however, treasury balances accumulated in the Treasury and were disbursed by Secretary Guthrie through purchases of government securities in the open market.

Although Guthrie and some of his predecessors carried out significant monetary policies before 1860, very little central banking doctrine as such emerged. The specie standard seemed to discourage discretionary monetary experiments. The policies that occurred were primarily circumstantial. They were necessary at the time in order to disburse residual cash balances that resulted from unforeseen fiscal surpluses. No special doctrine followed them.

The real opportunities for central banking innovation became much more favorable when specie payments were suspended in 1862, and the United States economy had to operate on an inconvertible paper standard until 1879. Contraction of the stock of paper money seemed the most straightforward answer to the inflation that the paper money had created. But this diet was too austere for public tolerance, and was discontinued in 1868.

Secretaries of the Treasury during the suspension used balances of gold and greenbacks to influence the monetary system. Even such an avowed contractionist as Secretary McCulloch argued for discretionary manipulation of the Treasury's gold balance to discourage conspiracies that might attempt "to bring about fluctuations [in the price of gold] for purely speculative reasons." He acknowledged the use of gold as an open-market device "to prevent commercial panics."[27]

Monetary control arose primarily because the paper currency was not redeemable in specie. If it was not redeemable, the monetary system could not be self-regulating. If it was not self-regulating, someone had to regulate it—Congress ideally and constitutionally, but the Treasury Department practically and realistically.

The abandonment of the contraction policy in 1868 coincided with the appointment of George Boutwell as secretary of the Treasury. Boutwell's administrative experience with the existing irredeemable paper currency prompted him to favor a certain amount of discretionary policy. He saw no reserve in the private economy that could provide seasonal elasticity, a new norm for the monetary system, and he concluded that the Treasury Department should have the power to alter the volume of paper currency in circulation in order to take care of this problem.[28]

After his election to the Senate in 1873 Boutwell presented another extensive argument for the Treasury to have central banking powers. He commented on the flow of currency to New York City in the summer and the difficulty of getting it back in the fall. Elasticity of the currency in commercial countries tended to be perverse, he observed, "without special intervention from the [monetary] authorities." He also discussed in considerable detail the Bank of England's general policy for insuring elasticity. The policy was not automatic but required official intervention.

To several queries about the extent of treasury responsibility, Boutwell replied that the Treasury should keep the real relationship between debtor and creditor undisturbed, by which he implied the goal of a stable price level. The means of effecting this responsibility was the discretion to issue temporarily the $44 million of greenbacks in the reserve and to maintain permanently the statutory minimum stock of $356 million.[29]

Despite Boutwell's arguments, Congress resisted all schemes that would have thwarted the progress of the monetary system toward resumption of specie payments. It also rejected any further discretion for the secretary of the Treasury in monetary affairs. So the system functioned until resumption with neither a bank nor a treasury department acting as a central bank.

Resumption occurred on schedule in 1879, but it did not return the monetary system to its 1860 status. By this time the quantities of United States notes, national bank notes, coined silver, and silver certificates were either significant or would become so during the next decade. Since all these currencies were guaranteed by the federal government to be redeemable in gold, the monetary system remained mixed and subject to Treasury policy in the short run. In the long run the international gold standard was again dominant.

In England the same mixture of paper money and gold prevailed. However, the only paper currency of consequence there was Bank of England notes. Thus any actions undertaken by the Bank of England significantly affected the British monetary system.

The most famous treatise on central banking doctrine to appear in the latter half of the nineteenth century was Walter Bagehot's analysis of Bank of England policies. Bagehot's book, *Lombard Street*,[30] appeared some seventy years after Henry Thornton's *Paper Credit*. It was written when the pound sterling was the king-pin currency and in no danger of sustained suspension.

The major governmental policy applicable to the bank at this time was still the Bank Act of 1844, which separated the Bank of England into the Issue and Banking Departments. The Issue Department did nothing but regulate the volume of Bank of England notes. The maximum amount it could issue was equal to the sum of its gold bullion holdings plus £15 million in government securities. Since the bank earned interest from the securities, it had every inducement to keep its portfolio close to the maximum. Gold flows then altered the currency in practical accord with the currency principle.

The Banking Department was the prototype for all hybrid central banks. It was commercial in its dealings with discount houses and bill-brokers; it was a public bank because of its fiscal relationship to the government; and it was at times a central bank in the ad hoc manner typical of that era.[31] Despite the obvious public interest that the bank maintained, as exemplified by its significant policy actions in 1847, 1857, and 1866, its directors never acknowledged its central banking functions and frequently denied them. Parliamentary committees and government officials also made similar disclaimers. Bagehot observed that these denials strained a reasonable man's credulity. Such self-deprecation, he argued, also hampered policy initiative in times of crisis. The bank might do the right thing and make advances to the money market despite a commercial predisposition to do just the opposite; but under such circumstances it could not carry out its relief policies to their best advantage.[32]

Bagehot documented his criticisms by referring to a controversy between the *Economist* news weekly and one of the principal directors of the bank. (Since Bagehot was the editor of the *Economist*, he was simply citing his own arguments.) The article in the *Economist* analyzed the bank's actions during the panic in the spring of 1866. It observed that the bank had used its reserve with commendable discretion when it made advances to the other banks during the panic and that the governor of the bank, Mr. David Salomons, had admitted as much at a recent proprietors' meeting.[33]

Mr. Salomons's remarks indeed implied that the bank had a central banking facet. While other banks were seeking accommodation, the Bank of England was granting it. "I am not aware that any legitimate application made for assistance to this house was refused," Mr. Salomons stated firmly, "and if accommodation could not be afforded to the full extent which was demanded, no one who offered proper security failed to obtain [some] relief from this house."[34]

Bagehot (via the *Economist*) considered this statement a clear admission of responsibility. The directors of the bank disagreed. Their spokesman for the rebuttal was Mr. Thomson Hankey. Mr. Hankey's case, though positive and dogmatic, was unconvincing. It demonstrated again that the Bank of England could be a bank at one moment and something quite different—a central bank—at another.

In his remarks Mr. Hankey offered what might be called the fair-share doctrine of central banking: "I consider it to be the undoubted duty of the Bank of England," he stated, "in the event of a sudden pressure in the Money Market . . . to bear its full share of a drain on its resources." This disposition was not to admit that the bank should retain unemployed cash to meet such an emergency. "The more the conduct of the affairs of the Bank is made to assimilate to the conduct of every other well-managed bank in the United Kingdom," he concluded brusquely and positively, "the better for the Bank, and the better for the community at large."[35]

Hankey's implication that the bank's commercial character gave it its only responsibility—returning a profit to its stockholders—was clearly inconsistent with the bank's actual practices over many decades. His contention that the Bank should not admit to a central banking function was on firmer ground. If the bank were to advertise the retention of a reserve to meet panics, he argued in a more comprehensive work, knowledge of this fact would presuppose its necessity. The availability of a reserve would encourage laxity and prodigality in the discounting policies of other commercial banks. Another argument against such a policy, he stated, was that it would require someone with discretion to authorize its use and some recognizable signal for taking positive action. His only prescription for policy was that the bank should not lend below the market rate of interest.[36]

Bagehot did not deal directly with these latter points. He only replied that Hankey's disclaimer put the whole question of policy during a crisis in an "unsatisfactory and uncertain condition . . . Mr. Hankey leaves us in doubt altogether," Bagehot remonstrated, "as to what will be the policy of the Bank of England in the next panic, and as to what amount of aid the public may then expect from it. His words are too vague. No one can tell what a 'fair share' means; still less can we tell what other people at some future time will say it means."[37]

Bagehot then prescribed his explicit rules for central bank behavior during a panic. First, the reserve should be advanced freely and promptly. Second, the advances should be made only at very high rates of interest. The high rates, he felt, would "operate as a heavy fine on unreasonable timidity" and would ration the limited reserves among the most eager demanders in the same way that a high price rations any scarce commodity in a free market. Third, the attitude of the bank should be to make advances, not on good securities, but on securities that would be good under normal conditions. To reject bad bills or bad securities would do no harm; this class of securities was small and would have been rejected even in prosperous times. "But if securities, really good and usually convertible, are refused by the Bank," he warned, "the alarm will not abate, the other loans made will fail in obtaining their end, and the panic will become worse and worse." Should the bank find its reserves depleted before it stopped the panic, then it would simply have to run before the wind in fashion similar to ordinary commercial banks. "The only safe plan for the Bank," he emphasized, "is the brave plan . . . This policy may not save the Bank; but if it does not, nothing will save it."[38]

Bagehot's prescriptions were at least compatible and often identical with those of Thornton. Both observed that Bank of England notes, not gold coin or bullion, were the principal reserve currency and the currency that should be supplied in a panic to satisfy an internal drain. Both emphasized the necessity of extending credit early in a panic—in contrast to the normal reaction of commercial banks which would be to restrict credit. The extension of paper money by a central bank, both believed, would temporarily restrain the external gold drains that might occur because of unfavorable expectations.

No official documents record that Bagehot's crusade was a success. But it was. As Fetter concluded, "The Bank, although officially silent, was taking to heart the advice of Bagehot, and the ever increasing importance of deposit banking made it less likely that the special note issue restrictions . . . would present any problems.[39]

Central banking doctrine that calls for active intervention by a monetary authority makes little headway in the presence of an automatic, self-regulating specie standard. Consequently, the United States' resumption of specie payments in 1879 retarded the trend toward what Boutwell had expounded as the personal intervention of men possessing power.

Resumption retarded this trend, but the free-silver movement and the government's silver-purchase programs kept it going. Silver was monetized in limited quantities at a mint price that was at a greater and greater premium over the market price. Silver money was thus in the same class as greenbacks. It was a fiat government issue, kept in circulation by legal tender provisions and redeemable in gold at the Treasury. Whereas greenbacks were 100 percent fiat, silver was 3 percent to 45 percent fiat. But this difference was irrelevant. If currency is legal tender, it circulates at its monetary value as long as its commodity value is lower.

Throughout the Silver Era (1878-1893) Congress wrote its own monetary policies. Most of these policies attempted to use silver as the vehicle for altering the quantity of money, although one secretary, Charles Fairchild, deliberately deposited treasury balances in national banks in order to stimulate the economy. This action received much censure from Congress as well as from the next secretary, William Windom, who gradually reversed the policy until all the treasury's balances were again in its own offices.[40]

The use of silver as a policy vehicle finally ended in 1893. When the chips were down and the gold standard seemed threatened by silver-purchase policies, silver was demonetized. Gold became the only standard. Its quantity then increased throughout the commercial world due to new discoveries and technological advances in refining gold ore.

The gold boom at the turn of the century had the same effect on treasury receipts as the one in the 1850s. The large excess reserves that accumulated in Treasury and subtreasury offices between 1902 and 1906 provoked overt policy actions by Secretary Leslie Shaw. His major policy was the deposit of the Treasury's excess balances in national banks in the fall to encourage a seasonal expansion of the money supply—the same policy that had received so much congressional censure fifteen years earlier. Treasury balances were then allowed to reaccumulate in treasury offices by means of fiscal surpluses during the following winter.

Academicians, politicians, and journalists were almost unanimous in condemning Shaw's policies, even though Shaw argued that he assumed this power only in response to the major monetary problem of the time— lack of seasonal elasticity in the money supply. Shaw had no quarrel with the gold standard; in fact, he was one of its champions. Thus he did not try to influence the secular growth in the stock of money. He was only concerned with controlling the seasonal variation of the money stock in order to prevent panics and crises arising from temporary technical stringencies in the banking system.[41] He proposed a supplemental bank-issued currency capable of immediate and widespread issue. The massive amount of work involved in evaluating the collateral the banks offered for treasury deposits, he thought, argued for the job to be done wholly by the commercial banks. The additional currency would be retired routinely and promptly once "the demand therefore ceases."[42]

The Treasury had managed the greenbacks before resumption. After resumption it kept a discretionary gold balance as a reserve for a fixed quantity of greenbacks and a declining volume of national bank notes. It bought silver to be coined. Through the comptroller of the currency, it administered the national banking system. It managed the sinking fund for bond redemptions. With all these routine powers, it naturally could and would assume some extraordinary powers, for example the deposit of treasury balances in national banks. Thus the Independent Treasury Act of 1846 that was designed to take the Treasury out of policy and politics came full circle sixty years later. By 1906 the Treasury was more a central bank in its deliberate attempts to influence the monetary system than the Second Bank had ever been.

This much intervention and discretion again proved unpopular. But this time Congress could not retreat to an independent treasury system because the independent treasury itself was the offending institution. Besides, bank panics and crises of recent decades seemed to demonstrate the need for reform; so a more sophisticated institution was conceived—the Federal Reserve system.

Creation of the Federal Reserve system was a clear reaction to the treasury policies, mild as they were, that Shaw had developed. Equally important was the anticipation that the new system would promote form-seasonal elasticity in the money supply—the monetary problem publicized by Boutwell and Shaw—not through the discretion of a government official, but on the initiative of commercial bankers themselves through a supercommercial (Federal Reserve) bank. The emphasis on action thus shifted from discretionary policy by a government agency to automatic and self-regulatory policy in the market. Indeed, the early Federal Reserve system, operating on a real-bills principle and on the doctrine of maintaining its discount rate above market rates of interest, was to be a self-regulating appendage to a more fundamental self-regulating system, the operational gold standard.[43]

One can argue that Congress in fashioning the Federal Reserve system was far from single-valued either about the means or ends of policy. However, congressmen offered no arguments that would have had the new institution usurp the functions of the gold standard. In giving the Federal Reserve only limited powers, Congress did not feel the need to proscribe its activities with explicit rules and goals.

Power was always the issue of central bank existence, and the consensus of polity during the nineteenth century was an abhorrence of power. Virtually every central banking institution that emerged during this period had its powers proscribed either by the act creating it or by implications in the arguments of its founders. Whenever central banking discretion was recognized, it was rebuffed and denied by subsequent political action. Only in the twentieth century has the general philosophy of laissez faire and its use as a principle for curbing the power of central banks been abandoned.

Central banking was not primarily the evolution of a sophisticated theory on the management of money. Rather, it was a circumstantial emergence—an "unpredicted appearance of new characteristics in the course of . . . social evolution." It was derived from institutions endowed with the powers that could provoke and nourish the central banking function. Such a declaration is not the same as saying that central banks happened because they happened. It is not tautological. The central banking function appeared because the financial environment in which certain institutions operated favored its development and because circumstances such as a bank crisis, a depression, or a war thrust these institutions into new roles.

The creation of a Bank of the United States, or for that matter a Bank of England, was no more than governmental chartering of a commercial banking institution that would also act as a banker for the government. Such an institution was first a commercial bank and second a public bank, and that was all so far as its founders were concerned. Its status as the government's bank suggested and encouraged its intervention in monetary affairs. Numerous currencies—diverse currencies issued by many different banks—went through its hands, and the magnitude of its branch operations as the government's depository set it apart from other commercial banks.

In practice the government-sponsored bank made loans to the government, otherwise assisted in fiscal operations, and kept the government's balances. Because government balances were often sizable, it also felt some public responsibility to assist ordinary commercial banks at times of crisis, an action that enlarged its public banking function into a central banking function. Since crises were infrequent and random while public fiscal actions and the necessity for commercial profit were routine and constant, the commercial-public bank functions dominated its activities. The central banking role was as infrequent, but also as spectacular, as the appearance of a new comet in the night sky.

A bank panic or liquidity crisis immediately thrust the commercial-public institution into prominence because it had the only reserves that could save anyone and everyone. However, the institution's managers usually had little experience with or precedent for undertaking positive and sophisticated policies. In fact, what they had to do to offset panics and restrain crises was contrary to all their commercial banking instincts. As commercial bankers they confined loans, discounts, and advances to paper that promised a very low risk of default. In a bank crisis no such paper is available. The very nature of a crisis turns good paper, that is, short-term self-liquidating, bona fide loans, into highly questionable investments. In addition, a nineteenth-century quasi-central bank had to restrain itself during prosperous periods from lending on all good paper, which would have maximized its earning assets, so that it would have some metallic reserves to parlay among commercial banks if they were threatened by liquidity drains. When a panic occurred, the now-central bank had to lean into the wind, and, as Bagehot prescribed, lend on what might be called subjunctive paper—paper that would be good when general business conditions were again normal. Thus the commercial-public-central bank had to be more conservative than its fellows during a boom, and radical to the point of foolhardy in a crisis! No wonder the directors of these institutions had such difficulty afterwards explaining their operations to governmental investigating committees. Central banking policies could never be rationalized by recourse to commercial banking principles.

This explanation does not cover the independent treasury. It obviously was not a commercial bank by any definition, but it was the government's bank, and it shared at least one feature with institutions such as the Bank of England and the Bank of the United States. It kept the financial accounts of the government and from time to time had a workable reserve of high-powered money. Here was common ground—the existence of a strategic monetary stock that could be used to shore up financial weak spots at critical times. Whereas the commercial-public bank faced the disagreeable prospect of using its uncommitted reserves on questionable paper under unfavorable circumstances, treasury officials had only to repurchase government securities having little or no profit-and-loss characteristics.

The independent treasury's strategic position for carrying out countercyclical policies was fairly good even if it did not try to do so—even if it acted only as a good fiscal housekeeper. For when a business downturn developed, receipts to the Treasury would fall off and a fiscal deficit would appear. To cover this deficit the Treasury could either disburse specie balances, accumulated when business had been properous, or get Congress to authorize an issue of treasury notes. In either case, it added high-powered money to the system. Secretaries of the Treasury might then assume the credit for having taken the initiative to relieve a panic or prevent a crisis; but simple fiscal necessities would have obtained the same response from any pedestrian administrator.

When a gold boom developed, the increase in business activity resulted in greater Treasury receipts than expenditures. The fiscal surplus then formed a balance in the Treasury that could be used in a subsequent downturn. In fact, it would have to be used up before a tightfisted Congress would authorize any new government debt.

Such a Treasury-central bank was not technically incompatible with a gold standard, nor was a Bank of England or a Second Bank of the United States. All these institutions could operate as central banks, but only within a limited scope and for short periods. Too pervasive or too chronic a depression would deplete the central institution's gold reserves, leaving the institution impotent and returning the gold standard to dominance. Prices, wages, incomes, and the stock of ordinary money would tumble until the price level and its supporting money stock were again compatible with the operating equilibrium of the gold standard. Falling prices would encourage new discovery and better exploitation of the precious metals, because falling commodity prices increased the real value of gold. But this solution could not be expected to furnish short-run relief.

The intellectual weakness of the independent treasury was its lack of a real-bills connection to the stock of money. Its relationship to the money market was based on government bonds issued because of fiscal necessities as long-term investments rather than as short-term, self-liquidating securities to encourage the production and marketing of real goods. A Treasury-central bank was thus toxic to the belief that the production of goods generated money. The organization of the Federal Reserve system in place of the independent treasury was the overt manifestation of the ascendance of the real-bills doctrine to policymaking eminence.

Independent treasury, Bank of England, or Bank of the United States: Is a central banking institution necessary to the monetary environment of a specialized economic system? One could argue that the appearance of such institutions presupposes the answer. But if such an argument were true, then everything in existence would be necessary. So it really begs the question. It also leaves unanswered another question. What alternative arrangements to a discretionary governmental agency for managing the monetary system might be desirable?

Two alternatives are, first, a monetary system in which the provision of money is left entirely in the hands of private individuals or business firms and, second, one in which the government specifies the rules for a commodity standard and does nothing more. Experience has not adequately tested the first possibility, but it has intuitive appeal. The second alternative was adopted by laissez faire societies believing in limited government because it was considered impervious to undesirable intervention. Random circumstances that provoked monetary crises frequently led to government involvement. Political intervention, it may be observed, stimulates the penchant to regulate. Still, regulation was resisted throughout the nineteenth century. Even the Federal Reserve system was seen by many of its founders as an institution that would reduce the Treasury's influence on the monetary system by setting up a quasi-scientific, self-regulating machine for responding only to form-seasonal variations in the demand for money. If its growth to an omnipotent monetary agency had been anticipated in 1913, the bill to create it would never have been reported out of the House Banking and Currency Committee.

The performance of central banks has not confirmed their necessity. Their policies in the twentieth century have resulted in much more variation in business activity than was witnessed in the nineteenth century under specie standards.[44] This record suggests that a market system for handling random or even periodic disturbances to the monetary system is more stable than one managed by authorities. Since the self-interest of private persons in business firms and households governs a market system, and since it is in their interest to have a stable system, these people will develop market machinery to stabilize the system. The use of clearinghouse certificates during certain nineteenth-century bank crises and the restriction on the conversion of bank deposits into currency demonstrate how private institutions may stop the momentum of a potentially unstable monetary development.[45] Only when government institutions overissued paper currency during wars or underissued it during recessions was some initial instability aggravated and made fundamental.

In the twentieth century specie standards have become a dead letter; central banks have become omnipotent; a laissez faire monetary system looks politically impossible. The only hope is that legislatures will recognize the absolute powers assumed by most central banks and will impose rules for central bank behavior that result in monetary expansion approximately the same as what was achieved under specie standards. This change would imply a fifth stage of monetary control that would provide inestimable benefits to society.

Notes
Index

Notes

1. The Genesis of Monetary Control

1. Fritz Redlich, *The Molding of American Banking, Men and Ideas*, part 1, 1781-1840 (New York: Hafner Publishing Co., 1951), pp. 96-100. Redlich argues, I think correctly, that the First Bank of the United States could not have been created as a central bank because no commercial banking system to be controlled was in existence. No commercial banking system presupposed no central banking functions.

2. Two concepts of the stock or quantity of money are used by contemporary econononmists. The "narrow" stock, or M_1, includes currency (coin and paper money) held outside banks, plus demand deposits of commercial banks, minus interbank and government deposits. The "wide" stock, or M_2, includes everything in the narrow stock, plus time deposits in commercial banks, also adjusted for interbank balances. One can think of an even "wider" stock M_3 that includes *all* time and savings deposits whether in commercial banks or not. Although any of the concepts is satisfactory, this study uses the "wide" stock M_2, if only because accounting procedures during most of the nineteenth century did not distinguish between time and demand deposits. Current practices for reviewing the monetary systems of the nineteenth century should not be confused by the early (normative) nineteenth-century view that regarded only gold and silver as money.

3. The arguments in all passages that discuss the gold standard system apply equally to both silver and bimetallic standards.

4. A gold dollar was defined as containing 25.8 grains of gold 0.9 fine, which implies 23.22 grains of pure gold. Since 480 grains equals one ounce, one ounce of gold equaled $20.67 (480 ÷ 23.22).

5. Frederick Soddy, *Wealth, Virtual Wealth and Debt*, 2nd ed. (New York: E. P. Dutton and Co., 1933), p. 179.

6. Gerald T. Dunne, *Monetary Decisions of the Supreme Court*, (New Brunswick, N. J.: Rutgers University Press, 1960), p. 1.

7. Bray Hammond, *Banks and Politics in America*, (Princeton, N. J.: Princeton University Press, 1957), p. 139. This work is recommended for its rich detail of monetary and banking development in this period.

8. *Annals of Congress*, 1st Cong. 2nd sess., 14 December, 1790, "Report on a National Bank." (*Annals of Congress* hereafter cited as *AC*.)

9. Adam Smith, *The Wealth of Nations*, ed. Edwin Cannan (New York: Random House, Modern Library Edition, 1937), p. 304.

10. *AC*, "Report," pp. 2082-2111.

11. Smith, *Wealth of Nations*, pp. 304-305; *AC*, "Report", pp. 2082-83.

12. Smith, *Wealth of Nations*, p. 305.

13. *AC*, "Report," p. 2095.

14. Smith, *Wealth of Nations*, p. 308.

15. *AC*, "Report," p. 2095.

16. Ibid., p. 2101. Hamilton was at just the right age to have read and been impressed with Smith's *Wealth of Nations*. Hammond (p. 133) noted that Hamilton "followed an explanation of the utility of banks which Adam Smith had presented in the *Wealth of Nations*." His "Report" in places reads like a copy of Smith.

17. *AC*, "Report," pp. 2095-2103. The bank's notes were to be limited legal tender, that is, "receivable in all [public] debts of the United States."

18. Ibid., p. 2109.

19. Ibid.

20. Exchequer bills were issued as interest-bearing temporary debt of the government. Frequently, however, they were payable on demand and always receivable for all public dues. Bank of England notes differed only in that they were more permanent and did not bear interest. One observer has argued that the Bank of England's administration of these currencies "served as a bond between the State and the Bank, which bound the two together in ever closer relations." (Eugen von Philippovich, *History of the Bank of England and Its Financial Services to the State*, National Monetary Commission, 61st Cong., 2nd sess., Sen. Doc. No. 591, 1911, p. 107.) The general acceptance of both currencies was, of course, due to their acceptability for all debts owed the government.

21. *AC*, 1st Cong., 3rd sess., p. 1919.

22. Ibid., pp. 1895-96. Madison cited some other minor factors, such as the consequences of a run on the bank.

23. Ibid., p. 1897. He mentioned a Virginia law that prohibited the circulation of notes payable to bearer.

24. Ibid., p. 1916.

25. Ibid., p. 1898.

26. Ibid., pp. 1904 and 1907. Theodore Sedgwick and Elbridge Gerry, both of Massachusetts, also argued for the bank in terms of the expediency it would provide the government as a borrower (pp. 1913 and 1948-49).

27. See James Willard Hurst, *A Legal History of Money in the United States, 1774-1970*, (Lincoln, Neb.: University of Nebraska Press, 1973), pp. 12-13. Hurst argues that the clause "regulate the value" reflected the desire of Congress to achieve "formal standardization of the monetary system." This view presumes too much ex post facto rationalization of subsequent congressional action. All that the Constitution left to Congress was the discretion to stipulate the metallic contents of gold and silver coins in terms of their legal tender monetary values. This was sufficient discretion for establishing a stable and certain monetary system.

28. *AC*, 1st Cong., 3rd sess., p. 1957.

29. Ibid., p. 1906.

30. John Thom Holdsworth, *The First Bank of the United States*, 61st Cong., 2nd sess., Sen. Doc. No. 571, National Monetary Commission, 1910, pp. 123-125, 136-137, 116. The balance sheet shown in this source is one of the few that were preserved. Most of the records were lost in the fires of 1814 and 1833.

31. Ibid., p. 123. A "memorial" in this context is a written statement of facts presented to a legislative body in the form of a petition or remonstrance.

32. Hammond, *Banks and Politics*, pp. 115-116, 198-200.

33. *AC*, 11th Cong., 3rd sess., p. 22, "Petition of President and Directors of the Bank of the United States for Re-charter," 18 December 1810. This statement was signed "David Lenox, President." The stockholders thought of the bank only as an orthodox aid to the Treasury.

34. Ibid., p. 32. This memorial was signed "Condy Raguet and one hundred others."

35. Ibid., pp. 212-213.

36. The Democratic party of this day was the anti-Federalist party of Jefferson, Madison, Gallatin, and Crawford, even though they then called themselves Republicans. I reserve this latter appellation for the descendants of the Whig-Federalist group.

37. *AC*, 10th Cong., 2nd sess., p. 458.

38. *AC*, 11th Cong., 3rd sess., pp. 394-395.

39. Ibid., pp. 122-125.

40. Ibid., pp. 142-143.

41. See speeches on these points by Clay and William B. Giles of Virginia, ibid., pp. 175-207 and 215-218. See also Redlich, *Molding of American Banking*, p. 100. Redlich's discussion of the First Bank includes many details on its operations that have been abbreviated here. His conclusions about the growth of the First Bank into an embryonic central bank are in substantial agreement with what I have found using different source material.

2. Treasury Policy, 1811-1820

1. This part of the story is certainly true even though neither the Constitution of 1789 nor the debates of the Congress in 1790-91 indicated that the First Bank *ought* to regulate the state banks or financial markets. The regulatory function just grew without official sanction.

2. R. C. H. Catterall, *The Second Bank of the United States* (Chicago: University of Chicago Press, 1902), p. 4. Catterall's reference to treasury notes as a medium of exchange should be borne in mind for much of the later analysis.

3. The references for this account are legion. An incomplete but sufficient list includes Catterall, *Second Bank*; W. B. Smith, *Economic Aspects of the Second Bank of the United States* (Cambridge, Mass.: Harvard University Press, 1953), ch. 7, especially pp. 114-115; Hammond, *Banks and Politics*, pp. 200-201 and 227-250; E. R. Taus, *Central Banking Functions of the United States Treasury, 1789-1941* (New York: Columbia University Press, 1943), pp. 24-27; Murray N. Rothbard, *The Panic of 1819* (New York and London: Columbia University Press, 1962), ch. 1, pp. 1-23. This last work, while complete and well done on most aspects of its subject, does not mention the existence of treasury notes, let alone acknowledge their high-powered monetary influence on the inflation of 1814-1817.

4. John Jay Knox, *United States Notes*, 3rd ed. (New York: Charles Scribner's Sons, 1899), p. 22

5. Knox, *United States Notes*, p. 23.

6. United States Treasury Department, *Reports of the Secretary of the Treasury of the United States*, vol. 1, 1790-1814, p. 529. Campbell's reference to the notes "in circulation" was typical affirmation of their monetary character. (Hereafter an annual report of the secretary of the Treasury is cited simply as *Treasury Report*.)

7. Ibid.

8. *American State Papers: Finance*, 3, p. 18 (hereafter cited as *ASPF*).

9. Given a significant increase in bank reserves, the number of banks could be expected to grow. The creation of bank credit, and the issue of bank notes that the new reserves would induce, would require additional bank administrations. In short, one big bank could expand credit and notes in a theoretical model; but the frictions of printing and signing the notes and negotiating loans would require an extension of banking offices.

10. *ASPF* 3, p. 131 (*Treasury Report*, 1816).

11. Ibid. The last issue of treasury notes (act of 24 February 1815) included over $3 million in "small" notes (under $20) that did not bear interest.

12. Ibid., p. 132.

13. Ibid., p. 116. Dallas to House of Representatives, 19 March 1816.

14. *AC*, 14th Cong., 1st sess., appendix, p. 1640 (*Treasury Report*, 1815).

15. Ibid., p. 1643.

16. *ASPF* 3, p. 59. Dallas to John C. Calhoun, Chairman of the Committee on the National Currency, 24 December 1815.

17. Ibid., pp. 316-317. Crawford to William Jones, 29 November 1816.

18. Ibid., p. 60. Dallas to Calhoun. The emphasis of the secretary continued to be on bank paper rather than on the treasury notes used as reserves that gave rise to such paper. Thus was symptom conveniently transposed into cause.

19. Ibid., pp. 60, 58.

20. Ibid., p. 59.

21. David Ricardo, "The High Price of Bullion," in *Economic Essays*, ed. E. C. K. Gonner (London: G. Bell and Sons, 1923), p. 41.

22. *ASPF* 4, p. 764. Jones to Crawford, 9 January 1817.

23. *ASPF* 3, pp. 316-317.

24. *ASPF* 4, pp. 283 and 360-362. Government revenues were supposed to be deposited in the Bank of the United States in accordance with the act creating the bank.

25. Ibid., pp. 499, 536, 577.

26. U. S. Bureau of the Census, *Historical Statistics of the United States, Colonial Times to 1957* (Washington, D. C., 1960), series E-I, p. 115.

27. *ASPF* 4, p. 769. See also Leon Schur, "The Second Bank of the United States and the Inflation after the War of 1812," *Journal of Political Economy* 68 (1960): 120.

28. See *ASPF* 3 for an extended correspondence between Crawford and Jones, and between Jones and the state bank executives, on this issue.

29. Ibid., pp. 539-540. Crawford to Directors of the Bank of the United States, 3 July 1817.

30. Ibid., p. 845. Jones to Crawford, 29 May 1818.

31. Ibid., pp. 853-854. Jones to Crawford, 23 June 1818.

32. Ibid., p. 586. Crawford to Jones, 30 June 1818.

33. *ASPF 2*, p. 275 (*Treasury Report*, 1818).

34. *ASPF* 3, p. 508. Crawford to House of Representatives, 24 February 1820.

35. Ibid., p. 496.

36. Ibid., p. 501.

37. Ibid., p. 504. This same "principle" was also stated by Dallas (see epigraph at beginning of chapter). In view of the limitations explicitly set forth in the Constitution, the validity of this "principle" may be questioned.

38. Ibid., pp. 507, 505.

39. Hammond, *Banks and Politics*, p. 249.

3. Central Banking Growth of the Second Bank

1. Hammond, *Banks and Politics*, ch. 11, especially p. 305.

2. Smith, *Economic Aspects of the Second Bank*, p. 263.

3. Redlich notes that the Second Bank performed certain functions not part of the usual operations of a commercial bank: (1) It acted as a fiscal agent for the federal government. (2) It provided a national paper currency. (3) It held the metallic reserves of the monetary system (*Molding of American Banking*, part 1, p. 98). While every central bank has these functions, they are only the administrative side of central banking. At least a fourth characteristic is necessary: deliberate and purposive actions on the monetary system.

4. *AC*, 18th Cong., 1st sess., p. 926.

5. *Register of Debates in Congress* (Washington, D.C.), 18th Cong., 2nd sess. (*Treasury Report*, 1824), appendix, pp. 40-41 (hereafter cited as *RDC*).

6. David McCord Wright, "Langdon Cheves and Nicholas Biddle: New Data for a New Interpretation," *Journal of Economic History* 13, no. 2, 1953: 305-319. Also Hammond, *Banks and Politics*, p. 278.

7. Hammond, *Banks and Politics*, pp. 301, 323. Biddle in 1819 expressed only the opinion that the government should not trust its funds in the hands of the state banks. He implied no ideas of control over the banks or the money supply.

8. Ibid., p. 305.

9. *RDC*, 20th Cong., 2nd sess. (*Treasury Report*, 1828), appendix, pp. 21-22.

10. Ibid., p. 22.

11. Jacob Meerman, "Nicholas Biddle on Central Banking" (Ph.D. diss., University of Chicago, 1961), pp. 14-15.

12. The performance of the Federal Reserve system's policymaking officials in 1929-1933 is a good example of a central bank-inspired disaster.

13. Hammond, *Banks and Politics*, pp. 324, 307-309. See also Meerman, *Nicholas Biddle*, pp. 9 and 26; Redlich, *Molding of American Banking*, part 1, p. 136.

14. Hammond, *Banks and Politics*, p. 305.

15. Ibid., p. 311.

16. Rush himself had run for vice-president and had been defeated by John C. Calhoun. Calhoun was probank and Jackson was antibank; but the bank issue

had not crystallized at all, so the positions of the candidates on the bank's role could not have been substantive factors in their political successes and failures.

17. Hammond correctly underscores the significance of the adverb "well" (p. 374). Use of "well" before "questioned" was propaganda; and the further declaration that the bank had not furnished a sound and uniform currency, implying that it had done just the opposite, was absurd. This argument does not say that the currency necessarily would have suffered without the bank.

18. U.S. Congress, 22nd Cong., 1st sess., *Reports of Committees, House Report No. 283*, 9 February 1832 (hereafter cited as the McDuffie report).

19. Ibid., pp. 10, 11. The first quotation suggests that the circumstances of the times were extending the concept of money beyond gold and silver coin. If other things such as bank notes were in fact treated and used as money, then Congress had the power to regulate their values by means of specific rules.

20. Ibid., pp. 13, 14. Mill's *Principles* was not published until 1848. The similarity of language between this passage and his chapter 8 is striking.

21. McDuffie report, p. 12.

22. Ibid., p. 18.

23. Ibid., pp. 29-31. They affirmed here that the treasury notes of 1812-1816 were an example of government-issued currency.

24. Ibid., pp. 25, 19.

25. Ibid., p. 49.

26. Ibid., p. 55.

27. Ibid., p. 52.

28. Ibid., pp. 52, 57.

29. U. S. Congress, 22nd Cong., 1st sess., *Reports of Committees, House Report No. 460*, 14 March 1832, submitted 30 April 1832 (hereafter cited as the Clayton report).

30. Ibid., pp. 15-20.

31. Ibid., p. 299.

32. Ibid., p. 309.

33. Ibid., p. 311.

34. Ibid., pp. 404, 406, 52.

35. Ibid., p. 29.

36. Ibid., p. 319.

37. Ibid., p. 320.

38. Ibid., pp. 334, 336-337.

39. Ibid., p. 362.

40. Ibid., p. 363.

41. U. S. Congress, 22nd Cong., 1st sess., *Executive Documents, Doc. No. 300*, "Message from the president of the United States returning the bank bill with his objections to the Senate," 16, July 1832, pp. 5-6.

42. Ibid., pp. 9, 10.

4. Decline of the Second Bank and Rise of the Treasury

1. Hammond, *Banks and Politics*, p. 345.

2. Carl B. Swisher, *Roger B. Taney* (New York: Macmillan Company,

1935), p. 214. According to Swisher, McLane was the one who had proposed Duane for the secretaryship.

3. William J. Duane, *Narrative and Correspondence concerning the Removal of the Deposits, and Occurrences connected therewith* (Philadelphia, 1838), pp. 42 and 58.

4. For an analysis of Jackson's hostility to the Second Bank and Taney's influence on Jackson's actions, see Redlich, *Molding of American Banking*, part 1, pp. 173-177.

5. *RDC*, 23rd Cong., 1st sess., appendix, pp. 60-70.

6. *RDC*, 23rd Cong., 1st sess., pp. 206-223.

7. Ibid., p. 147.

8. Ibid., pp. 81, 758, 2336. Senator Hill pointed out that to deny the secretary the power to contract or expand the circulation of bank paper was to claim it for the Second Bank.

9. Ibid., pp. 58-59, 4467-69, 1541. Presentation of these "memorials" by congressmen can be found anywhere in the *Register of Debates* for 1833-1834.

10. Ibid., appendix, p. 160.

11. Ibid., pp. 60, 74.

12. Ibid., appendix, p. 159, pp. 1076-78, 1713, 1797.

13. Binney in the House was almost the only one who seemed to be aware of the possibility of raising the silver content of the silver dollar. But silver, he said, was the basis of the current metallic currency (since no gold was in circulation), and therefore the value of the gold dollar should be changed (ibid., p. 4663).

14. *Treasury Report*, 1835, p. 24.

15. *RDC*, 23rd Cong., 1st sess., appendix, p. 160. Taney's letter to House Committee, 15 April 1834.

16. George Macesich, "Sources of Monetary Disturbances in the United States, 1834-1845," *Journal of Economic History* 20 (1960): 412, 430. Comparable spending and price level stimulation did not occur one hundred years later (1934-37) under a much greater devaluation. First, the monetary and banking policies of the Federal Reserve system, based as they were on faulty central banking theory and suffering from other constraints, not only aggravated the depression but also inhibited the recovery. Second, the radically interventionist policies of the New Deal seriously discouraged private spending. See Milton Friedman and Anna J. Schwartz, *A Monetary History of the United States, 1867-1960*, National Bureau of Economic Research (Princeton, N.J.: Princeton University Press, 1963), pp. 299-492 passim.

17. *RDC*, 23rd Cong., 2nd sess., p. 1300.

18. *RDC*, 23rd Cong., 1st sess., pp. 92, 183, and 3232.

19. *RDC*, 23rd Cong., 2nd sess., pp. 621-630, 721, 1349.

20. Ibid., p. 1437. Polk noted that such a provision "had never been imposed upon the Bank of the United States or its branches."

21. Since the "surplus" was in the form of a treasury deposit in the depository banks, it could be provided for in the same bill.

RDC, 24th Cong., 1st sess., p. 1763.

Chances are that Jackson had indicated that he would not sign a distribution bill if the "pet bank" system were jeopardized. Since the desire for some sort of distribution was almost unanimous, those who wanted genuine bank restrictions had to yield. Possibly many also felt that distributing the surplus would leave no money in the Treasury for them to be concerned about. No money would require no restrictions.

22. Ibid., p. 1599. Wright stated: "We should, as far as may be in our power, so regulate that use [of banks] as to promote, not to disturb, the great moneyed interests of the country" (p. 1612).

23. Ibid., p. 1808. Benton's dissatisfaction with what occurred here had much to do with his promotion of the Specie Circular.

24. *Treasury Report*, 1835, p. 23. This statement was made before the Deposit Act and thus indicates that Woodbury had some awareness of what was needed.

25. *Treasury Report*, 1836, p. 77.

26. Ibid., pp. 79-80.

27. *Treasury Report*, 1834; pp. 95, 108.

28. *RDC*, 23rd Cong., 1st sess., p. 219.

5. The Specie Circular and Distribution of the Surplus

1. The term "pet" has often been applied to the banks chosen to hold the government's deposits. Such an adjective implies that the banks were selected on a basis of political favoritism. Political compatibility with the Jackson administration probably was a determinant in selecting some of these banks. Just as important was the location of the banks in places where the volume of government revenues (from tariffs and public lands) was likely to be greatest. In view of the crusading zeal with which the hard-money Jacksonians attacked banks, the chosen banks might well have been skeptical of any favors offered by the government. In any event, the "pet" thesis has no utility in an analysis of the economic situation of the period. All the banks were fractional reserve, and this feature is the one that was instrumental in provoking the bank panic. (See, however, Frank Otto Gattell, "Spoils of the Bank War: Political Bias in the Selection of Pet Banks," *American Historical Review* 70 (1964): 35-58. Gattell concludes that political considerations were prominent in the selection of depository banks.)

2. The "surplus" was defined as the cash over $5 million in the Treasury as of 1 January 1837. The amount finally determined to be "surplus" was $37.5 million. In fact, only three-fourths of this amount, $28.1 million, was distributed to the states. The money, while distributed in fact, was "deposited" in name. This nomenclature was adopted to avoid a veto from Jackson, who had become opposed to distribution. See E. G. Bourne, *The History of the Surplus Revenue of 1837* (New York, 1885), pp. 20, 21.

3. *RDC*, 24th Cong., 1st sess., p. 1649.

4. Under the independent treasury system, which came into existence a few years later, balances of specie did accumulate in the Treasury and subsequently had an effect when expended that corresponded to what Webster implied here.

5. Thomas Hart Benton, *Thirty Years View*, 2 (New York, 1854-1856), pp. 652-655.

6. Ibid., pp. 685, 677. Benton's report of this action is justifiably authorita-

tive. He indicated that Woodbury and the rest of the cabinet were actually opposed to the Specie Circular. Apparently only Benton and Jackson were in favor of it.

7. A. Barton Hepburn, *A History of Currency in the United States* (New York: Macmillan Company, 1924), p. 122.

8. The stock of money was between $200 million and $300 million. The Treasury Department in 1840 estimated the total of manufactured products to be $1,006 million. Thus an income estimate of $1,000 million is conservative.

9. I am indebted to Milton Friedman for this observation.

10. *Treasury Report*, 1836, p. 86.

11. Ibid., p. 81.

12. Bourne, *History of the Surplus;* R. C. McGrane, *The Panic of 1837* (Chicago: University of Chicago Press, 1924); and Bray Hammond, *Banks and Politics*, are just a few of these analyses.

13. *Treasury Report*, 1836, p. 81. Woodbury reported later that $25.13 million had been transferred from bank to bank by his orders between 1 July 1836 and 1 January 1837 in order to make the distribution smooth. If a mere transfer of funds could provoke a crisis, the crisis surely would have occurred in late 1836, not in the middle of 1837.

14. Ibid., pp. 77-78. This statement was made before the actual distribution.

15. Quoted in Benton, *Thirty Years View*, 2, p. 11.

16. *RDC*, 24th Cong., 1st sess., pp. 3259-61.

17. Ibid., pp. 27, 36, 37.

18. *Treasury Report to Special Session*, 1837, p. 17. This report by the secretary was in addition to his regular report at the end of the year.

19. This is the sum of the negative values in the third column of table 5.4. If either Mississippi or Louisiana is included in the South, the southern surplus states would also have covered the amount due the southern deficit states.

20. National Archives and Records Service, Record Group. No. 56, *Letters on State Deposits* (27 June 1836 to 11 September 1837) (Washington, D.C.). These data were also published as U.S. Congress, 25th Cong., 1st sess., *House Document No. 30*. (I am indebted to Peter Temin for calling my attention to this latter document.)

21. *Treasury Report*, 1836, p. 78, and *Treasury Report*, 1837, p. 73. These values are losses from all *three* installments of the distribution and from ordinary fiscal expenditures.

22. *Treasury Report*, 1836, p. 14.

23. *House Document No. 30*, p. 78.

24. *Treasury Report to Special Session*, 1837, p. 17.

25. Specie in banks increased from $30 million in May 1837 to $35 million in May 1838. (See *Treasury Report*, 1838, exhibit F, pp. 41-44.)

26. Evidence of this reaction was seen in the congressional debates, already mentioned, which attempted to prescribe reserve requirements.

27. *Treasury Report to Special Session*, 1837, p. 16.

28. *Treasury Report*, 1835, p. 23.

29. For a contrary opinion see Harry N. Scheiber, "The Pet Banks in Jacksonian Politics and Finance, 1833-41," *Journal of Economic History* 23 (1963):

196-214. For a comprehensive supporting opinion, see Peter Temin, *The Jacksonian Economy* (New York: W.W. Norton and Co., 1969), pp. 120-128.

30. Money in the specie-money ratio is the stock of bank-issued currency and deposits. A change in the specie-money ratio at this time had approximately the same effects that a change in the currency-deposit ratio would have today, because specie was legal tender then as central bank currency is now.

31. Temin, *Jacksonian Economy*, pp. 172-173. Gold also played a significant role, especially after the devaluation of 1834. See ch. 4.

32. Ibid., p. 81.

33. Ibid., p. 135.

34. Ibid., p. 146.

6. The Independent Treasury System before the Civil War

1. *Treasury Report*, 1838, p. 45, exhibit G. Woodbury reported that $8.5 million of this amount came between April and July of 1838.

2. Ibid., pp. 1-5.

3. For a fuller discussion of economic conditions, see Temin, *Jacksonian Economy*, pp. 148-171.

4. *RDC*, 23rd Cong., 1st sess., p. 4641.

5. See William M. Gouge, *A Short History of Paper Money and Banking in the United States* (Philadelphia, 1833). The hard-money men, unlike Gordon, favored the scheme because they honestly wished the federal government to operate independently of all banks.

6. The Democrats passed an independent treasury act in 1840, the last gesture of a lame-duck administration. The Whigs repealed this act in the summer of 1841, and the ultimate Independent Treasury Act did not pass until 1846.

7. *Congressional Globe*, 26th Cong., 1st sess., p. 495 (hereafter cited as *CG*).

8. In his message to the special session Tyler had indicated that he would favor some kind of national bank scheme (*CG*, 27th Cong., 1st sess., p. 6).

9. *CG*, 27th Cong., 1st sess., appendix, p. 6.

10. "Stability" as an ideal for governmental policy was not confined to the Whigs. Woodbury frequently used the word, as did almost every secretary before the Civil War.

11. Section 16 of the bill provoked a great deal of opposition from the states' right group in Congress. The intent of this section was that Congress might establish a branch of the bank in any state whether that state wanted it or not. The Virginia delegation, of which Tyler had been a part, particularly objected to it.

12. Benton, *Thirty Years View*, 2, p. 319.

13. Ibid., p. 343. William M. Gouge wrote disgustedly: "The President has signed the bill to repeal the 'Sub-Treasury act' and *vetoed* the bill to incorporate a fiscal bank. The result is THE REVIVAL OF THE PET BANK SYSTEM—the *worst* of all possible systems" (*Journal of Banking* 1841, 1, no. 4, p. 59).

14. Benton, *Thirty Years View*, 2, p. 345. Calhoun, although a South Carolinian, was apparently the ringleader of this group. Benton remarked that Calhoun "had that ascendancy over Mr. Tyler which it is the prerogative of genius to have over inferior minds."

15. Ibid., p. 350.

16. Webster was involved in negotiating what became the Webster-Ashburton Treaty. When this item was finished, he also resigned and Calhoun became secretary of state.

17. Ibid., p. 354.

18. Ibid., p. 343.

19. *Treasury Report*, 1841, p. 18.

20. U.S. Congress 27th Cong., 2nd sess., *Report to Congress on a Board of Exchequer, Senate Doc. No. 18*, 1841, p. 8.

21. Ibid., pp. 10, 13.

22. Benton, *Thirty Years View*, 2, p. 395.

23. Ibid., p. 33.

24. *CG*, 26th Cong., 1st sess., appendix, p. 305.

25. An amendment to the treasury note bill was offered in the House that would have prohibited the secretary from engaging in this practice, but it failed to pass, 69-90 (*CG*, 26th Cong., 1st sess., p. 293). Congressmen apparently felt that such inflationary impetus at this time (1840) would be helpful.

26. U.S. Congress, 26th Cong., 1st sess., *Senate Doc. No. 359*, vol. 6, 25 March 1840; and *Senate Doc. No. 476*, vol. 7, 19 May 1840. Woodbury's reply to the March request was unenlightening and undetailed, so another request was made in May.

27. U.S. Congress, 26th Cong., 1st sess., *Senate Doc. No. 476*, vol. 7, p. 4.

28. Ibid., p. 6.

29. Ibid., table A, p. 9.

30. Ibid., pp. 21-22.

31. Ibid., p. 89.

32. *CG*, 26th Cong., 2nd sess., p. 227.

33. *RDC*, 23rd Cong., 1st sess., p. 219.

34. *CG*, 25th Cong., 2nd sess., p. 386.

35. John J. Knox, *United States Notes*, 2nd ed. rev. (New York: Charles Scribner's Sons, 1885), pp. 52-62.

36. *CG*, 29th Cong., 2nd sess., p. 30. Many other congressmen observed the central banking character invested in the Treasury Department by the note authorizations.

37. *CG*, 29th Cong., 1st sess., p. 1115.

38. *CG*, 35th Cong., 1st sess., pp. 96, 67. At the same time he piously declared that the issue of treasury notes was not a "monetary measure."

39. Ibid., p. 75. Again congressmen observed that issues of treasury notes would make the Treasury a quasi bank. See ibid., p. 100, for the remarks of Senator Preston King of New York.

40. *Treasury Report*, 1857, p. 17.

41. *CG*, 35th Cong., 1st sess., p. 94.

42. Ibid., appendix, p. 533.

43. See James Polk, *The Diary of a President, 1845-1849*, ed. Allen Nevins (New York: Longmans, Green and Co., 1929), pp. xix and 26.

44. *CG*, 29th Cong., 1st sess., appendix, p. 13; 29th Cong., 2nd sess., appendix, p. 10.

45. *CG*, 29th Cong., 1st sess., appendix, p. 13. "A just and permanent set-

tlement" referred to the resolution of monetary policy Walker hoped would be fabricated by the independent treasury.

46. To a real hard-money man, Walker's ideas were very "soft." See *CG*, 29th Cong., 1st sess., p. 820, for a speech by Thomas Hart Benton, who despised Walker.

47. *Treasury Report*, 1848, pp. 28-29. Also *CG*, 30th Cong., 1st sess., p. 901.

48. *CG*, 30th Cong., 2nd sess., p. 355.

49. Ibid.

50. *Treasury Report*, 1848, p. 24.

51. One Whig secretary, George Bibb, suggested in 1844 a top-executive open-market committee composed of the Chief Justice of the Supreme Court, the secretaries of state and the Treasury, and the attorney general, who would have decided when and at what price the debt should be repurchased. Nothing came of his proposal.

52. *CG*, 32nd Cong., 2nd sess., appendix, p. 350.

53. *Dictionary of American Biography*, vol. 8, pp. 60-61.

54. *CG*, 33rd Cong., 1st sess., appendix, p. 2.

55. Ibid.

56. Margaret G. Myers, *The New York Money Market*, vol. 1 (New York: Columbia University Press, 1931), pp. 140-141.

57. *CG*, 33rd Cong., 2nd sess., appendix, pp. 6-9.

58. *CG*, 34th Cong., 1st sess., appendix, p. 12.

59. *Treasury Report*, 1854, p. 282.

60. *CG*, 33rd Cong., 1st sess., appendix, p. 3.

61. *CG*, 34th Cong., 1st sess., appendix, p. 16.

62. Judge George Bibb to Guthrie, July 1854. Guthrie Papers, Box 17, Filson Club, Louisville, Kentucky.

63. *Treasury Report*, 1856, p. 31.

64. *Treasury Report*, 1857, p. 11.

65. Ibid., pp. 17, 9. Cobb to J. Glancy Jones, chairman of the House Committee on Ways and Means.

66. Hammond has shown that such emotions were important in the fight against the Second Bank of the United States. See *Banks and Politics*, pp. 371, 381, and passim.

67. The operations of the specie standard did in fact significantly determine the path of monetary events at several points in time: first in 1817-1820, then during the mild gold inflation of 1850-1860, and third, between 1892 and 1914, when a gold scarcity was followed by a gold bounty. (See ch. 11 and 12, and Friedman and Schwartz, *Monetary History*, pp. 89-188.)

7. Civil War Inflation and Postwar Monetary Policies

1. Hepburn, *History of Currency*, p. 180.

2. Hugh Rockoff, "The Free Banking Era: A Reexamination," *Journal of Money, Credit and Banking* 6 (1974): 151, 143.

3. David Kinley, *The Independent Treasury of the United States* (New York, 1893), pp. 160-161.

4. These alternatives are very clearly discussed and evaluated in Bray Hammond, "The North's Empty Purse," *American Historical Review* 67 (1961): 1-18.

5. Some of the sources for information on the income tax are George S. Boutwell (who became a secretary of the Treasury and a senator from Massachusetts), *A Manual of the Direct and Excise Tax System of the United States* (Boston, 1863 and 1864); idem, *The Tax Payer's Manual* (Boston, 1865); C. N. Emerson, *Emerson's Internal Review Guide* (Springfield, Mass., 1866); and H. E. Smith, *The United States Federal Internal Tax History from 1861 to 1871* (Boston: Houghton Mifflin, 1914. These sources are given in Anna J. Schwartz, "Gross Dividend and Interest Payments by Corporations at Selected Dates in the 19th Century," *Trends in the American Economy in the Nineteenth Century,* Studies in Income and Wealth, vol. 24, National Bureau of Economic Research (Princeton, N.J.: Princeton University Press, 1960), p. 407, n. 1.

6. Hepburn, *History of Currency,* pp. 306-312.

7. The total value of notes issued could not be greater than 90 percent of the par or market value of the securities, whichever was lower.

8. James K. Kindahl, "Economic Factors in Specie Resumption: The United States, 1865-79," *Journal of Political Economy* 69 (1961): 30-48.

9. James M. Blaine, *Twenty Years of Congress* (Norwich, Conn., 1886), p. 320.

10. Bank notes and deposits increased by $117 million, but government currency declined by $252 million. A large part of government currency was held by banks as reserves; and since the data on government currency are much better than the data on bank deposits, such a large decline in currency indicates a strong presumption that net increases in bank obligations could have occurred only if the banks had held "excess" reserves in 1865 and then let these reserves run down as they issued their own currency (national bank notes and deposits). An excellent treatise on the political-monetary developments of this period is Robert P. Sharkey, *Money, Class, and Party* (Baltimore, Md.: Johns Hopkins University Press, 1959). Sharkey errs when he assays the decrease in the currency at "only $45 million" and fails to note that the decrease in the total money stock was much greater.

11. Blaine, *Twenty Years of Congress,* p. 328.

12. *Congressional Record,* 43rd Cong., 1st sess., p. 704 (hereafter cited as CR).

13. *Dictionary of American Biography,* vol. 2, pp. 489-490.

14. The complete history of this bizarre episode is contained in U. S. Congress, 41st Cong., 2nd sess., *The Gold Panic Investigation, House Report No. 31,* by the Committee on Banking and Currency, James A. Garfield, Chairman. See pp. 1-4. See also L. Wimmer, "The Gold Crisis of 1869," *Explorations in Economic History* 12 (1975): 105-122.

15. *The Gold Panic Investigation,* pp. 19 and 342-353.

16. Ibid., pp. 468-469.

17. Ibid., p. 470.

18. *CG*, 38th Cong., 2nd sess., appendix, p. 1358.

19. *Report of the Comptroller of the Currency*, 1868, House Exec. Doc. No. 4, 40th Cong., 3rd sess., p. iii.

20. *Treasury Report*, 1865, p.x; *Report of the Comptroller*, 1865, House Exec. Doc. No. 4, 39th Cong., 1st sess., p. 65.

21. *Treasury Report*, 1865, pp. 52-54. McCulloch was disgruntled when Congress stopped his retirements of United States notes in February 1868. He had almost an obsession for contraction in order to obtain resumption of specie payments.

22. *Report of the Comptroller*, 1866, p. xi. Also, *Treasury Report*, 1868. See also Redlich, *Molding of American Banking*, part 2. Redlich argues that the so-called National Bank Act was really a national currency act, which originally would have promoted a national currency by the existing state banks. The bill that Secretary of the Treasury Salmon P. Chase foresaw would have left the chartering of such banks with the states. This idea gave way in the final bill to national chartering but with preference given to existing state institutions (pp. 101-102 and 118).

23. *Report of the Comptroller*, 1867, 40th Cong., 2nd sess., House Exec. Doc. No. 4, p. 11. See also *Treasury Report*, 1865, p. 4.

24. See, for example, *CG*, 41st Cong., 2nd sess., appendix, pp. 525-528, in which E. C. Ingersoll of Illinois discussed not only currency per capita, but also currency per acre of territory in which it was issued. He also compared per capita currency quantities of the United States with those of France and Germany and found the U.S. values wanting.

25. *CG*, 41st Cong., 2nd sess., p. 4949. Sentiment in the Senate was to hold the total stock of currency constant. It was said that the Senate would not pass a bill that would increase the currency, and the House would not allow a bill to pass that would contract it (ibid., p. 4950).

26. Ibid., p. 4950.

27. Ibid., p. 543.

28. Ibid.

29. Ibid., p. 544.

30. Congressmen correctly approximated the average national bank reserve requirement at 20 percent. Thus the additional $45 million of national bank notes would require about $9 million of United States notes as reserves in national banks.

31. Ibid., p. 5303. Also appendix, p. 700.

32. The reason for the paucity of national banks in the South has never been satisfactorily investigated. An hypothesis that looks more and more appealing and is suggested by the large volume of publicity it received at the time is the relationship between state usury laws and the payment of interest on deposits. By a provision of the National Bank Act, state regulations governed maximum rates of interest that national banks could pay and receive. State usury laws differed from state to state. Some New England states had no maxima, while in many southern states the maximum rate was only 6 percent. As it was, about two-thirds of the national banks paid interest on deposits. In 1870, 1,064 national

banks paid $6.5 million, while 540 paid no interest (*Report of the Comptroller,* 1870, p. 28). Thus, to compete for reserve funds many national banks felt compelled to pay interest on deposits. If the maximum rates they could charge were constrained such that the spread between what they could charge for loans and what they paid on deposits was not profitable, they could not continue issuing notes and they had little reason to remain as national banks. (See *Report of the Comptroller,* 1872, pp. 89-90.)

33. "Country" national bank balances in New York national banks increased from $50 million to $63 million, and other reserve city national bank balances with New York national banks increased from $24 million to $31 million.

34. *Treasury Report,* 1872, pp. xix-xxii. He discussed bank-induced inflation and depression. He recognized almost explicitly that note elasticity was perverse as "provided" by the commercial banking system.

35. Ibid., p. xxii.

36. *Treasury Report,* 1874, pp. 26-30. The act of February 25, 1862, pledged repurchase of at least 1 percent per year of the outstanding interest-bearing debt to be held as an interest-earning asset by the Treasury Department.

37. U. S. Congress, 42nd Cong., 3rd sess., *Report to the Committee on Banking and Currency on the Increased Issue of Legal Tender Notes,* House Exec. Doc. No. 42, December 1872.

38. U. S. Congress, 42nd Cong., 3rd sess., *Senate Report No. 275,* 1872, pp. 1-5.

39. *Report on the Increased Issue of Legal Tender Notes,* pp. 1 and 2. (See also *CR,* 43rd Cong., 1st sess., p. 704.) McCulloch had set the precedent Boutwell referred to by reissuing notes several times between 1866 and 1868. "In answer to remonstrance against this practice," wrote James G. Blaine, "the Secretary maintained that the authority . . . [was] within his discretion. This was unquestionably the law of the case" (Blaine, *Twenty Years of Congress,* p. 329).

40. *Senate Report No. 275,* pp. 8-10. The minority consisted of G. W. Wright and T. W. Ferry of Michigan. Ferry, especially, was a greenbacker who treated the idea of a metallic standard cavalierly. Their opinion would have had more substance if applied specifically to those periods when Congress was not in session, especially the fall.

41. Eugene M. Lerner, "The Monetary and Fiscal Programs of the Confederate Government, 1861-65," *Journal of Political Economy* 62 (1954): 506-522; idem, "Money, Prices, and Wages in the Confederacy, 1861-65," *Journal of Political Economy* 63 (1955): 20-40; idem, "Inflation in the Confederacy, 1861-65," in *Studies in the Quantity Theory of Money,* ed. Milton Friedman (Chicago: University of Chicago Press, 1956), pp. 163-175.

42. John M. Godfrey, "Monetary Expansion in the Confederacy," (Ph.D. diss., University of Georgia, 1976). This work will be published in 1978 as a book by the Arno Press.

43. Ibid., pp. 54-58.

44. Ibid., p. 122.

45. Ibid., pp. 118-119.

46. Ibid., p. 123.

47. See table 7.1.
48. Godfrey, p. 14.

8. The Panic of 1873 and Resumption

1. *Dictionary of American Biography,* vol. 15, p. 578.
2. *Treasury Report,* 1878, p. xi.
3. *Report of the Comptroller,* 1874, House Exec. Doc. No. 2, p. 159
4. *Treasury Report,* 1872, p. xx.
5. *Treasury Report,* 1873, pp. xv-xvi. One can hardly imagine a more pusillanimous and vacuous observation. By inflation Richardson did not mean rising prices but a price level that was still too high to allow convertibility of greenbacks for gold at the prewar parity.
6. Ibid., pp. xii-xx, xxx.
7. Ibid., pp. 95 and 111. This observation emphasizes that United States notes were reserves of the national banks and served to redeem national bank notes. In fact, the inability of some national banks in New York City to pay out United States notes for national bank notes is what triggered the panic in the first place.
8. *CR,* 43rd Cong., 1st sess., p. 700.
9. Ibid., appendix, pp. 17-19.
10. Ibid., appendix, pp. 20-22. David Mellish, a Republican congressman from New York, had substantially the same opinion as Boutwell on the morality of changes in the price level. His policy ideal, however, waived resumption in favor of a fixed stock of $800 million in United States notes (ibid., pp. 1097-1103).
11. See ibid., pp. 974-975, for a statement by Thomas Bayard of Delaware.
12. Hepburn, *History of Currency,* p. 313.
13. *CR,* 43rd Cong., 1st sess., pp. 13-15. The differences in per capita currency holdings between, say, New England and the South were startling—approximately $30 per person in New England to $3 per person in the South.
14. Ibid., p. 455.
15. Ibid., p. 165.
16. See Irwin Unger, *The Greenback Era,* (Princeton, N.J.: Princeton University Press, 1964), pp. 251-254, for a discussion of the political climate in which the Resumption Act was wrought. The abrupt about-face from monetary indulgence to apparent monetary austerity still presents some puzzles.
17. Blaine, *Twenty Years of Congress,* pp. 563-565.
18. See *Report of the Comptroller,* 1874, House Exec. Doc. No. 2, pp. 123-133. Even if the states that were entitled to additional notes did not want their share, provision still had to be made to redistribute the notes in case these states ultimately called for them. Redistribution, of course, would provoke other problems.
19. *CR,* 43rd Cong., 2nd sess., p. 188.
20. Ibid. This passage is followed by the provision that states the date (January 1, 1879) for redemption of United States notes in coin. Since national bank

notes were convertible by law into United States notes, this date for resumption also applied to coin redemption of national bank notes.

21. Unger, *Greenback Era*, p. 253.

22. *CR*, 43rd Cong., 2nd sess., p. 195.

23. Ibid., p. 196. Additional statements by Schurz and others at this point again made clear the antipathy to the use of a reserve of United States notes issued at the discretion of the secretary of the Treasury.

24. Ibid., p. 204.

25. This result would have been contingent on the ability of the national banks to attract deposits of United States notes, not an impossible task since banks in many states were allowed to pay interest on deposits.

26. By this time deposit banking was so well developed that circulation of notes was unnecessary.

27. See Unger, *Greenback Era*, p. 264. Unger notes the significance of the 80 percent clause and correctly assesses its impact.

28. United States notes outstanding are not shown in the table. They were $383 million in early 1875 and were fixed forever at $346 million on May 31, 1878. So they were reduced by $36 million during this interval. The working of the formula in the Resumption Act thus resulted in a decrease in United States notes and an approximately equal decrease in national bank notes.

29. *CR*, 43rd Cong., 2nd sess., pp. 206-208.

30. Ibid., p. 197.

31. Free banking, in this era, meant abolition of the statutory limitations on national bank note issue. It is not used here in the sense of banking firms free to enter the industry so long as certain rules were followed. (I am indebted to the late Bray Hammond for this caution.)

32. *Treasury Report*, 1877, pp. xv-xx.

33. U.S. Congress, 44th Cong., 2nd sess., *Report and Hearings of the Silver Commission, Senate Report No. 703*, 1877.

34. Ibid., p. 1.

35. Ibid., pp. 127 and 133. The verb "repealed" implied "amended so as to include silver."

36. Ibid., pp. 134-138. Boutwell wanted an international conference that would reestablish silver as a universal legal tender and so prevent the United States from absorbing the world's silver.

37. Ibid., pp. 155-156 (their italics).

38. Ibid., pp. 159-160.

39. Ibid., pp. 129-131. The proposed silver dollar of 412.5 grains was already at a 3 percent discount in gold. The silver revaluation suggested by these three men would have promoted an additional 3 percent discrepancy, even though their ratio of 15.5 to 1 was more realistic in the rest of the world.

40. Ibid., pp. 131-133.

41. Kindahl, "Economic Factors," p. 47. Hepburn, while he specifically mentioned the Silver Commission, neither admitted the recommendations for devaluation nor pointed out the pressure for silver remonetization as a political price for resumption.

42. *Treasury Report*, 1877, p. xxxiv.

43. Kindahl estimates that the money stock in the hands of the public declined from $1,703 million to $1,557 million between 1875 and 1878, while the index of wholesale prices fell from 130 in 1874 to 99 in 1878 ("Economic Factors," p. 40).

44. Hepburn, *History of Currency*, p. 238.

45. Hindsight suggests that the gold dollar should have been devalued to accommodate the market price of gold no later than 1869 or 1870, when the price level and the nominal price of gold were only 12 to 15 percent higher than their 1860 values. Such a move would not have seriously compromised any moral codes of polity.

46. The speech in early 1874 by George Boutwell, who had returned to a seat in the United States Senate after his term as secretary of the Treasury, reveals this acceptance of constancy in the money stock. "We have a citadel," he said, by which he meant a majority that could successfully resist the contractionists on the one hand and the inflationists on the other, "and we had better keep in it. If we are driven out, we shall then only be in the position which the Senator from Missouri [Carl Schurz] advises us voluntarily to accept" (*CR*, 43rd Cong., 1st sess., appendix, p. 27). Schurz had suggested to Boutwell that the true way to prevent inflation was to go for contraction.

47. The three secretaries were Benjamin Bristow, Lot Morrill, and John Sherman, all of whom had been congressmen.

48. Friedman and Schwartz, *Monetary History*, p. 82. Friedman and Schwartz had the company of Senator Allen Thurman of Ohio who made the same observation in 1874.

9. Controversy over Currency Denominations

1. For example, Adam Smith, *Wealth of Nations*, pp. 307-309. Also, Henry Thornton, *The Paper Credit of Great Britain*, ed. F. A. von Hayek, (New York: Rinehart, 1939), p. 189.

2. An exception is Redlich, *Molding of American Banking*, part 2, p. 89. He observes without elaboration that the ideas for prohibiting small notes were "as old as they were incorrect."

3. See W. Philip Gramm, "The Optimum Nominal Stock of Money and Cheap Money' Movements in the United States," forthcoming.

4. Charles F. Dunbar, *The Theory and History of Banking* (New York: C. P. Putnam's Sons, 1922), pp. 62-63.

5. Davis R. Dewey, *State Banking before the Civil War*, National Monetary Commission, Sen. Doc. No. 581, 61st Cong., 2nd sess. (1910), p. 64.

6. Lloyd W. Mints, *History of Banking Theory* (Chicago: University of Chicago Press, 1945), p. 148.

7. See Dewey, *State Banking*, pp. 65 and passim. See also Hepburn, *History of Currency*, pp. 84, 90, 94, 163, 181, 308.

8. Smith, *Wealth of Nations*, p. 308.

9. Henry Thornton, *Paper Credit*, p. 189.

10. Smith, *Wealth of Nations*, p. 306, note.

11. Jacob Viner, *Studies in the Theory of International Trade* (New York: Harper and Brothers, 1937) p. 179, and Ricardo, *Economic Essays*, p. 213.

12. Viner, *Studies*, p. 182.

13. Knox, *United States Notes*, pp. 37-38.

14. Hepburn, *History of Currency*, p. 89 (my italics).

15. *ASPF* 3. See also ch. 2.

16. Hepburn, *History of Currency*, p. 163. The use of the word *barter* by Hepburn is revealing. Silver was undervalued at the mint and therefore a commodity during this period. Without bank-issued small notes, many transactions undoubtedly were barter.

17. Dewey, *State Banking*, pp. 66-83, and Hepburn, *History of Currency*, pp. 166-167.

18. A few writers recognized this truth. See Richard Hildreth, *Banks, Banking and Paper Currencies* (1840), reprinted by Greenwood Press (1968).

19. Neil Carothers, *Fractional Currency* (New York: Reprints of Economic Classics, Augustus M. Kelley, 1967), pp. 76-78. A common device was to cut the half dollar into four more-or-less equal pieces (p. 81).

20. Ibid., p. 92.

21. Ibid., pp. 110-111.

22. Ibid., p. 160. This example should have proven beyond all doubt that the inflation and disappearance of metallic currency came first and were followed by innovations of substitute paper currency. Knox also reported that premiums of 10 to 12 percent over its commodity value were offered for small amounts of silver coin "by businessmen who desired it for convenience in making change" (Knox, *United States Notes*, p. 100).

23. Hepburn, *History of Currency*, p. 308.

24. *Report of the Comptroller of the Currency*, 1872, House Exec. Doc. No. 1562, pp. 96-97. The Alabama notes were in five denominations which read: "The State of Alabama: Receivable as ____ dollars in payment of all dues to the State. Montgomery, May 1, 1867." They were signed by the governor and the comptroller of public accounts.

25. *Report of the Comptroller*, 1873, House Exec. Doc. No. 1603, p. 109.

26. Ibid.

27. House of Representatives, 43rd Cong., 1st sess., *Miscellaneous Document No. 48*, 19 Dec. 1873, pp. 1-2.

28. *Report of the Treasurer*, 1874, House Exec. Doc. No. 1641, p. 353.

29. Charles Moran, *Money, Currencies and Banking* (New York, 1875), p. 4.

30. Ibid., p. 39. While Moran was correct in his evaluation of denominational factors, he was as an antibullionist wrong in his assessment of quantitative factors. His case demonstrates how quantity of the total can get mixed up with quantities of specific denominations. The former can be overabundant, while a specific denomination can be distressingly short, for example small denominations in 1862.

31. Richard Selden, "Monetary Velocity in the United States," in *Studies in the Quantity Theory of Money*, ed. Milton Friedman (Chicago: University of Chicago Press, 1956), p. 189 and passim. Also Clark Warburton, "The Secular

Trend in Monetary Velocity," *Quarterly Journal of Economics* 63 (1949): 68-91; reprinted in Clark Warburton, *Depression, Inflation and Monetary Policy* (Baltimore, Md.: Johns Hopkins Press, 1966), pp. 199-209. Selden's data sources for his V-39 velocity values are the same as those for his V-27 estimates. These latter were taken from Warburton's study and used income data compiled by Robert F. Martin, *National Income in the United States, 1799-1938*, National Industrial Conference Board (New York, 1939). (Warburton, *Depression, Inflation and Monetary Policy*, p. 201, note 3.)

32. Friedman and Schwartz, *Monetary History*. See also Warburton, *Depression, Inflation and Monetary Policy*, p. 212.

33. Friedman and Schwartz treat at length the question of secular change in velocity. Their data show a slight downward trend from 1900 to 1914, a rough constancy from 1914 to 1929, a sharp decline in the early thirties followed by a rise to 1941, another sharp decline to 1946, and then a constant rise to 1960 (pp. 136, 197, 494, 641). The post-World War II figures, they note, show a "clear upward trend" (p. 643). Later studies on velocity measurement indicate that the upward trend has continued through the sixties and into the seventies. Therefore no clear-cut *secular* decline can be inferred for the twentieth century, the short-run effects of the depression and World War II notwithstanding.

34. Let M be the stock of money, P the price index value for goods and services exchanged for money, R the volume of goods and services exchanged for money, r the volume of goods and services bartered or exchanged by means of unaccounted money, $V_{R'}$ apparent velocity, and V_R real velocity. Then apparent velocity is $V_{R'} = (PR + Pr)/M$, while real velocity is $V_R = PR/M$. Obviously, $V_R > V_R$. But over time as barter exchange is replaced by monetary transactions, PR will come to include the value of goods and services formerly valued as Pr, and $V'_R \rightarrow V_R$ as $Pr \rightarrow 0$.

35. Warburton, *Depression, Inflation and Monetary Policy*, pp. 208-210.

36. The reliability of Martin's estimates of income is subject to some serious doubts. Aside from questionable methods and some obviously spurious results, he gives no indication of how much nonmonetary income is included in his estimates. In all fairness, it was not his intention to do so. Therefore his income estimates are for the *value* of that income but do not give any indication of how much of this income was exchanged for money. Selden unaccountably reports that Martin's estimates (not identified by name, but just by reference to Warburton) exclude nonmonetary income ("Monetary Velocity," p. 244), but Martin clearly does not make any such adjustment. His estimates are simply projections of production figures from the census of manufactures multiplied by price relatives.

37. Fractional currency is not included here. The fractional paper currency in existence from 1862 to 1876, although explicitly recorded in treasurers' reports, is subject to extraordinary error due to unaccounted losses and destructions such as the currency destroyed in the Chicago fire. After 1877 metallic fractional currency replaced the paper currency of the earlier years. The totals of this latter currency are not readily calculable because of the reimportations after 1876 of millions of United States coins that had been exported in 1861 and 1862. No constraints on fractional currency were noticeable after resumption. Also these data

include neither the very largest denominations ($100 and over), nor state and national bank deposits. However, the denominations listed in the table contain about 90 percent of the high-powered money stock.

38. The price data are from Warren and Pearson's Wholesale Price Index (1910-1914 = 100). This index is very sensitive, so it may exaggerate somewhat the fluctuation in the general price level.

39. The data for 1879 are counted as the end values for the first period and as the beginning values for the second period.

40. Growth of real output and the behavior of velocity do not lend themselves to accurate measurement before 1890. See Friedman and Schwartz, *Monetary History*, pp. 36-44, 87, and passim.

41. Richard Sylla argues that note and deposit issues by private (unincorporated) banks provided another significant core of unaccountable moneys. This contention is both complementary to and compatible with the analysis that refers to scrip, barter, and trade credit. (See Richard Sylla, "Forgotten Men of Money: Private Bankers in Early U. S. History," *Journal of Economic History* 36 (1976): 173-188.)

10. The Golden Cloud with the Silver Lining

1. In 1882 Congress passed a law implying, but not specifying, that the Treasury should maintain a minimum gold reserve of $100 million against outstanding currency obligations. This responsibility was made explicit and the amount was increased to $150 million by the Gold Coin Act of March 14, 1900.

2. Friedman and Schwartz, *Monetary History*, p. 21.

3. Even though national bank notes were specified only as legal tender for all government dues and payments, they were almost always exchangeable for United States notes at par and were treated for the most part as if they were full legal tender. Occasionally—for example, during a panic—a small premium might appear between them and other legal tender.

4. The marketable bullion value of silver in the silver dollar was $0.93 in 1878 and fell constantly until it was only $0.49 in 1894. During all this time, it was legal tender for one dollar just as were United States notes which had no bullion value. Thus the bullion value of the silver in the silver dollar could not have been responsible for any of its monetary value. Silver dollars would have circulated as exchange media worth one dollar each, even if they had had no bullion value, so long as the government invested them with the legal tender feature.

5. The market price of silver was already below its mint price at this time. Therefore $24 million expended on silver purchases bought more than enough silver to produce $24 million worth of coined silver. The difference (or "profit") between the total value of the coined silver and the cost of acquiring it (seigniorage) was realized by the government.

6. F. W. Taussig, *The Silver Situation in the United States* (New York, 1893), p. 8.

7. The desirability of increasing the silver content of the silver dollar was recognized by many secretaries and legislators; see, for example, Sherman's report for 1880, p. xix. In fact, the real price of silver did not fall before 1894, but

its gold price did because of the appreciation in the real value of gold.

8. *Treasury Report*, 1881, p. x. The ratio, he said, had fluctuated between 36 and 45 percent. At this time almost no silver had been issued, so no gold balance was considered to be held against outstanding silver.

9. *Treasury Report*, 1882, pp. xix-xx.

10. Ibid., p. xxix.

11. Ibid., pp. xxvii-xxviii. At this time the so-called 3 percent debt was callable. It amounted to about $130 million.

12. See *Report of the Comptroller*, 1884, pp. 149-154.

13. Redlich, *Molding of American Banking*, part 2, p. 158. See also pp. 159-167.

14. *Treasury Report*, 1885, p. xiv.

15. Ibid., pp. xlvi, xxxvi (his emphasis).

16. *CR*, 48th Cong., 2nd sess., pp. 238-244.

17. Ibid., pp. 245-246.

18. Ibid.

19. Ibid., p. 247.

20. Ibid., p. 248.

21. Horace White, *Money and Banking*, new ed. (Boston: Ginn and Co., 1935), p. 272. The authority and obligation to issue silver certificates in these lower denominations were made explicit in an appropriation act passed July 1, 1886 (*CR*, 49th Cong., 1st sess., p. 6421).

22. *CR*, 49th Cong., 1st sess., pp. 6877-78.

23. Ibid., p. 6879.

24. Ibid., pp. 6923-25.

25. Ibid., pp. 6884, 6887. Warner's speech confirmed that he was very familiar with the writings of Colonel Torrens and Lord Overstone. "The 'honest' dollar," he said further on in his speech, "is the dollar that has the same value—purchasing power—when one parts with it as when he received it" (ibid.). All through the congressional debates on monetary affairs during the nineteenth century, an amazing number of congressmen displayed a keen understanding of prices, the value of money, and the relationship of these variables to the quantity of money.

26. Ibid., p. 6931.

27. The House had a majority of Democrats, but the Senate was still Republican.

28. Ibid., p. 6935.

29. Ibid., p. 6937.

30. A lot of argument developed over just how much of a surplus there was and what items constituted it. The Senate debate over the resolution dealt more thoroughly with these questions.

31. Ibid., p. 6946.

32. Ibid., p. 7675. The separation of purse and sword as a principle of democratic government was noted frequently in debates throughout the nineteenth century.

33. Ibid., p. 7687.

34. Ibid., appendix, pp. 355-359. Jones included in his speech a statement on

the impossibility of general overproduction, à la Jean Baptiste Say. "Whoever produces anything for sale creates thereby a new demand for something else, and the power of the world to consume depends upon the extent to which it produces" (ibid., p. 361).

35. Ibid., p. 7682. He cited the *London Economist* as authority for his Bank of England data.

36. Ibid., p. 7684. Sherman was surely the most experienced and probably the most sophisticated congressman in financial affairs. He was the only speaker who recognized explicitly the semifiat nature of the silver dollar.

37. Ibid., pp. 7738-40. The trade-dollar provisions were inappropriate to the bill and were taken out later. The trade dollar was then repealed by means of a separate act.

38. Ibid., pp. 7736-37, 7742.

39. The senators on the Committee were Allison of Iowa, Aldrich of Rhode Island, and Beck of Kentucky. The representatives were Morrison of Illinois, Breckenridge of Kentucky, and Hiscock of New York.

40. *CR*, 49th Cong., 1st sess., p. 7939. "Suspension" was adopted rather than the "postponement" inserted by the Senate.

41. Ibid., p. 7986. Weaver claimed that a caucus of senate Republicans, who met at the home of a former secretary of the Treasury (Hugh McCulloch?), did the actual amending.

42. Ibid., pp. 7988, 7990, 8002. See statements by Bland of Missouri and Warner of Ohio.

43. Ibid., p. 7998. Statement by Benjamin Butterworth of Ohio. The Treasury reserve of $100 million, Butterworth stated, "is the ballast which keeps our monetary ship steady as she moves through the sea of financial troubles which constantly threaten. [Applause.]" (ibid.)

44. *Treasury Report, 1887*, pp. xxii-xxvii. The three percent certificates had been issued in 1882, and were callable at the pleasure of the government. About $130 million were purchased and retired in the two year-period 1887-1889, even though President Cleveland never signed the resolution.

45. Between October 1885 and October 1887, national bank notes were reduced by $107 million (*Report of the Comptroller*, 1889, p. 412).

46. *Report of the Comptroller*, 1889, p. 399.

47. *Treasury Report*, 1887, p. xxviii.

48. Ibid.

49. Ibid., p. xxxiii.

50. *Report of the Treasurer*, 1895, p. 34.

51. *Report of the Comptroller*, 1888, p. 453.

52. *CR*, 50th Cong., 1st sess., index, p. 753.

53. Ibid., pp. 1596, 1597. Thomas Reed of Maine made the same allegation in the House of Representatives (ibid., p. 1600).

54. Ibid., pp. 1597, 1598.

55. Ibid., pp. 1601-1602. He noted that open-market purchases of some significance had been conducted by James Guthrie, a fellow Kentuckian, during the administration of Franklin Pierce some thirty-five years earlier.

56. Ibid., pp. 1606, 2394-2398, 2739, 2779.

57. *Treasury Report*, 1888, p. xxvi. He stated that the Treasury had paid out $44 million for the purchase of bonds during October and November 1888. However, he did not mention the fact that this action occurred at election time.

58. *Treasury Report*, 1889, pp. lxxxvii and lxxxix.

59. Ibid.

11. The Fall of Silver

1. Hepburn, *History of Currency*, pp. 342-366 and passim. Also Charles Hoffman, "The Depression of the Nineties," *Journal of Economic History* 16 (1956): 137-164.

2. White, *Money and Banking*, pp. 88-89.

3. All secretaries without exception bought only the minimum, $2 million a year.

4. Harrison had 90,000 fewer popular votes than Cleveland but won the electoral vote 233 to 168.

5. *Treasury Report*, 1889, p. lxxiv.

6. Ibid., pp. lxxiii and lxxiv.

7. *CR*, 51st Cong., 1st sess., p. 6167.

8. Ibid., p. 6172. At a price of $0.4444 an ounce for silver, the expenditure on 4.5 million ounces would have been just equal to the $2 million a month currently being purchased. The price of silver averaged $1.05 an ounce in 1890, which meant a monthly purchase of almost $5 million under the terms of the Silver Purchase Act passed that year. The price dropped rapidly thereafter, reaching $0.78 an ounce in 1893 and $0.60 an ounce in 1897.

9. Ibid., p. 6182.

10. Ibid., p. 6982.

11. Ibid., p. 7018.

12. Ibid., p. 7103.

13. Ibid., pp. 7226 and 7264.

14. Friedman and Schwartz, *Monetary History*, p. 705.

15. Ibid., p. 104.

16. Hepburn, *History of Currency*, p. 304.

17. J. Rogers Hollingsworth, *The Whirligig of Politics* (Chicago: University of Chicago Press, 1963), p. 2.

18. *CR*, 53rd Cong., 1st sess., pp. 205-206.

19. Ibid., p. 242.

20. One ounce equals 480 grains.

21. Ibid., p. 320.

22. A 28-to-1 ratio in the market implied a divergence from par of thirty-one cents per ounce, if par was a mint price for silver that resulted in a 20-to-1 mint ratio. With the mint ratio at 16 to 1 (a mint price of one dollar for 371.25 grains of pure silver), the market divergence from par was 55 cents per ounce.

23. Ibid., pp. 307-309.

24. See statement by John Warner of New York, ibid., p. 325.

25. Ibid., p. 553.

26. Ibid., p. 310.

27. Ibid., pp. 363-364.

28. Ibid., p. 276.

29. For example, William Stewart of Nevada (ibid., p. 294).

30. Ibid., p. 496. Data were furnished by Charles Morgan of Missouri.

31. Ibid., p. 463. Sibley had an interesting description of "intrisic value." This concept, he said, was meaningless. The intrinsic value of a wooden plank 24' x 1' x 2" was worth more than a million dollars to a drowning man.

32. Hollingsworth, *Whirligig*, p. 16.

33. *CR*, 53rd Cong., 1st sess., p. 561.

34. Ibid.

35. *Treasury Report*, 1893, p. lxxv.

36. *CR*, 53rd Cong., 1st sess., p. 1004.

37. House rules of procedure prevent filibuster. It has always been possible in the Senate, although subject to cloture action by a two-thirds majority.

38. Ibid., p. 1102.

39. See statement by Henry Teller of Colorado, ibid., p. 1350.

40. Ibid., appendix, pp. 606-705.

41. Ibid., p. 618.

42. Ibid., p. 1251. The predicted division was 53 to 32 for repeal. The actual vote two months later was 43 to 32. The silver Republicans included Wolcott and Teller of Colorado, Stewart and Jones of Nevada, Dubois of Idaho, Pettigrew of South Dakota, and Hansbrough of North Dakota. They were joined by several Populists: Allen of Nebraska, Kyle of South Dakota, and Peffer and Martin of Kansas.

43. Ibid., p. 1092.

44. Ibid., p. 1309.

45. Ibid., p. 705. This same article was reported in the Senate by Richard Coke of Texas the same day.

46. Hollingsworth, *Whirligig*, p. 17.

47. *CR*, 53rd Cong., 1st sess., p. 2910. Cited in the Senate 28 October 1893 by Arthur Gorman of Maryland.

48. Ibid., p. 2597.

49. Ibid., p. 2917.

50. Ibid., p. 2821.

51. Ibid., pp. 2947 and 2933-36.

52. Ibid., pp. 2886-88. Those who had changed from yea to nay were Faulkner (W. Va.), Hill (N.Y.), Mills (Tex.), Ransom (N.C.), Turpie (Ind.), Voorhees (Ind.), Squire (Wash.), and Gordon (Ga.). Most of these men had been outspoken advocates of free silver until 1893.

53. Ibid., pp. 2917-20.

54. Ibid., p. 2953. Stewart's plea for devaluation of the gold dollar was one of many times in the century that such a change had been seriously considered. In 1834 the gold content of the dollar was reduced 6 percent; and in 1878 one minority report of the Silver Commission recommended devaluation of the gold dollar by 2.6 percent. (See chs. 4 and 8.) Stewart's proposed devaluation of 25 percent was too large to be politically feasible even though it was economically reasonable.

55. Ibid., pp. 2930-31.

56. Ibid., p. 2946.

57. Ibid., p. 3066.

58. See Hoffman, "The Depression of the Nineties," and W. Jett Lauck, *The Causes of the Panic of 1893* (Boston: Houghton Mifflin, 1907).

59. Alfred Marshall, *Money, Credit and Commerce* (London: Macmillan, 1929), p. 64.

60. World gold production fell gradually but steadily until about 1885. It then rose gradually until 1893, but more rapidly to the end of the century and for many years thereafter. In the two years 1899-1900 production equaled or exceeded that for almost any five-year period from 1870 to 1890 (Marshall, *Money, Credit, and Commerce,* p. 70).

61. Friedman and Schwartz, *Monetary History,* pp. 131-134. See also Rendigs Fels, *American Business Cycles* (Chapel Hill, N.C.: University of North Carolina Press, 1959), pp. 209-212 and passim.

62. Friedman and Schwartz, *Monetary History,* p. 134, note.

63. Alfred Marshal suggested in 1888 a scheme that he labeled "symmetallism." The mint would fashion ingots of gold and silver. The silver ingot would weigh, say, twenty times as much as the gold ingot, if the current market ratio of value was 20 to 1. The government would maintain the mint price of a *pair* of ingots. The price of one metal could then fall if the price of the other rose (*Money, Credit and Commerce,* pp. 64-67). Marshall's scheme had much to recommend it, but it was never discussed in Congress, so far as I could ascertain, as a possible alternative to either monometallism or bimetallism. Its principal interest seemed to lie in academic circles.

12. Monetary Policy in the Golden Era

1. See *Historical Statistics of the United States,* p. 127. A 10 percent decline in prices does not imply a severe depression. However, the peak of prices in 1892 was already 20 percent below the peak for 1872, while prices by 1897 were almost down to their level of 1860.

2. Hepburn, *History of Currency,* p. 351.

3. Ibid., pp. 351-352.

4. Hollingsworth, *Whirligig,* pp. 84-107.

5. Ibid., p. 102.

6. *Treasury Report,* 1896, p. lxxiii. No vestige of Carlisle's former free-silver principles can be found in any of his secretarial writings.

7. *Treasury Report,* 1897, p. lxxiv.

8. Ibid., pp. lxxvi-lxxvii.

9. Ibid., p. lxxvii.

10. *Treasury Report,* 1899, pp. lxxxvii-xciv.

11. Indianapolis Monetary Commission, *Report of the Monetary Commission of the Indianapolis Convention,* (Indianapolis, Ind.: Hollenbeck Press, 1900), pp. 60-74. The convention was composed of "boards of trade, chambers of commerce, commercial clubs, and other similar bodies of the United States." Some of the better-known members were H. H. Hanna, A. Barton Hepburn, and J. Lawrence Laughlin, the academic economist from the University of Chicago.

12. *Treasury Report*, 1900, pp. lxxii-lxxiii.

13. Ibid., p. xxviii.

14. Ibid., p. xxiii.

15. *Treasury Report*, 1901, p. 22.

16. Ibid., pp. 74-75 (his italics).

17. Ibid., p. 76. Gage never seemed to associate changes in bank credit and deposits with changes in the gold base. He never included in his analyses any awareness of the price-specie flow mechanism.

18. Ibid., p. 77. Gage cited the appealing analogy between a federated United States of America and a federated central bank. This was an image that would enlist a lot of political support in the future.

19. *Dictionary of American Biography*, vol. 17, pp. 43-44. He was also in favor of high tariffs in contrast with his chief, President Theodore Roosevelt. See *Nation* 81 (1905): 272; 82 (1906): 502-503.

20. This kind of transfer had been carried out by at least two previous secretaries—Fairchild and Gage. Gage had done it in 1898 when cash balances had risen exceptionally due to the lack of synchronization between the sale of securities to finance the war with Spain and actual expenditures on the war effort. Fairchild had done the same thing for policy purposes during 1887. Congress censured his action and passed legislation that countermanded it.

21. A. Piatt Andrew, "Treasury and Banks under Secretary Shaw," *Quarterly Journal of Economics* 21 (1907): 540-541.

22. L. M. Shaw, *Current Issues* (New York: D. Appleton and Co., 1908), p. 322. Comment on Report of American Bankers Association (30 November 1906). Also *Treasury Report*, 1904, pp. 40-41.

23. *Treasury Report*, 1902, p. 58.

24. *Treasury Report*, 1905, p. 34; and 1906, pp. 37, 39, and 40. Most of Shaw's remarks were directed at the call loan rate of interest. "The sure indication of world-wide money stringency," he stated in 1906, "is the fact that legitimate interest rates on commercial paper everywhere are higher than for many years" (p. 40).

25. *Treasury Report*, 1902, p. 58.

26. Ibid., p. 2.

27. Ibid., pp. 58-60.

28. *Treasury Report*, 1905, p. 34. This idea of special issues of currency subject to a nominal tax was widespread at this time.

29. *Treasury Report*, 1904, p. 8. When government securities were repurchased, the Treasury's balance in the subtreasuries diminished appreciably, but its deposit accounts with the national banks did not increase the way they would when cash reserves were deposited with them. Bank reserves in general would be influenced equally by either method, although a direct treasury deposit was more immediately realized as reserves.

30. *Treasury Report*, 1905, pp. 8 and 9.

31. *Treasury Report*, 1906, p. 42.

32. *Nation* 83 (1906): pp. 216-217.

33. The following analysis refers primarily to the articles by Patton and Andrew and to Kinley's book on the independent treasury: Eugene B. Patton, "Secretary Shaw and Precedents as to Treasury Control over the Money Mar-

ket," *Journal of Political Economy* 15 (1907): 65-87; Andrew, "Treasury under Shaw," pp. 519-568; David Kinley, *The Independent Treasury of the United States and Its Relation to the Banks of the Country*, Sen. Doc. No. 587, 61st Cong., 2nd sess., National Monetary Commission, 1910.

34. Patton, "Precedents," p. 86.

35. Andrew, "Treasury under Shaw," pp. 520-523.

36. Ibid., pp. 524 and 538.

37. *Nation*, amusingly enough, by 1906 allowed that Shaw's policy of depositing the public money in banks was justifiable because it "would have followed precedent." The editor did not seem to remember how strongly this same policy had been criticized a few years before as unprecedented! This article went on to attack Shaw's gold-import policy because "the use of Government money, avowedly to influence a financial market with whose movement the Treasury is not itself concerned, is something new" (*Nation* 82 (1906): 315).

38. Shaw, *Current Issues*, pp. 352 and 358. Address before Bankers' Association of Washington, D. C., September 1905.

39. Andrew, "Treasury under Shaw," pp. 522-523.

40. Patton, "Precedents," p. 86. Kinley made almost exactly the same criticism. See *Independent Treasury*, p. 271.

41. Andrew, "Treasury under Shaw," pp. 559-566.

42. Shaw, *Current Issues*, p. 370. Address before State Bankers' Association, Louisville, Kentucky, 10 October 1906.

43. Ibid., p. 279. Address before the Ohio Bankers' Association, September 1905. Also *Treasury Report*, 1905, p. 8.

44. Andrew, "Treasury under Shaw," p. 547.

45. *Treasury Report*, 1906, p. 49.

46. *Treasury Report*, 1908, pp. 20-22.

47. Kinley, *Independent Treasury*, p. 280. In 1907, Kinley observed, "the surplus was all deposited in banks. The Treasury could do nothing more." Other factors, such as aggressive gold policies by the Bank of England in the first half of the year, also provoked trouble. See O. M. W. Sprague, *History of Crises under the National Banking System*, Senate Doc. No. 538, 61st Cong., 2nd sess., National Monetary Commission, 1910, pp. 241-243.

48. U.S. Congress, 60th Cong., 1st sess., *Response of the Secretary of the Treasury . . . In Regard to Treasury Operations*, Senate Doc. No. 208, p. 32.

49. Kinley, *Independent Treasury*, pp. 326-338.

50. *Treasury Report*, 1906, p. 37. In 1903 he noted that a stock market decline had not been an issue in treasury policymaking. The decline had had no effect on general business due to treasury support of legitimate trade (*Treasury Report*, 1903, p. 45).

51. Shaw, *Current Issues*, p. 295.

52. Remark made during lecture, University of Chicago, 1952.

53. Friedman and Schwartz, *Monetary History*, p. 150.

13. Advent of the Federal Reserve System

1. Friedman and Schwartz, *Monetary History*, pp. 189-196.

2. See Hepburn, *History of Currency*, pp. 397-410.

3. J. Lawrence Laughlin, "Currency Reform," *Journal of Political Economy* 15 (1907): 609.

4. *CR*, 60th Cong., 1st sess., pp. 6323 and 6375.

5. Ibid., pp. 7063-7064.

6. Ibid., p. 7069.

7. Ibid., p. 7074.

8. Ibid., p. 7077.

9. Ibid., pp. 7146-7244.

10. Ibid., p. 7250. Gore's idea preceded Einstein's general theory of relativity.

11. Ibid., p. 7252.

12. Ibid., p. 7260.

13. Ibid., p. 6320. Sections 11 and 12 created the commission.

14. Nelson W. Aldrich, *The Work of the National Monetary Commission*, *Senate Doc. No. 406*, 61st Cong., 2nd sess., 1910, pp. 3-29.

15. *CR*, 62nd Cong., 2nd sess., p. 587.

16. Ibid., appendix, p. 483.

17. Ibid., pp. 484-487.

18. *CR*, 62nd Cong., 3rd sess., pp. 1775-79.

19. Ibid., p. 1779.

20. Ibid., pp. 1779-83.

21. *CR*, 63rd Cong., 1st sess., pp. 4642, 4644.

22. Ibid., p. 4644.

23. Ibid., p. 4783, remarks by Robert Bulkley of Ohio. See also speech by Gilbert Hitchcock, ibid., p. 6015.

24. Ibid., p. 6021.

25. Ibid. (Glass), p. 4643.

26. Ibid., p. 4644.

27. Ibid., p. 4645.

28. Ibid.

29. Ibid., p. 4768.

30. Ibid., p. 4790.

31. Ibid., 63rd Cong., 2nd sess., p. 703.

32. Ibid., 63rd Cong., 1st sess., p. 4692. Mondell understood perhaps, but the chronic growth of regulatory government would seem in retrospect to have refuted his faith in the people.

33. Ibid., 63rd Cong., 2nd sess., p. 1137. The two cabinet officers were the secretaries of the Treasury and agriculture. In a final conference before the bill passed, the secretary of agriculture was dropped. Not until 1935 were the secretary of the Treasury and the comptroller of the currency removed from the board, and this change did not by any means restrain their subsequent unofficial influence.

34. Ibid., 63rd Cong., 1st sess., p. 4646.

35. *CR*, 63rd Cong., 2nd sess., pp. 1480-81.

36. *CR*, 63rd Cong., 1st sess., p. 4865.

37. *CR*, 63rd Cong., 2nd sess., p. 762.

38. *CR*, 63rd Cong., 1st sess., p. 4865.

39. Ibid., p. 4691.

40. Ibid., pp. 4651, 4661. See also statement by Richard Austin of Texas, ibid., p. 5089.

41. Ibid., pp. 4661-63.

42. *CR*, 63rd Cong., 2nd sess., p. 1072.

43. *CR*, 63rd Cong., 1st sess., p. 6016. A similar view was given by Knute Nelson of Minnesota.

44. *CR*, 63rd Cong., 2nd sess., p. 523. Joseph Bristow of Kansas also made this argument (ibid., p. 530).

45. Ibid., p. 525.

46. *CR*, 63rd Cong., 1st sess., p. 6001.

47. Ibid.

48. *CR*, 63rd Cong., 2nd sess., p. 1440.

49. *CR*, 63rd Cong., 1st sess., p. 6016.

50. *CR*, 63rd Cong., 2nd sess., pp. 667-668.

51. Hepburn, *History of Currency*, pp. 501-504.

52. *CR*, 63rd Cong., 1st sess., p. 6018.

53. Ibid., p. 5998.

54. *CR*, 63rd Cong., 2nd sess., p. 279.

55. *CR*, 63rd Cong., 1st sess., p. 4680.

56. See statement by Knute Nelson of Minnesota, for example, in which he denounced treasury monetary policy as "discretionary" and subject to favoritism (*CR*, 63rd Cong., 2nd sess., pp. 445-453).

57. *CR*, 63rd Cong., 1st sess., p. 5109. See also p. 6024 for statement by John Shafroth of Colorado.

58. *CR*, 63rd Cong., 2nd sess., p. 279.

59. Ibid., pp. 5100-6.

60. Ibid., pp. 5507-10.

61. Ibid., p. 6018.

62. Ibid., pp. 1063 and 1081.

63. This freeze on United States notes was imposed in 1878, while the statutory reserve provision appeared in the Gold Coin Act of 1900.

64. Ibid., p. 6018.

65. *CR*, 63rd Cong., 2nd sess., p. 880.

66. Ibid., p. 904.

67. Ibid., p. 466.

68. Ibid., p. 905.

69. *CR*, 63rd Cong., 1st sess., p. 4661.

70. Ibid., p. 829. The original bill stated that the Federal Reserve Banks could allow "such discounts . . . as may be safely and reasonably made with due regard for claims and demands of other member banks" (ibid., p. 1063). This statement implies a quantitative limitation based on the discretion ("due regard for") of the bank's discounting managers.

71. Ibid., pp. 966-967.

72. Ibid., p. 1037.

73. Ibid., p. 877.

74. Ibid., p. 979.

75. Ibid., p. 903.

76. Ibid., p. 968.

77. Ibid., p. 1074.

78. Ibid., p. 1116.

79. Ibid., pp. 1358, 1196. Carter Glass cited this same argument in the House.

80. Ibid., p. 1200.

81. Ibid., appendix, p. 564. Glass indicated that the House conferees threw out this provision.

82. Ibid., p. 1226.

83. Ibid., pp. 1294, 1352-56.

84. Ibid., p. 1482.

85. Ibid., appendix, p. 562.

86. Ibid., p. 564.

87. Ibid., pp. 1447-86.

88. Ibid., p. 702. Hitchcock, being a part of the loyal opposition, could say that the Federal Reserve system was a central bank and thereby justify his vote in favor of the institution on final passage. But none of the Democratic sponsors could agree because the Democratic party's platform had spoken out against a central bank.

89. See Mints, *History of Banking Theory*, p. 9. Mints derived this term from a passage in Adam Smith's *Wealth of Nations*.

90. *CR*, 63rd Cong., 2nd sess., p. 904.

91. *CR*, 63rd Cong., 1st sess., p. 4652.

92. *CR*, 63rd Cong., 2nd sess., pp. 537-538.

93. Ibid., p. 1446.

94. Ibid., p. 1225.

95. Ibid., p. 546.

96. This argument is elaborated in ch. 14.

97. Ibid., p. 1447.

14. Emergence of Central Banking Doctrine: Recapitulation

1. For an account of monetary evolution see White, *Money and Banking*, pp. 6-20.

2. I do not intend these few remarks to exhaust the arguments for and against this theoretical system. All I mean to imply is that private production of money is as likely to arise in a private enterprise system as is private production of any commodity or service that reduces costs by economizing resources.

3. R. A. Radford, "The Economic Organization of a P. O. W. Camp," *Economica* 12 (1945): 194-198.

4. The Constitution stated (backhandedly) that nothing except gold or silver would be legal tender; but it also gave Congress the power "to coin money and regulate the value thereof." So specification of the gold and silver values of the unit of account was implied but not mandated.

5. For an account of monetary events and policies during the restriction see Viner, *Studies*, pp. 122-170, and Frank W. Fetter, *Development of British Monetary Orthodoxy* (Cambridge, Mass.: Harvard University Press, 1965), pp. 26-63.

6. Thornton, *The Paper Credit of Great Britain*, p. 90. For analysis of Thornton's monetary theory see Mints, *A History of Banking Theory*, pp. 52-56 and passim. Many of his contemporaries also contributed arguments on the issues, but Thornton was exemplary in furnishing a sophisticated monetary policy as a distillate of monetary issues and events. (See Fetter, *British Monetary Orthodoxy*, p. 45.)

7. Thornton, *Paper Credit*, pp. 90 and 123.

8. Ibid., pp. 127, 163.

9. Ibid., p. 128.

10. Ibid., pp. 123, 116, 124.

11. Ibid., p. 152.

12. Ibid.

13. Ibid., p. 259.

14. See ch. 2 and Rothbard, *The Panic of 1819*, for a detailed account of this inflation.

15. *ASPF* 3, pp. 494-508.

16. Ibid., p. 498.

17. Hammond, *Banks and Politics*, pp. 199-301.

18. Ibid., p. 307.

19. Ibid., p. 324.

20. Viner, *Studies*, pp. 254, 324, 368 (my italics).

21. See, for example, *AC*, 1st Cong., 3rd sess., pp. 1895-1957.

22. Fetter, *British Monetary Orthodoxy*, pp. 23, 24.

23. Hammond, *Banks and Politics*, p. 324.

24. Fetter, *British Monetary Orthodoxy*, pp. 152-164 and passim.

25. Luke 14:1.

26. Viner, *Studies*, pp. 255-269, and Fetter, *British Monetary Orthodoxy*, pp. 165-197.

27. *Treasury Report*, 1866, pp. 9 and 10.

28. *Treasury Report*, 1872, pp. xx-xxi.

29. *CR*, 43rd Cong., 1st sess., appendix, pp. 17-20.

30. Walter Bagehot, *Lombard Street*, rev. ed. (London: Kegan Paul, Trench, Toubner and Co., 1906).

31. In Bagehot's time deposits of commercial banks and other private parties in the Banking Department of the Bank of England were about £18 million and government deposits £8 million, while note reserves were about £10 million. Gold was only £0.9 million. The Issue Department had £33 million notes outstanding, against which it had £18 million in bullion and £15 million in securities.

32. Bagehot, *Lombard Street*, pp. 162-170.

33. Ibid., p. 168. I am indebted to Frank W. Fetter for calling my attention to Bagehot's editorship of the *Economist* and for other helpful suggestions.

34. Ibid.

35. Ibid., p. 172.

36. Thomson Hankey, *The Principles of Banking* (London, 1867), p. 19.

37. Bagehot, *Lombard Street*, p. 175.

38. Ibid., pp. 200, 201.

39. Fetter, *British Monetary Orthodoxy*, p. 282.
40. *Treasury Report*, 1889, p. lxxxviii.
41. Shaw, *Current Issues*, p. 279.
42. Ibid., pp. 293-295.
43. Hepburn, *History of Currency*, pp. 500-504.
44. See Friedman and Schwartz, *Monetary History*, pp. 698 and passim.
45. Ibid., pp. 693-695.

Index